STRUCTURE AND MEANING
IN TONAL MUSIC

Festschrift in Honor of
CARL SCHACHTER

Carl Schachter

STRUCTURE AND MEANING IN TONAL MUSIC

Festschrift in Honor of CARL SCHACHTER

L. Poundie Burstein and David Gagné,
Editors

HARMONOLOGIA SERIES No. 12

PENDRAGON PRESS

HILLSDALE, NY

Other Titles in the Series **HARMONOLOGIA: STUDIES IN MUSIC THEORY**

Thomas Christensen, General Editor

No. 1 *Heinrich Schenker: Index to Analyses* by Larry Laskowski (1978)

No. 3 *Between Modes and Keys: German Theory 1592-1802* by Joel Lester (1990)

No. 4 *Music Theory from Zarlino to Schenker: A Bibliography and Guide* by David Damschroder and David Russell Williams (1991)

No. 5 *Musical Time: The Sense of Order* by Barbara Barry (1990)

No. 6 *Formalized Music: Thought and Mathematics in Composition* (revised edition) by Iannis Xenakis (1992)

No. 7 *Esquisse de l'histoire de l'harmonie: An English-language Translation of the François Joseph Fétis History of Harmony* by Mary I. Arlin (1994)

No. 8 *Analyzing Fugue: A Schenkerian Approach* by William Renwick (1995)

No. 9 *Bach's Modal Chorales* by Lori Burns (1995)

No. 10 *Treatise on Melody* by Anton Reicha (2001)

No. 11 *A Topical Guide to Schenkerian Literature* by David Carson Berry (2004)

This publication was made possible by generous contributions from David and Eugenia Ames and from David P. Goldman.

Library of Congress Cataloging-in-Publication Data

Structure and meaning in tonal music : Festschrift for Carl Schachter / edited by L. Poundie Burstein and David Gagné.
    p. cm. — (Harmonologia series ; no. 12)
 Includes bibliographical references (p.   ).
 ISBN 1-57647-112-8 (alk. paper)
 1. Music—History and criticism. I. Schachter, Carl. II. Burstein, L. Poundie. III. Gagné, David. IV. Series.
 ML55.S3565 2005
 780'.9—dc22
                        2005008366

Copyright 2006 Pendragon Press

CONTENTS

VI FORM

VII TRIBUTES AND REFLECTIONS

VIII BIBLIOGRAPHY OF CARL SCHACHTER'S WRITINGS

I — INTRODUCTION

Carl Schachter is widely acknowledged to be one of the leading music theorists of his generation. His influence, both as a teacher and through his writings, is incalculable. Yet as known to his colleagues, students, and friends, Carl Schachter the man is equally remarkable. The essays in this book reflect both aspects of his influence.

During his salad days, Carl Schachter—like many other youthful keyboard players—worked as an accompanist to anyone who would hire him. Among the many people he worked with in this regard was a lady who was particularly lacking in musical talent. This woman took up singing as therapy, on the advice of a psychiatrist who evidently thought that her moaning and complaining might as well be done to piano accompaniment.

At the practice sessions, the singer would occasionally take breaks from her vocalizing in order to give young Carl some meddling advice. Although he could have done without her counsel, his ears always welcomed the brief respite from her singing. "Why does your mother allow you to be a musician?" the woman whined. "You're smart; couldn't you find a more lucrative career?" She then noted that her own son had once wanted to become a musician—but she put a stop to that! "One day, I threw out his violin! He's hated me ever since, but if I didn't do it, he would not be the successful surgeon that he is today!"

To our great fortune, Carl Schachter ignored her advice and continued in a field that—while perhaps not as lucrative as some others—has nonetheless brought him and his field much success. He is one of the most admired music theorists and analysts of our time. His path breaking essays, books, lectures, and teachings—which take the theories of Heinrich Schenker as their starting point— have brilliantly demonstrated the interaction of harmony, rhythm, form, and performance in contributing to the dramatic expression in the masterworks of the tonal concert repertoire. While his command of pure theory is exceptional, what makes Schachter's contribution particularly notable is his almost unparalleled ability to use music theoretic concepts to enlighten the masterworks of the Western tonal repertoire.

Schachter's influence, particularly strong among American theorists and performers, has an international reach as well. He is frequently invited to teach and lecture in Europe and Asia, and musicians and scholars heavily and directly indebted to Schachter may be found in Canada, England, France, Belgium, Netherlands, Germany, Austria, Spain, Finland, Estonia, Israel, China, Korea, Japan, Columbia, Mexico, and elsewhere. Indeed, one might well speak of a "Schachter school of music analysis."

The present volume is a collection of essays from some of the members of this school, including a number of Schachter's long-time colleagues and students. The Festschrift concludes with some reminiscences and tributes by some of his friends and admirers, though it should be noted that many of the essays themselves include tributes as well. In a larger sense, of course, all of the essays herein offer indirect testimony to Carl Schachter's inspiration and guidance.

Many of the essays in this volume stemmed from presentations given at a symposium in honor of Carl Schachter that was sponsored by Queens College, City Universty of New York, on May 2, 1999.

We wish to acknowledge the generous support from David P. Goldman, a member of the Mannes Board of Governors, from Eugenia Ames, Mannes College of Music alumna and member of the Mannes Board of Governors, and from David Ames, Mannes College of Music alumnus and Com-muications Consultant, who made possible the publication of this volume.

Poundie Burstein and David Gagné
New York City, 2004

II. EXPRESSION

For Carl

The Two Curious Moments
in Chopin's E-Flat Major Prelude

Charles Burkhart

The delicious E-flat Major Prelude from Chopin's Op. 28 is not particularly well known, perhaps because it is so hard to play.[1] Recently I was drawn to it anew upon re-reading George Perle's citation of a curious moment in it—measures 43–44, which is composed entirely of diminished-seventh chords in contrary motion, and which Perle sees, together with other similar nineteenth-century cases, as a precursor of the "inversionally complementary interval cycles" typical of the compositional practice of early twentieth-century composers, notably Alban Berg.[2] While I have no quarrel with Perle's view, I am at the same time persuaded that these bars, together with another curious diminished-seventh spot at measures 29–32, relate to the tonal structure of Chopin's prelude. How they do so is my primary topic. In looking for answers—and they are not obvious—I have had help from an unexpected source—Heinrich Schenker. My paper is essentially a gloss on Schenker's analysis.

Schenker published not a single word on this prelude,[3] but on Nov. 25, 1916, he did fill a half page of music manuscript paper with analytic jottings on it, a number of which pertain to the passages in question. Before giving my own ideas, I will report on this document, which is now located in the New York Public Library's Oster Collection (Kosovsky 32/125), and is reproduced below as Example 1.[4] Starting with the words "Prel. 19 / Es dur," it consists of brief sketches and comments on various details. Apparently

---

[1] For listening, I recommend Rubinstein's recently reissued performance in AR's *The Rubinstein Collection*, Vol. 16.

[2] See George Perle, *Twelve-Tone Tonality*, 1ˢᵗ ed. (Berkeley: University of California Press, 1977), p. 171; 2ⁿᵈ ed. (1996) p. 166. Perle adduces the beginning of Berg's Op. 2, No. 2, with its contrarily moving "French sixths," as a case in point. See also his *The Listening Composer* (Berkeley: University of California Press, 1990), pp. 91-92. The Chopin passage is also quoted by Mark DeVoto in his revision of Piston's *Harmony*, 4ᵗʰ ed. (New York: Norton, 1978), p. 482, where it is listed under "The Whole-Tone Scale."

[3] At least the Laskowski index of Schenker's published analyses lists not a word. Analytic comment by other authors is also sparse.

[4] My thanks to John Shephard of Special Collections, New York Public Library, for permission to reproduce this document.

Example 1. Schenker's jottings.

Schenker was going through the piece from beginning to end, jotting down observations as they occurred to him—a style typical of other unpublished items of this time (e.g., the F♯ major prelude, Kosovsky 32/120). In the left margin (and some other places) he has written measure numbers, some preceded by "T." for *Takt*. Though the page contains examples of brief foreground reductions, there is no *Urlinie-Tafel* or any other kind of all-inclusive structure, concepts Schenker had not yet developed.

In studying this document (or any similar one), one must of course bear in mind that it was written for Schenker's eyes only, not intended for publication, and consists only of first thoughts that might well have been modified later. One must also remember that Schenker surely knew more about the piece than he took the trouble to write in these hasty notes. Still, it is not without interest, especially when it deals with the curious diminished-seventh spots. I will discuss it as shown in Example 2, which is a diplomatic copy of Example 1, plus an overlay of boxed segments A through R, and with each line (stave) numbered 1 through 8. The date, "25/11 1916," will be seen in Box N.

Schenker's Jottings[5]

<u>Line 1</u>. The first words in Box A, "3.4. Brch," mean that bars 3–4 are to be understood as *Brechung*, or arpeggiation, that is, as a downward E♭–B♭–G, in reply to the upward arpeggiation of bars 1–2.[6]   Box B is bars 5–8.

---

[5]I am grateful to Hedi Siegel and John Rothgeb for their generous help in both deciphering Schenker's very personal mixture of Sütterlin and cursive scripts and pondering his meaning.
[6]This is an interpretation of John Rothgeb's.

The brackets in Boxes A and B denote repetitions of a one-bar motive. Apparently Schenker heard them consistently as dactylic. However, it is easy for the listener to hear amphibrachs, that is, weak-strong-weak, or, in music notation, ♪| ♪♪. (Perhaps there is a kind of ambiguity in the composition here, but the case for dactylic rhythm seems supported by the way Chopin drew the relevant decrescendo wedges in his manuscript: They are only one measure in length, and consistently drawn entirely *within* the bar lines, never crossing a bar.[7])

The equal sign before Box C, together with the word "auch" (also), means that C is a reduction of B (bars 5–8). Schenker is showing that these bars initiate a downward 4th-progression $eb^2–d^2–c^2–bb^1$ that ends in bar 9. He is following his usual analytic practice of discounting a repetition (in this case the return to E♭ in bar 7) in favor of the continuation of the progression, here shown by his arrow from the pitch D to C. Above the arrow, he writes a d^2 in parentheses, as though the two notes E♭–D were both repeated. And under this 4th-progression, on Line 2, he shows in Box G (see "T. 5. 6") the full voice leading of bars 6 and 8, complete with figured bass.

What about the equal sign between Boxes A and B? Perhaps Schenker is saying here that, starting already in bars 3–4, the space from E♭ down to B♭ is stated (E♭–C–B♭), then reiterated, stretched out, in 5–9.

At Box B, bottom, the words "dann: 16, 24" may mean that the bracketed motive—falling step plus leap—returns at bars 16 and 24 as C–B♭–F.

Box D contains two general statements: "[The] left hand [part] is a composing-out," and "[it is] also parallel with the melody." Both apply to Line 2. The first statement in Box D refers to Boxes E and F. Schenker is saying that in bars 2–3 (not 3–4, as he mistakenly wrote) the bass and "tenor" are to be understood as in Box E, not ("u[nd] nicht") as shown in Box F^1 (where the bass rises E♭–G–B♭—Schenker's hypothetical bass for bar 2), but as in Box F^2, where the bass is shown as simply a composing-out ("blos[s] ausk[omponierung]"*)* of the fifth E♭–B♭. The second of Box D's statements refers to bars 1–2, where E♭–G–B♭ is actually composed in the "tenor" voice. In sum, bars 1–2 are conceived as in Example 3.

(For Box G see under Line 1, above.)

Line 3. Boxes H and I go together. Schenker writes: "[In bar] 17 no fifths—see soprano and neighboring voices." In other words, the parallel fifths Chopin wrote in the right hand's lower two voices—F–C♭, E♭–B♭, D♭–A♭—are not faulty since they are not caused by the essential voice leading. Rather, they are the fortuitous result of the elaboration of the essential voices, which are shown in Box I.

---

[7]Thomas Higgins (*Chopin, Preludes, Op. 28*, Norton Critical Scores, 1973, p. 67-68) also has noted this. He points out that not only Chopin's dynamics but also his pedal marks make clear that the final beats in bars 4 and 8 (and similarly throughout) are not sensed as anacruses. The only other authors I know of who treat this issue are Cooper and Meyer in *The Rhythmic Structure of Music* (Chicago: University of Chicago Press, 1960), pp. 151 ff. and 185 ff., who do read anacruses, and thus amphibrachs.

8

Example 2. Transcription of Schenker's jottings.

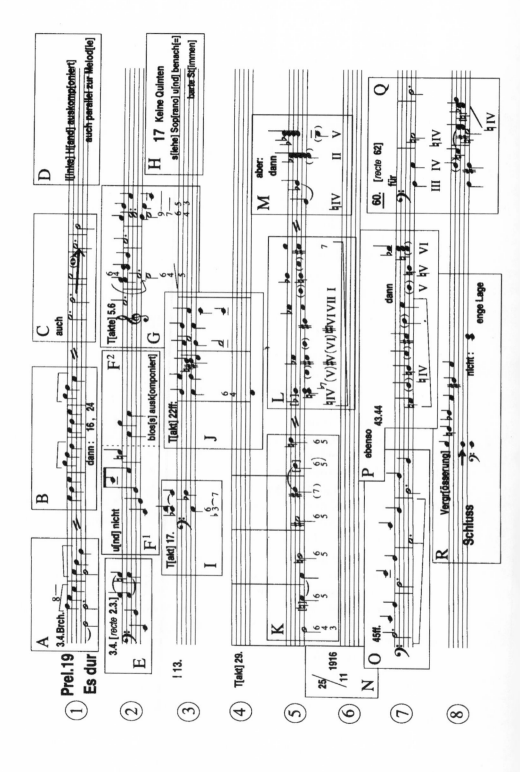

Example 3. Schenker's conception of bars 1-2.

One wonders what Schenker might have said about the *three* naked outer-voice fifths in bars 12–13. The exclamation point he wrote before the "13" in the left margin shows he was struck by something here, left room to comment on it, then didn't.

Box J shows the voice leading of bars 22–23. Schenker's "6/4" begins to uncover a deeper level, the complete figures of which would be:

$$
\begin{array}{cc}
8 & 7 \\
\\
6 & 5 \\
\\
4 & 3
\end{array}
$$

<u>Line 5</u> brings us to the first of the curious diminished-seventh passages (bars 29–32). (For easy reference I shall henceforth refer to this as Passage 1 and to bars 43–44 as Passage 2.) Schenker's bar lines suggest he first intended to analyze all voices, then confined himself to the bass.

Boxes K, L, and M each traverse mostly the same material, but only M completely covers the entire 4-bar stretch. K shows the hemiola rhythm caused by the changes of chord every two beats. Beyond this Schenker merely adds figures to each of the six chords.

Box L aims at a deeper interpretation. Here Schenker writes each chord in *root* position, then assumes for each a resolution which, because it is elided, he encloses in parentheses. The construct in L does not have a one-to-one relation with that in K. Instead, L is a rising chromatic line representing only the first *four* chords of K. While I think Schenker's approach in L is open to question, it apparently led him to one overarching insight symbolized by the bracket placed beneath. This is explained in Box M, which, as though dropping some of the excess baggage of L, sums up the first four chords of the passage (all of L's bracket) *as a single prolonged* ♮IV$^{(♭7)}$ *harmony* in the prevailing key of B♭ major. With the words "however: then" (*"aber: dann"*), Schenker separates the passage's two final harmonies (that is, the ones that apply to bar 31, third beat, through bar 32) from what has gone before. *These* diminished sevenths are interpreted in a different way—as having implied roots that give them dominant function, namely, "II$^{(♭9)}$–V$^{(♭9)}$" in the home key of E♭. (Though Chopin composed a bass B♭ only on the last quarter of bar 39, Schenker's parenthesized B♭ here is understood to govern the last *two* quarters.)

Line 7. The even more astonishing Passage 2 (the one that interests Perle) is analyzed in Box P. Here again are just six chords, but since they go by at a quarter- instead of a half-note rate, they take up only two measures. Again the lowest voice rises in major seconds, again Schenker (dubiously) sees hypothetical resolutions, but again (happily) reads a prolonged ♮IV$^{(♭7)}$ (now in E♭ major) embracing the first four chords. And again the last two chords are special (see *"dann"*). For the first one (the fifth chord of the six) Schenker writes both "V" and " ♮V." Here the idea of an elision—in which the potential B♭^{7} is replaced by a B♮^{o7} (bar 44, second beat)—is persuasive. The "♮V" then points to "VI$^{(♭7)}$," an applied dominant of the coming cadential II.

Schenker placed the material of Box P under that of L to show their relationship, which is why he wrote "ebenso (similarly) [Takte] 43–44." In the composition P then proceeds to O. Here Schenker's upward- and downward-slanting brackets seem to point to the correspondence between two subdominant harmonies—the chromaticized IV of P, and the diatonic II^6 of O.

In Box Q Schenker is saying that at bar 60 [*recte* 62] the bottom staff's chromatic harmonies with the bass G–G♯–A♮ are composed "instead of," or substitute for (*"für"*), the progression written on the staff above, with its more conventional G–A♭–A♮. While some might take this observation as downgrading a colorful passage from unusual to humdrum, I believe that, on the contrary, Schenker is pointing to the chromatic version as an interesting variation of the basic progression.

Line 8. Starting with bar 65, Box R is devoted to the "Schluss," or close (actually the codetta of the coda), and is notated in the bass clef. The upward-stemmed notes represent the top notes of 65–68, composed two octaves higher.   Schenker's *"Vergr[össerung]"* says this is an "augmentation," or better, a rhythmic enlargement. But of what? Surely of the falling 3rd-progression B♭–G that starts the coda at bars 49–51. But what does he mean by the two harmonic intervals shown at the bottom— E♭–B♭ followed by E♭–G—and by the cryptic comment on them? Perhaps they refer to the left-hand part, and the meaning is something like "It's B♭ (see arrow)—the main interval here is a fifth—E♭–B♭. The diminution does not reduce to a third—E♭–G, that is, it is *nicht enge Lage*—not close position." But this seems obvious, and there is no question of close position in the left hand. Still, that is exactly the point Schenker made about the left hand in the first two bars (recall Boxes E–F). Is he making the same point here?

View of the Whole

With the benefit of concepts that Schenker developed *after* 1916, I offer Exx. 4 through 6, my view of the structure of the entire prelude. The reader will notice elements I have taken over from Schenker's jottings on the piece, especially his harmonic analysis of the two diminished-seventh passages—Passages 1 and 2.

The interruption scheme $\hat{3}\,\hat{2} \parallel \hat{3}\,\hat{2}\,\hat{1}$ is familiar. I take the structural (obligatory) register to be the one that starts on g³, though the wide instrumental range, so typical of Chopin, promotes an elaborate play between the 3- and 2-line registers. As shown in Example 4, the top line moves at the outset between g³ and g². At bar 8 it moves to f², but this is only a lower-rank $\hat{2}$. The main $\hat{2}$ occurs at 16 *on the ultimate background level*, but it cannot be prominently composed there because of the need to end the A¹ section on a strong cadence in B♭. Therefore bar 16 ends with top-line b♭² (a very prominent tone throughout the composition). However, f² does appear on bar 16's third beat. This represents $\hat{2}$, but in the lower register. The B section now stays in that register for much of its time, during which the neighbor tone g♭² is prominent. Finally, at bar 29 begins the rise that will culminate at bar 32 with the long-delayed f³, which "answers" the opening g³.

The A² section (Example 5) starts like the beginning. At Passage 2 I have attempted to capture something of its "weightless," transitory quality by expressing Schenker's "♮IV♭⁷" in purely *linear* terms, that is, as neighbor tones within the prevailing tonic (see especially Example 5b) . And I show that tonic as enduring through bar 44's last beat, where it is chromaticized. A², like A¹, closes (at bar 49) in the 2-line register. Though the coda, like B, continues much of the time in the lower register, registral balance with the main body is achieved by the two prominent returns to g³ (54 and 62) and the high E♭'s in the penultimate bar.

There are two striking design features that integrate the main body with the unusually long coda. First, as shown in Example 6a, the chromatic descent in Passage 2, though cut off by the structural close, is continued in the coda. The second, shown in Example 6b, is the important role played by the pitch b♭²—so prominent throughout the composition, as noted. Its most crucial moment occurs at the structural close—bars 45–49—when the c³ of 45–47 is suddenly abandoned at 48 with a leap down to f² to close the section with f²–e♭². This event casts an unsettled air over the close. It also leaves the c³ "unresolved," and a gap—c³–f²—that cries to be filled. So bar 49 brings back b♭² (see the curved arrow), which initiates the motive B♭–C(♭)–B♭–A♮–A♭–G, which in turn fills the gap with steps. However, a fully persuasive cadence on e♭² remains to be reached. Bars 64–65 bring a full cadence, but again b♭² is left hanging, creating a need for a codetta to the coda. Here the vehement syncopations of the enlargement of the motive (65ff.), underscored with *cresc.*, finally succeed in displacing the persistent b♭² and winning a fully stable e♭² (bar 69).

Several other motivic events in the prelude deserve mention. The opening rising arpeggio B♭–E♭–G re-echoes in the coda at bars 53–54 and 61–62 (after which bars 62–64 seem to faintly re-echo Passage 2). Also, a remarkable enlarged motivic repetition occurs as follows: See again the B-section, recalling its two 8-bar phrases. In the first phrase, note at bar 21 the upward arpeggio E♮–B♭–D♭ which occurs on the way to a cadence on b♭². But in the second phrase, at the analogous place—bar 29ff.—the E♮–

Example 4. Multi-layered view of bars 1-32.

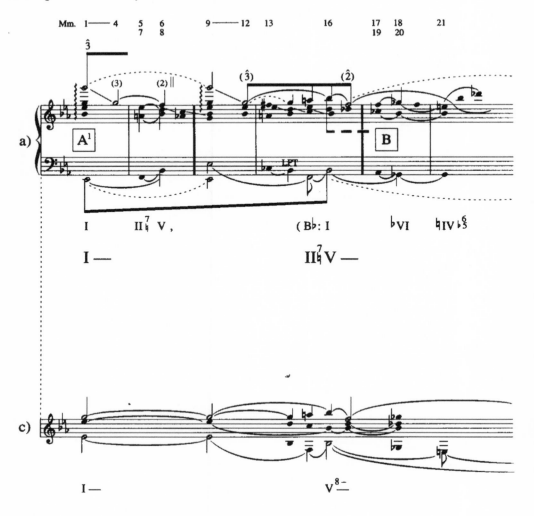

B♭–D♭ is enlarged to span three measures, as shown in Example 7. The enlargement is embedded in Passage 1, which regains the 3-line octave and culminates on f³ as full-fledged 2̂ in bar 32.

The prelude's outer form is an utterly conventional ABA plus coda. Equally conventional is its phrase rhythm: There is not a single break in the regularity of the 8-bar (4 + 4) hypermeasures (marked with heavy bars lines in Exx. 4–6), all of which are commensurate with 8-bar phrases until the structural close brings the typical phrase overlap into strong bar 49, which starts the coda (with its again typical overlaps at 57 and 65). Except for the overlap at 49, which creates a 9-bar phrase, all three form-sections are exactly the same length—two 8-bar phrases.

The regularity of the phrase lengths is relieved by subtler rhythmic features. In addition to the above-mentioned issue of the one-bar dactylic

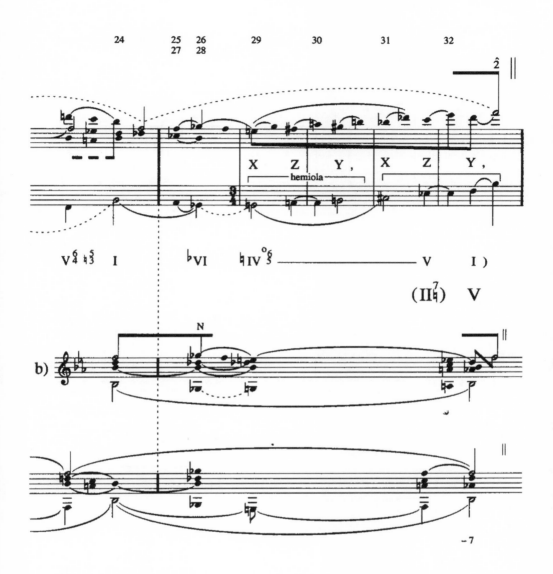

rhythms, the two-bar hypermeasures—so metrically regular throughout (all odd bars strong, evens weak)—sometimes interact with the *tonal* rhythm[8] such that the opposite accentual pattern is projected. Can bars 5–6 and 7–8 be heard as weak-strong? Perhaps here the applied dominants in 5 and 7 will more likely be heard as "appoggiatura harmonies," that is, as strong. But, as shown in Example 8, much of the B section (bar 17ff.) is quite susceptible to being heard the opposite way—until Passage 1 arrives, where the switch to hemiolas causes bar 29 to be heard as strong. Again, all this

[8]The very useful concept of tonal rhythm is presented by Carl Schachter in his "Rhythm and Linear Analysis," *The Music Forum* Vol. 4 (New York: Columbia University Press, 1976), p. 313; repr. in *Unfoldings* (New York: Oxford University Press, 1999), p. 37.

Example 5. Multi-layered view of bars 33-49.

seems supported by Chopin's dynamics—now pairs of wedges covering two-bar groups.[9]

Finally, Passages 1 and 2 occur in somewhat analogous places within the two-part interruption structure, that is, just prior to the cadential chords that conclude the pre- and post-interruption segments, each a moment of tonal suspense that finally yields to the gravitational pull of stronger functions.

[9]Is it significant that at bar 29 Chopin switches from wedges to "cresc. . . ."? Could this be another of those cases where wedges are intended to suggest a degree of rubato as well as dynamics? If so, the *non*-rubato "cresc." over Passage 1 surely makes musical sense. See also the switch to "cresc.....dim." at 65-69.

Example 6. The role of $b^{\flat 2}$ (see * *, particularly in the Coda).

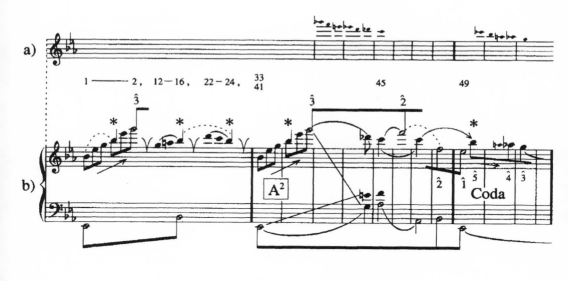

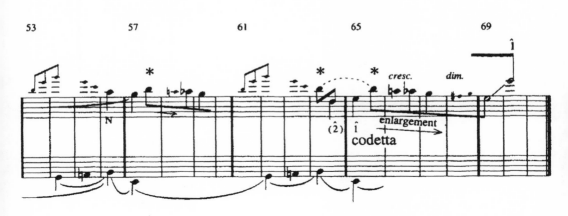

Example 7. A motivic enlargement.

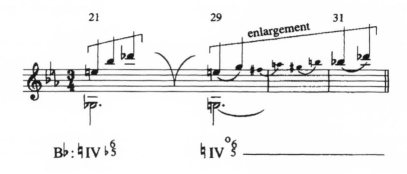

Example 8. Alternate hearing of the B-section's hypermeasures.

Tonal and Atonal

Both of our curious passages are examples of "equal (symmetrical) division of the octave (or octave-segment)," which is to say, division of the pre-compositional pitch material—a phenomenon frequently exploited in nineteenth-century music.[10] Such passages have been described as "lying on the boundary of tonality,"[11] and equal division itself described as "one of the nineteenth-century sources of a basic premise of twentieth-century music: that all twelve tones of the chromatic scale are available to the composer as elements of potentially equal status."[12] Such passages are of course tonal "in the large" in that they either prolong a single tonal harmony or connect one large harmony to another, but their internal construction may be seen as "atonal" because pitch symmetry is foreign to the basic materials of tonality. Our two passages will bear looking at from a "12-tone" point of view.

There are only three content-distinct members of the set-class 0369. Let us arbitrarily name these three X, Y, and Z, as in Example 9a, and conceive of them as forming all together a 12-tone set (S). As pictured in Example 4a at bars 29–32, the six chords of Passage 1 are disposed over the four bars so as to form two successive statements of S (as XZY), which are related to each other as S^0 to S^6. Now notice that the top voice of bars 29–32 is composed of a series of six dyads (E–G, F♯–A, etc.) that produces a secondary 12-tone row (and in exactly twelve beats!). This comes about because 1) the top two and bottom two pitches of 0369 lie a tritone apart, and 2) S^0 and S^6 lie a tritone apart.

[10]The seminal study of this subject is Gregory Proctor's well-known *Technical Basis of Nineteenth-century Chromatic Tonality: A Study in Chromaticism*, Ph.D. diss., Princeton, 1977. He does not discuss the Chopin E-flat prelude.

[11]Oswald Jonas, *Introduction to the Theory of Heinrich Schenker* (1934), trans. Rothgeb (New York: Longman, 1982), p. 81.

[12]Edward Aldwell and Carl Schachter, *Harmony and Voice Leading*, 2nd ed. (San Diego: Harcourt Brace Jovanovich, 1989), p. 543.

In Passage 2, the two chord streams are inversionally complementary such that a move down one semitone in the upper stream leads to the same chord as does a move up two semitones in the lower. In short, -1=+2 (mod 3). Passage 1 is actually based on the same process: It expresses one step at a time what Passage 2 expresses simultaneously (see Example 9b).

Example 9. Set-class 0369.

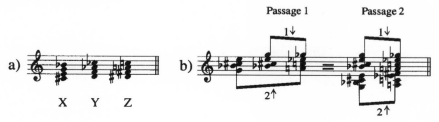

Most symmetrical passages in tonal music are forced to relinquish their rigid repetition at or near their end in order to conform to a tonal goal (often a cadence), but Passage 1, like clockwork, adheres to its top-line pattern to the very end (bar 32, 3rd beat), where the twelfth note, f^3, produces the structural 2 at the last possible moment—and in the structural register to boot. At this point the bass has the single tonal adjustment—B♭ (to provide the root of the cadential dominant) instead of the expected sequential A♭.[13]

Can such symmetrical constructs as our two passages have tonal meaning? Schenker of course found they did. The surprising thing to me is that he read a stream of four diminished sevenths (the first four chords in each passage) as a *prolongation.* Not only is this a prolongation of a dissonant chord, but a prolongation effected by means of other, mutually exclusive, dissonant chords that have no *interior* tonal relationship threading them together. To read a prolongation here Schenker had to invoke primarily the parameter of rhythmic emphasis—that is, in Passage 1's opening "X Z Y | X," for example, because the two X's fall on metrically emphasized points, the four chords as a whole are generalized as a "prolongation of X." Such a reading seems to me remarkable—for Schenker. I recall no similar one elsewhere in his work—but of course passages like these are rare in the composers Schenker favored.[14]

Passage 1 requires a final comment. Conceiving its first four chords as *ascending in major seconds* (as in Box K) does not fully represent the voice leading *from chord to chord.* The change of chord in bar 29, for example, takes place more decisively from beat *2* to 3 rather than from beat *1* to 3—that is, it is better understood as a *falling half step* rather

---

[13]To my knowledge, the sequential pattern of Passage 1 (bars 29-32) is generally rare in the repertory. However, it occurs rather frequently in Wagner's *Tristan* (see Schirmer piano score, page 10/1/1 to 10/3/2, and also the simpler example on page 118/1/3f.).

[14]This example of a dissonant prolongation is remarkable in its own right, not because Schenker later proscribed them in *Der freie Satz,* Par. 169.

than a rising whole step (and likewise for the rest of the passage). In Ex. 4a, my "XZY's" symbolize this essentially falling half-step structure.

This raises the possibility of an alternative analysis of the passages—interpreting them in terms of descending consecutive diminished sevenths *that function in the manner of interlocking applied dominants.*[15] Schenker analyzes the last two chords in Passage 1 as precisely that (Box M). Could the rest of the series be likewise interpreted? I leave it to the reader to toy with this possibility. My own experiments all seem more like reharmonizations than analyses.[16]

The voice leading superiority of falling half over rising whole steps is clearly demonstrated in Passage 2, where both occur simultaneously. Here the top line "leads" and the lower "follows" (reminiscent of Schenker's "leading" and "following" linear progressions). The lower is not a true bass voice, but a kind of free-floating voice that merely accompanies the top. What a daring idea!—as Schenker might say. Indeed, the composer who could write such a passage, not to mention the famous E♭ at the end of the F-major prelude, or the long chain of parallel fifths near the end of the mazurka Op. 30/4, and who could structure the entire Op. 25 F-major etude on tritone-related keys—to name only the most obvious of his audacious flights—was surely, in Schumann's famous phrase, "the boldest poetic mind of the age."

---

[15]*Harmony and Voice Leading*, pp. 530-532.

[16]Since writing this I have discovered that Celestin Deliege hears Passage 1 in this way. In his "Pertinence du metre musical" (*Cahiers du CREM*, vol. 1, 1986, p. 13) he writes under the six chords "[♮] IV, VII, III, VI, II, V." But then he is probably following a tradition that always sees diminished sevenths as dominants.

Circular motion in Chopin's late B-major Nocturne (Op. 62, No. 1)

William Rothstein

The last of Chopin's three nocturnes in B major, composed in 1845–46, is among the most remarkable of the composer's later works.[1] Although based, like most of his nocturnes, on the Italian vocal style of Chopin's youth and early adulthood, this is a comparatively restrained work: it contains only a few elaborate *fioriture*, for example, and its surface rhythms are distinctly, even determinedly plain. Nor is there any hint that Chopin intended these plain rhythms to be embellished in any way—unlike his procedure, for example, in the early Nocturne in E♭ Major, Op. 9, No. 2.[2] In these respects, one might say of Op. 62, No. 1 what Rossini reportedly said of Bellini's *Il pirata* (1827): that its style is "philosophical" and, consequently, somewhat lacking in brilliance.[3] The melodic material, too, is less memorable than that of many other nocturnes by Chopin. Not surprisingly, this Nocturne is rather infrequently performed.

What, then, is so special about this piece? I hope that my analysis, incomplete though it is, will go part of the way toward answering this question, but I will anticipate my conclusions in broad terms. This Nocturne links a highly conventionalized formal plan—a compound ternary form, the phrases of which are mostly eight measures long or derived from eight-measure models—to a musical substance that partakes strongly of the Romantic urge toward boundlessness. As will be seen, the deep-level harmonic and linear structure of the Nocturne is based on a repeating pattern that, in principle, could go on forever, like the repetitions of a ground bass. These repetitions conflict, to varying degrees, with the formal plan. Like many works by Chopin, then, this Nocturne supports the distinction—here raised to the level of a dichotomy—between form and content in nineteenth-century music. In so doing, it illustrates the danger of any attempt to collapse the distinction between what, more specifically, I like to call outer form—the formal plan of a work, considered in conventional terms—and inner form, the patterns created by a work's voice-leading structure.[4] Just such

---

[1] The other two nocturnes in this key are Op. 9, No. 3 and Op. 32, No. 1.

[2] For Chopin's embellishments to Op. 9, No. 2, see Jean-Jacques Eigeldinger, *Chopin, pianist and teacher, as seen by his pupils*, trans. Naomi Shohet (Cambridge University Press, 1986), pp. 77–79 and 257–61. The pianist Raoul Koczalski, a pupil of Chopin's pupil Karol Mikuli, recorded Op. 9, No. 2 (Pearl GEMM CD 9472) with embellishments that purportedly stem from Chopin himself.

[3] Reported in Herbert Weinstock, *Bellini* (New York: Alfred A. Knopf, 1971), pp. 80–81.

[4] On outer and inner forms, see my book *Phrase Rhythm in Tonal Music* (New York: Schirmer Books, 1989).

19

an attempt has recently been made in a major study by Charles J. Smith.[5] The problem with equating inner and outer forms is that the analyst thus robs the composer of a most important resource: conflict between related but distinct musical domains.

We know, thanks to Jeffrey Kallberg, that the composition of Op. 62, No. 1 gave Chopin considerable trouble; the compositional process continued right up to the date of publication and even beyond.[6] For this reason, the textual situation is complicated even by Chopin's standards. There is, and probably can be, no definitive text of the piece, for reasons that Kallberg makes abundantly clear. I will not address textual issues further, except to note that the differences between extant versions of the Nocturne have little impact on the analysis presented here. However, the reader should have one of the better editions of the Nocturne on hand for the discussion that follows.[7]

Among the many wonderful things that Carl Schachter has taught us, one of the most important is that the voice-leading structures of tonal masterpieces are not merely intellectual constructions. They embody motion—motion that must be continually experienced and re-experienced by performer, listener, and analyst if genuine musical communication is to take place. Motion in tonal music is not uniform; it has infinitely varying qualities.[8] It can progress, for example, either upward or downward, or in both directions at once, moving within either a triad or a seventh chord, or from one composed-out chord to another. Linear motion normally confirms the larger-scale harmonies—for it is linear progression, along with arpeggiation, that primarily defines composing-out (Schenker's *Auskomponierung*)—but linear motion may also conflict with a composed-out sonority, giving rise to tension and at least momentary uncertainty.[9] Then there are the individual actors on the tonal stage, short motives and even single tones. These typically maintain

[5]Charles J. Smith, "Musical Form and Fundamental Structure: An Investigation of Schenker's *Formenlehre*," *Music Analysis* 15 (1996): 191–297. Smith further clarified his position in a prepared response to a paper by Peter H. Smith at the 2001 meeting of the Society for Music Theory (Philadelphia, Pa.). The form of a piece, Smith asserted—meaning what I would call its outer form—"provides our only access to the background" (Smith's designation for levels that Schenker would have assigned to the early middleground). It follows that an independent inner form cannot exist, as a listener would have no way of hearing it. If my analysis of Op. 62, No. 1 is accepted, Smith's thesis will have been disproved.

[6]See Kallberg, *The Chopin Sources: Versions and Variants in Later Manuscripts* (Ph.D. dissertation, University of Chicago, 1982), pp. 248–75 and 309–22.

[7]Recommended editions are: the Polish government edition (Krakow, 1995), edited by Jan Ekier; the Wiener Urtext Edition (Universal Edition, 1980), also edited by Ekier; and the revised Henle edition (1990), edited by Ewald Zimmermann.

[8]Several of Schachter's essays address the qualities of tonal motion in particular musical situations. See "The Triad as Place and Action," in *Unfoldings*, pp. 161–83; "The Adventures of an F♯: Tonal Narration and Exhortation in Donna Anna's First-Act Recitative and Aria," in *Unfoldings*, pp. 221–35; "The Prelude from Bach's Suite No. 4 for Violoncello Solo: The Submerged *Urlinie*," *Current Musicology* 56 (1994): 54–71.

[9]Schachter addressed this issue in a keynote address, "Foreground *vs.* Background," delivered to the 1983 meeting of the Society for Music Theory (New Haven, Conn.). This paper has never been published, but a related discussion appears in "Either/Or" (*Unfoldings*, pp. 121–33).

their identities while their musical environments—harmonies, keys, and rhythms—change around them. Or they may find their identities challenged, either subtly or radically. All of these things happen in Op. 62, No. 1, but in such a way that its ends are always its beginnings; the completion of one idea gives birth to the next; the music seems to express the great cycle of being. Its motion, in short, is pervasively *circular*.

Circular motion, in our Nocturne, is not just a matter of frequent phrase overlapping, a technique that Chopin used in so much of his music (though never more than in this piece).[10] Circular motion is built into the music's phrase rhythm, its voice leading, and—to a remarkable degree—even into its motivic structure. Before describing any of these things, though, I will give a brief account of the work's formal plan, its outer form (see Example 1). Like most of Chopin's nocturnes, this one is in ternary or ABA' form. Both the first section, in B major, and the middle section, in A♭ major, are themselves composed as small ternary forms, so the larger form may be described as compound ternary. The final section, A', is an abbreviated and embellished recapitulation, consisting of a single period—corresponding, roughly, to the final period of the A section (bars 28ff.) but, unlike that period, reaching tonal closure in B major. As he does rather often, Chopin compensates for the abbreviation by expanding the recapitulation internally: in the present instance, he inserts a cadenza into the period's consequent phrase.[11] He thus de-emphasizes the symmetrical aspect of the recapitulation, making it the goal and climax of the piece despite its abbreviated length. (Embellishing nearly every note of the melody, mostly with trills, serves the same purpose.) A coda of fourteen measures intensifies one's sense of the piece as being end-weighted.

I have elsewhere described this Nocturne as "Chopin's most breathtaking venture into endless melody."[12] Rarely does Chopin avoid formal closes to quite the degree he does here. Within the compound ternary form there are seven subsections, which I have labeled with Greek letters in Example 1: α β α', γ δ γ', α". These do not include the two-measure introduction, two extensions (each over a bass pedal point), the interpolated cadenza, and the coda. Only two of the seven subsections end with a perfect authentic cadence (PAC). At bar 10, a PAC in B major marks the end of α, the A section's first period; but there is no slackening of the eighth-note rhythm, and a PAC in G♯ minor follows just two beats later. The G♯ cadence is more a beginning than an end, but it robs the B-major cadence of much of its effect. The next time a PAC marks the end of a subsection is at bar 81,

[10]See the present author's "Phrase rhythm in Chopin's nocturnes and mazurkas," in *Chopin Studies*, ed. Jim Samson (Cambridge University Press, 1988), pp. 115–41. The same essay appears, in slightly expanded form, as Chapter 9 of *Phrase Rhythm in Tonal Music*. The essay includes a brief discussion of rhythmic and metrical ambiguities in Op. 62, No. 1.
[11]For other examples of expansions shortly before the structural close of a piece, see Charles Burkhart, "Chopin's 'Concluding Expansions,'" in *Nineteenth-Century Piano Music: Essays in Performance and Analysis*, ed. David Witten (New York: Garland Press, 1996), pp. 95–116. On expansion in general see *Phrase Rhythm in Tonal Music*, especially Chapter 3.
[12]"Chopin's nocturnes and mazurkas," p. 139; *Phrase Rhythm*, p. 246.

Example 1. Chopin, Nocturne in B Major, Op. 62, No. 1, formal plan.

measures	1-3	3-10	11-21	21-28	29-36	37-44	45-52	53-61	61-68	69-75	76-81	81-9
subsections	introduction	α	β	extension	α'	γ	δ	γ'	extension	α"	cadenza*	
sections		A				B				A'		Cod

*The cadenza functions as an expanded cadence to subsection α" and, hence, to section A'.

the end of **α"** and the structural close of the piece; even there the rhythmic motion does not flag. The sole PAC in A♭ major, the key of the middle section, falls at bar 38, the second measure of that section. Although this is unequivocally a PAC—we will soon see that it forms the goal of an auxiliary cadence in G♯ minor—the cadence falls either too early or too late to mark an endpoint in the music's outer form. Cadences thus conflict with the Nocturne's formal plan at least as often as they reinforce it.

In a "typical" compound ternary form, one would expect half cadences to fall at the ends of central subsections, such as the ones labeled **β** and **δ** in Example 1, and perhaps in the retransition (if there is one) leading back to the A section; see the passage following **γ'** in Example 1. In Op. 62, No. 1, not one of these points features a half cadence in the main key, B major. **β** and **δ** end with minor chords—D♯ minor and D minor, respectively— making the interpretation of a half cadence impossible. Only subsection **γ'** ends with a half cadence, as does the following retransition, a cadential extension (or suffix) over a dominant pedal. But the half cadence and its extension are in A♭ major, not B major; the link back to B major (for the recapitulation) is thus made through an E♭-major triad, an enharmonic respelling of B major's major mediant (III♯).

Example 2 shows a five-chord formula which, I believe, governs the large-scale progression both of the A section and of the Nocturne as a whole. Between the staves of the formula there are two rows of measure numbers: the upper row refers to the A section, the lower row to the entire piece. Each number shows where the corresponding stage of the progression is reached in the score. The final cadence, shown in parentheses in Example 2, stands outside the formula and represents, in a sense, its resolution. Despite its somewhat unconventional format, Example 2 as a whole is intended to depict the deep-middleground structure of the Nocturne; it is offered here in lieu of more typically Schenkerian graphs of the "early" middleground (the first and second levels). It will be noted that the fundamental line, or *Urlinie*, is undivided, and that the middle section (bars 37–67) is based neither on an upper-voice neighboring note nor on mixture applied to the primary tone, $\hat{3}$. Thus the Nocturne does not conform to any of Schenker's models of ternary form. [13]

---

[13] See Schenker, *Free Composition (Der freie Satz)*, translated and edited by Ernst Oster (New York: Longman, 1979), pp. 132–3, and the discussion in Smith, pp. 216–31.

Example 2. Op. 62, No. 1, deep middleground (harmonic formula).

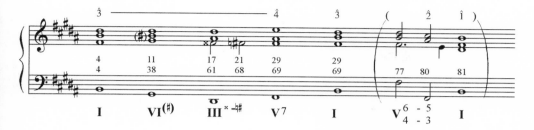

Example 3, a conventional Schenkerian graph, gives a more detailed account of the Nocturne's voice leading. [14] Read in conjunction with Example 2, the graph suggests how Chopin keeps harmonic and melodic motion active from the beginning of the piece to (at least) its structural close. Scale degree 3, D♯, is kept continuously alive in the upper voice. Every chord of the formula but one has D♯ as its top voice, and that chord—V7—merely moves D♯ to its upper neighbor, E. Return to the tonic harmony of B major thus entails resolution back to D♯ in the melody. The only exceptions occur at the two PACs in B major, bars 10 and 81, where the upper voice moves, at some level, down to the tonic note, B. If one examines bars 10–11 in Example 3, one sees that Chopin undermines the B-major cadence not only in the ways I have already described but in an additional and most ingenious way: he treats b[1] as though it were a passing tone on its way down to g♯[1]. A fifth-progression is outlined in bars 7–11, from d♯[2] to g♯[1], as though G♯ minor and not B major were the ultimate goal of the harmony. This presages a similar fifth-progression in bars 33–38; both fifth-progressions are accompanied by the auxiliary cadence III–V–I (or III–V–I♯) in G♯ minor. G♯ major—respelled as A♭ major—becomes the key of the middle section, much as G♯ minor governed the beginning of subsection β (the A section's middle part).

The heart of the five-chord formula in Example 2 is a four-chord progression, I–III–V7–I, which constitutes an ascending arpeggiation of the tonic triad in the bass. As the Roman numerals in Example 3 indicate, this progression governs even the internal structure of the middle section. Although D♯ is scale degree 5 in G♯ major, much of the middle section is governed melodically by the third scale degree, B♯; B♯ is, of course, spelled as C♮ in the score (and in Example 3). Notice how often C is regained from its upper neighbor, D♭ (4), so that the upper voice of the formula is maintained, albeit transposed, in the new key. At bar 61 e♭[2], the respelled primary tone, steps forward to reclaim its focal status in the melody and to prepare the recapitulation. Until then, E♭ has been content to remain in the one-line octave as the lower boundary of the melodic line, much as d♯[1] formed the lower melodic boundary in the A section. The question of melodic boundary points will become important as we proceed.

---

[14]The analysis in Example 3 is my own, but it incorporates a few ideas that the late Ernst Oster wrote into his personal copy of the score (Oster Collection, New York Public Library for the Performing Arts).

Example 3. Op. 62, no. 1, voice-leading graph.

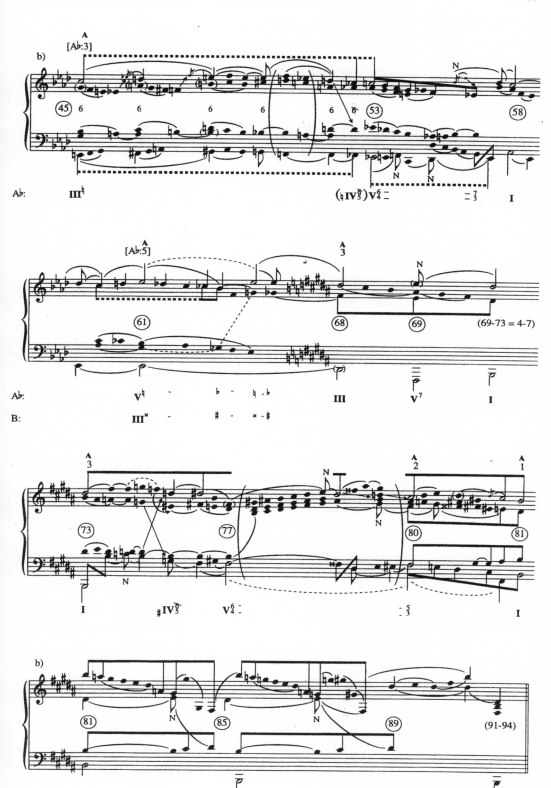

In his dissertation, Kallberg remarks upon the importance of the mediant harmony, D♯ minor, on both the large and small scales in this Nocturne. He even traces the mediant's influence to a scale that can only be called microscopic.[15] Chopin's sketch shows three different versions of what became the last four measures of the piece. Only the final version includes the dominant seventh chord, and thus the important neighboring motion D♯–E–D♯ in the upper voice. Once the final version had been determined, Chopin, in one of his autograph scores, placed accent marks on the fourth beats of bars 91 and 92. The accent in bar 91 emphasizes a fleeting D♯-minor sonority. Although, in a voice-leading sense, D♯ here acts as a suspension or retardation resolving upward to the dominant seventh, the result is a reminiscence of the progression I– III–V7– I, starting from the third beat of bar 91. In bar 92 Chopin's accent emphasizes IV7, another important sonority in the piece. Kallberg does not mention it, but perhaps it is not irrelevant, for so tactile a composer as Chopin, that the right hand in these measures, considered alone, plays first I–III–I, then I–VI–I—recalling, as it were, the upper and lower mediants of the harmonic formula in Example 2.[16]

If Chopin's use of a repeating harmonic formula reminds one of Baroque practice, the melodic dimension of the piece does much to reinforce that impression. This Nocturne, like several of Chopin's other works, draws heavily on the tetrachord descending from tonic to dominant, and to a lesser degree on the ascending form of the same tetrachord.[17] In this piece, unlike some others by Chopin, the tetrachord is often transposed, especially to the upper and lower mediants, D♯ minor and G♯ minor respectively. I will refer to the original tetrachord as *the B tetrachord*, and to its principal transpositions as *the D♯ tetrachord* and *the G♯ tetrachord*. The name refers, in each case, to the tetrachord's highest pitch. It should be noted that these tetrachords do not always function as voice-leading units—i.e., fourth-progressions—in the Nocturne. Often the tetrachord forms part of a fifth-progression, or a third-progression plus an upper neighbor. As Schachter has noted, motives and voice-leading units need not coincide in tonal music, even when the motives are scale fragments and thus potential linear progressions. However, there need to be good contextual reasons for a series of tones to be accepted as a discrete unit, even a purely motivic one. Rhythm and articulation can provide such reasons.[18]

[15]Kallberg, pp. 259–62.

[16]On the tactile element in Chopin's writing for the piano, see my essay "Chopin and the B-major complex: a study in the psychology of composition," in *Ostinato rigore, revue internationale d'études musicales* 15 (2000), pp.149–72.

[17]Some of the other pieces that belong to this group are the Fantasy, Op. 49; the F-minor Ballade, Op. 52; the F-minor Nocturne, Op. 55, No. 1; and the Polonaise-Fantasy, Op. 61.

[18]This is a summary of Schachter's argument in his 1983 keynote address (see note 9). He demonstrated his point most clearly in an analysis of Chopin's Mazurka in G♯ Minor, Op. 33, No. 1. In this piece, the fourth D♯– G♯ functions as a motive in the A section, where it forms part of the tonic triad; the same fourth is motivic in the B-major middle section, where it conflicts with the local tonic triad. Schachter was, in effect, rebutting a principal thesis of John Rothgeb's essay "Thematic Content: A Schenkerian View" (in *Aspects of Schenkerian Theory*, ed. David Beach [New Haven: Yale University Press, 1983], pp. 39–60). See also, in this connection, Richard Cohn's 1992 article "The Autonomy of Motives in Schenkerian Accounts of Tonal Music" (*Music Theory Spectrum* 14, pp. 150–70).

The B tetrachord is first heard in bar 3, as part of a fifth-progression prolonging V (see Example 3). This tetrachord recurs frequently in subsections α, α', and α''. The G$\sharp$ tetrachord is first heard in bars 5–7, in the lower notes of the right hand: first the tetrachord ascends, then it descends. In the second half of bar 9 the G$\sharp$ tetrachord descends again, concluding at the first beat of bar 10 and anticipating the subsequent move to G$\sharp$ minor. Here, at the final cadence of the first period (α), something crucial happens: the soprano voice drops out for the first eighth-note of the measure, but it is clear from the context that the omitted note is f$\sharp^1$. Omitting this note has several consequences, of which I will mention just two. The omission conspicuously denies the ascending form of the B tetrachord a complete statement, suggesting that such a statement might occur later. It also creates an abbreviated, three-note ascent, G$\sharp$–A$\sharp$–B, which Chopin immediately exploits in the following measures, mostly in the alto voice. This abbreviated ascent is, obviously, well suited to the local key of G$\sharp$ minor.

The complete tetrachordal motive is less in evidence in subsection β (bars 11–21); as Kallberg notes, the motive's appearances in this passage tend to be more or less disguised.[19] One of its more prominent occurrences (not shown in Example 3) is in the alto voice of bar 14, where it descends from $\hat{1}$ to $\hat{5}$ in F$\sharp$ major.[20] One can also discern a statement of the G$\sharp$ tetrachord, descending, in the upper voice of bars 15–17, with d$\sharp^2$ prolonged thereafter. As Example 3 shows, two descending fourths proceed from d$\sharp^2$ between bar 17 and bar 29. In fact there are more than two: the descending D$\sharp$ tetrachord is heard in the foreground of bars 22–23, 24–25, and 28–29—all in the extension following subsection β—in addition to the tetrachord's deeper-level statement in bars 17–21, within the subsection.

In bars 35–36, in subsection α'', the alto voice sounds the descending G$\sharp$ tetrachord much as it did in bars 9–10. Modulation to G$\sharp$—this time G$\sharp$ major—once again follows more or less immediately.

The middle section of the Nocturne again contains fewer statements of the tetrachordal motive, but those few are marvelous. The section begins with a descending tetrachord, stretching from the upbeat to bar 37 (c$\sharp^2$=d$\flat^2$) to the downbeat of bar 38 (a$\flat^1$); this is immediately followed by a descending tonic-to-dominant tetrachord in A$\flat$ major (see Example 3). A particularly clear statement is the descending fourth from f^2 to c^2 in bars 44–45, which bridges the boundary between subsections γ and δ (refer to Example 1). Less conspicuously, and at the same time, the bass begins a gradual ascent, rising first from E$\flat$ to E$\natural$ (bars 44–45), thence to F$\sharp$ (bar 47) and G$\sharp$ (bars 49–50). This is nothing other than the G$\sharp$ tetrachord in its ascending form, with E$\flat$ standing for D$\sharp$ and with most of the notes embellished (see Example

---

[19]Kallberg, pp. 254–55.

[20]The descending motion from the leading tone, e$\sharp^1$, helps the F$\sharp$ tetrachord to stand out in bar 14. This descending tetrachord crosses a more deeply embedded, *ascending* statement of the same tetrachord in bars 13–14. Only the latter statement appears in Example 3. The coexistence of these two statements, ascending and descending over the same four pitches, indicates something of the complexity to be found in Chopin's voice leading, especially in his later music.

3). The ensuing descent from G♯ back to D♯ uses somewhat different pitches, but it concludes with the motivic half-step E–D♯ in bars 52–53 (spelled F♭–E♭ in the score). In bars 61–66 the right hand sounds the descending D♯ tetrachord, spelled in flats and including a chromatic passing tone. The same tetrachord is immediately repeated, starting in bar 68, as a bridge to the A' section. Just before this point, in the tenor voice, a slightly altered form of the G♯ tetrachord is heard in bars 66–67, sounding mostly in parallel tenths with the upper voice. If spelled in sharps, this descent would read G♯–F♯–E♯–D♯.

The structural cadence in bars 80–81 demands special attention. The soprano and tenor voices are in canon, as Chopin emphasizes by writing a separate slur for the tenor. (This slur does not appear in all editions of the Nocturne.) As Example 3 shows, the bass descends by step from V to I. The soprano closes the fundamental line by leading $d{\sharp}^2$, $\hat{3}$, down to b^1, $\hat{1}$, while also touching on the motivic upper neighbor, e^2. (This descent was purposely omitted from bar 10, where the tonic note was reached from below.) The alto, having regained $g{\sharp}^1$ at the second quarter of bar 80, descends chromatically through the tones of the G♯ tetrachord, while the harmony includes a fleeting reference to the key of G♯ minor. The tenor, finally, fulfills the other unfinished business of bar 10 by ascending—in a slightly roundabout way—through the B tetrachord, now including its initial note, f♯.

The coda is based on the D♯-minor passage beginning at bar 21, but the key is now (naturally) B major. The voice leading is based largely on the descending B tetrachord, substituting the flatted for the diatonic seventh degree in the coda's traditional bow to the subdominant. The tetrachords are clearly spelled out in Example 3; the whole process is harmonized by repeated I–IV–V–I cadences over a tonic pedal. Here, as in so many other passages, the end of one cadential pattern becomes the beginning of the next. In the final measures, $d{\sharp}^2$ and $d{\sharp}^1$ have returned, as though the entire cycle were about to begin again.

The importance of the tetrachordal motive in the Nocturne has, I think, been sufficiently demonstrated, but an important question remains: How is Chopin's use of tetrachords implicated in the circular motion which, I have claimed, is a defining quality of this piece? Example 4 attempts to model an answer to this question. The example shows a set of three descending scales from $d{\sharp}^2$ to $d{\sharp}^1$; $d{\sharp}^2$ is embellished, in each case, by a diatonic upper neighbor. The first scale (Example 4a) is that of B major. The second and third scales (Examples 4b and 4c) each contain the same pitches, differing only in their tetrachordal subdivisions; both scales represent the key of the middle section, G♯ major. D♯, which forms the upper and lower boundary of each scale, is $\hat{3}$ in B major, $\hat{5}$ in G♯ major. The B-major scale—which is, of course, the main scale in this piece—is divided into three overlapping tetrachords; these are precisely those tetrachords to which I have already assigned the names B, G♯, and D♯ (see Example 4a). At the conclusion of the scale, the notes E–D♯ are transferred up an octave to become the initial neighboring-note motive; the entire descending scale could thus be repeated in circular fashion, *ad infinitum*. The G♯ and D♯ tetrachords, which overlap literally only on the pitch-class D♯, are thus given an artificially enhanced overlap, using the upper neighbor to D♯, so that an overlapping dyad is formed: E–D♯. Thus, any time that two tetrachords meet in Example 4a, there is an overlap, whether "natural" or "artificial," of two notes: B–A♯, G♯–F♯, or E–D♯. I have highlighted the overlapping dyads in each case with a square bracket, labeled either H (for half step) or W (for whole step). These dyads, especially the two half steps, play a special role in the melody of the two A sections, as may be ascertained by reviewing bars 3–12, bars 21–29, and related passages.

The scale in Example 4b is a hypothetical analogue to Example 4a, using the notes of the G♯-major scale. The tetrachordal subdivisions have been maintained in exactly the same places, although two boundary notes have undergone chromatic alteration (from B to B♯ and from F♯ to F✕). This is, in other words, a different octave species within the same D♯-to-D♯ ambitus. The species of the three tetrachords have all changed, because the whole and half steps are now in different places. The upper tetrachord in Example 4b belongs to a species not represented in Example 4a, the half step now falling in the middle. The three overlapping dyads, too, have all changed, either from half step to whole step (E–D♯ to E♯–D♯ and B–A♯ to B♯–A♯) or from whole step to half (G♯–F♯ to G♯–F✕). Perhaps it is the high degree of intervallic non-correspondence between Examples 4a and 4b that led Chopin not to use the latter as his subdivision of the G♯-major scale. Instead he uses the subdivision shown in Example 4c, at least up to bar 61; after that point he reverts to the pattern of Example 4a, in keeping with the retransitional function of bars 61–68. In the G♯-major section, Chopin "cheats" by including the upper neighbor to D♯ as the topmost note of a tetrachord (see Example 4c); but this is what allows him to maintain the same tetrachordal species, taken in the aggregate, that he used to subdivide the B-major scale (Example 4a), in which the half step falls at either the top or the bottom of each tetrachord. There are only two overlapping dyads in Example 4c, C♯–B♯ (spelled in the score as D♭–C) and E♯–D♯ (F–E♭ in the score). Chopin uses a short cut to connect the two registers of the latter dyad: twice, in the melody, he leaps downward a major ninth, from f² to e♭¹—closing the circle, as it were, with a single stroke. In both cases (bars 40–41 and 56–57) he avoids the pitch e♭² or d♯², the Nocturne's primary tone: as noted earlier, Chopin saves any emphasized occurrence of this pitch for bar 61, the beginning of the retransition.

I have chosen this rather abstract explanation of melodic events in Op. 62, No. 1 for two reasons. First, the melodies of the A and B sections occur, to a remarkable extent, within the same ambitus, d♯¹ to d♯², with an upper neighbor or upper third frequently appended to the latter pitch.[21] In fact, with the exception of a single *fioritura* (bar 71), it is only in inessential parts of the form—the extensions, cadenza, and coda—that Chopin ventures more than a fourth above d♯², reaching a♯²/b♭² in bars 21 and 62 and b² in

---

[21]On the significance of the d♯¹–d♯² ambitus in Chopin's B-major music, and of the note d♯² in particular, see the essay cited in note 16.

the coda. The relatively fixed nature of the melodic ambitus in this piece encourages a theoretical model that stresses octave and tetrachordal species, regardless of the keys involved. This surely reflects the origin of Chopin's "nocturne style" in the music of Italian opera.[22]

Secondly, the tetrachords featured in sections A and B relate in ways more complicated than simple transposition. Example 5 shows Example 4a transposed to G♯ major. While the most prominent tetrachord in the middle section, the G♯ tetrachord, may be derived as a transposition of the outer sections' B tetrachord—these are, of course, the upper tetrachords of the two respective major scales—the melodic ambitus used by Chopin stresses the identity of the boundary pitches, g♯¹–d♯¹, between the G♯ tetrachords used in the two sections, rather than the correspondence of scale degrees in the two keys. Similarly, when the D♯ tetrachord is heard in the retransition, it corresponds to the D♯ tetrachord of the A section (d♯²–a♯¹ in Example 4a) rather than to any transposed correlate in B major.[23] The D♯ tetrachord does not appear in Example 4c because I do not regard bars 61–68 as part of the B section proper; the tetrachord's appearance there is a link to the A' section, which begins precisely by overlapping the D♯ and B tetrachords in bars 68–69.[24] The same overlap occurs in bars 28–29, an analogous point in the form.

*   *   *   *   *

As we have seen, the inner form of Op. 62, No. 1 is based on a circular path (Example 2), involving repeated departure from and return to a tonic triad with D♯ on top. Since the path is round, might we reconcile inner and outer forms by classifying the piece as a rondo? Jeffrey Kallberg considers, and rejects, this possibility in his dissertation.[25] According to Kallberg, the motive of the descending fourth—the tetrachord—integrates the first three subsections of the piece, thus setting apart the A♭-major section as contrasting. Our analysis has revealed, however, that the tetrachordal motive occurs throughout the piece. And it must be said that the pattern of Example 2, with its crucial return from V7 to I at the end of each cycle, suggests rondo form more readily than it does a compound ternary. The relatively great length of subsection β might also support the attribution of rondo form, although at 18 measures (including the extension) it is still much shorter than section B, which is either 31 or 32 measures (depending on how one counts bar 68) if the retransition is included.

---

[22]Several authors, notably Pierluigi Petrobelli and Harold Powers, have stressed the importance of fixed pitches in the vocal lines of nineteenth-century Italian opera.

[23]The appearance of the tetrachord C♯–F♯ in the one-line octave (bars 13–14) occurs in a way that does not suggest a relation to bars 61–68.

[24]Poundie Burstein (personal communication) has pointed out that if the extension/retransition is included, the B section can be understood to emphasize the two secondary tetrachords of the A section (G♯ and D♯), in preparation for the return of the B tetrachord in section A'.

[25]Kallberg, pp. 254–55.

Example 4. Tetrachordal subdivisions of eighth-note scales (with upper neighbor).

          a) B major

          b) G♯ major; subdivision based on Example 4A

          c) G♯ major; subdivision used by Chopin

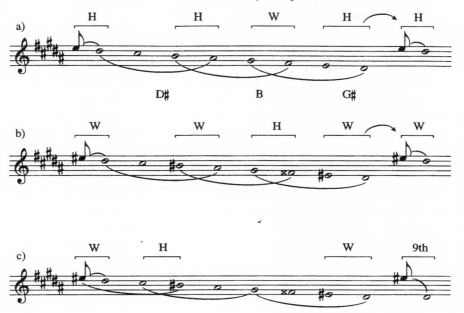

Example 5. Example 4a transposed to G♯ major.

       I agree with Kallberg, however, that such a reading of the outer form would be mistaken. Most obviously, sections A and B are contrasted by their patterns of accompaniment—steady eighth notes for section A, syncopations for section B. The disappearance of left-hand syncopations at bar 61 merely confirms that this is the beginning of the retransition.[26] The changes of key signature give visual confirmation of the ternary form; in Chopin, at least, such visual cues should not be disregarded.[27] It is also interesting that Chopin devoted a separate sketch to the A♭-major section;

---

[26]For reasons such as this, I believe that the definition of retransition offered by William Caplin in his book *Classical Form* (Oxford University Press, 1998) focuses too narrowly on harmony. A "standing on the [home] dominant" just prior to a recapitulation often reintroduces essential features of the theme that is about to return. There are, in other words, retransitional functions other than harmonic ones.

[27]See my essay "The Form of Chopin's Polonaise-Fantasy," in *Music Theory in Concept and Practice*, ed. James Baker, David Beach, and Jonathan Bernard (University of Rochester Press, 1997), p. 355.

there is no evidence that he did the same for subsection β.[28] What all of this suggests, it seems to me, is that Chopin *thought* he was writing a ternary form. In short, nearly everything having to do with the Nocturne's design points to a ternary form, even if we ignore the fact that Chopin's nocturnes are almost always ternary. "Nearly everything" includes phrase rhythm: the B section falls much more clearly into eight-measure units than does any other part of the piece.

We are left with an unusually sharp conflict between design and underlying structure—in other words, between outer and inner forms. And this, I submit, is exactly the way Chopin wanted it. It is part of what makes playing or listening to this Nocturne an exhausting experience, in the very best sense: Chopin gives neither pianist nor listener any place to "let down" until very nearly the end. As theorists continue to explore issues of form in tonal music, it would be well for them to maintain an ear for such ambiguities as exercised the ear, and the mind, of a Chopin.

---

[28]Kallberg, pp. 165–66 and 262–74; the sketch is transcribed on pp. 264–66. Kallberg comments most perceptively on the non-coordination of thematic and tonal plans in Op. 62, No. 1, especially in the middle section.

Of Species Counterpoint, Gondola Songs, and Sordid Boons

L. Poundie Burstein

The world is too much with us; late and soon,
/ . . .We have given our hearts away, a sordid boon!
// . . .
I'd rather be / A Pagan suckled in a creed outworn;

/ So might I . . .

/ Have glimpses that would make me less forlorn; /

Have sight of Proteus rising from the sea; / Or hear old
Triton blow his wreathéd horn.

William Wordsworth, 1806

Like many others, I first became acquainted with Carl Schachter through *Counterpoint in Composition*, the revolutionary textbook that he co-wrote with Felix Salzer.[1] My excitement over this book was a crucial factor in my decision to apply to Mannes College of Music, where I had the chance to study with both of its authors. In the classroom, as in the text, Salzer and Schachter taught me how the principles of species counterpoint can be applied to analyses of works not only from the Renaissance, but from later periods as well.

An analysis of my own that demonstrates such an application may be found in Example 1, which presents a close reading of the "gondolier's call" that opens Felix Mendelssohn's *Venetian Gondolied*, Op. 30, No. 6. The notes of this motive form dissonances that are not approached or left by step and which thereby violate the rules of strict counterpoint (Example 1a). Nevertheless, this passage may be related to a contrapuntal prototype in which the interval from F♯ to A is decorated by a passing tone and a neighbor tone (Example 1b). If this prototype were to be elaborated by an unfolding, the use of pauses, and implied tones (as in Example 1c), a structure is formed that is quite similar to the one found in the opening of the Mendelssohn piece (compare Example 1a and 1d).

Like many other analyses, Example 1 attempts to explain something that is relatively difficult and unfamiliar by comparing it to something simpler and more standard. Although this analysis is solidly grounded in the principles of strict counterpoint, we still might wonder how it benefits us. According to one possible train of thought, such an analysis can have a calming effect,

---

[1]Salzer, Felix and Carl Schachter, *Counterpoint in Composition* (New York: McGraw Hill, 1969).

33

Example 1. Felix Mendelssohn, "Venetian Gondolied" from *Song Without Words*, Op. 30, No. 6, bars 1-8 (a) excerpt; (b)- (d) strict counterpoint reduction and voice-leading analyses.

for it illustrates how a passage that seems to be unruly is actually quite "rule-y." In their surface appearance, the dissonances of Example 1a threaten us with their freedom. The contrapuntal analysis, on the other hand, allows us to tame and demystify the dissonances, for it contains them within the safe, logical boundaries of clearly defined rules. This in turn can give us a sense of empowerment, as we take control over the passage by means of contrapuntal reasoning.

But if this were in fact its primary goal, then such an analysis truly would be a "sordid boon," to borrow a phrase from the celebrated Wordsworth sonnet cited at the top of this essay. The narrator of this poem suggests (among other things) that the modern world's love of rationality numbs us to the beauties of Nature. In a similar vein, we might question whether a love of contrapuntal rationality numbs us to the beauties of music. This is especially true when dealing with a work like Mendelssohn's Op. 30, No. 6. After all, as a "Venetian Gondola Song," it is literally supposed to evoke something free floating and ungrounded, not something bound by severe rules.

It must be remembered, however, that an analytic reduction is but a type of metaphor for a piece of music. If a warning label were put on a species counterpoint analysis, it would read "For comparison purposes only!" An analysis that appeals to species counterpoint claims simply that a passage of actual music is in certain ways like a passage of strict counterpoint; it does not maintain that the music is indeed as orderly as a counterpoint exercise.

By noting that the passage from the Mendelssohn is like the species counterpoint of Example 1b, we in turn are invited to confront those ways in which it differs from its contrapuntal prototype. Within the strict counterpoint of Example 1b, the dissonances are neatly enveloped within consonant boundaries. In the Mendelssohn piece, however, the framing consonances are obscured. As a result, the dissonances seem disembodied, without a clear means of support. Like all such analyses, this one should not cause us to exclaim, "Aha! Now I see how this musical passage expresses but a simple contrapuntal figure!" Rather, one should exclaim, "Aha! Now I see how this simple contrapuntal figure is expressed in such a bold manner within this musical passage!" The excitement comes not in moving from the actual music to the contrapuntal reduction, but rather in moving from the reduction back to the actual music.

There has long been suspicion that voice-leading analysis seeks to reveal the logic of music and disentangle its ambiguities, at the expense of the individuality and intriguing paradoxes found in much great music.[2] To be sure, the many analytic studies devoted to examining tonal or motivic logic and coherence might well seem to suggest that these are considered to be the primary factors for determining the value of a composition. Yet surely this is a simplification. Indeed, a rigorous voice-leading analysis can often highlight tantalizingly illogical moments and ambiguities within specific works.

For instance, consider the passage shown in Example 2. The rhythm, articulation, and motivic structure suggest that the opening melodic note functions as a passing tone (as in Example 2a). Yet since it is the first note of the main theme, one might instead regard this pitch as initiating a tonic chord prolongation (as in Example 2b). This presents a paradox. According to a Schenkerian reading, a note cannot simultaneously function both as a chord tone and as a passing tone, at least not on the same level. A non-Schenkerian reading, however, could allow for such a contradiction.

It so happens such a non-Schenkerian reading of this passage has been proposed by a prominent theorist who is not normally thought of as a non-Schenkerian: namely, Heinrich Schenker. In a brilliant essay in Tonwille, Schenker claims that the opening pitch of this theme has "a peculiar double meaning" (*ein seltsames Zwielicht*). Accordingly, he reads this pitch as part of a prolongation of both dominant and tonic harmonies.[3]

One way we can come to grips with this contradiction is by understanding the opening note of the theme here as a type of anticipation. An anticipation, of course, is a dissonance that foreshadows an upcoming chord tone, so that the upcoming chord tone seems to be "projected back" into the space of the preceding harmony. An anticipation usually appears as a simple dissonance (as in Example 2c). In the Mendelssohn excerpt, on the other hand, matters are more

---

[2]Such a claim lies at the center underlies many criticisms of the approaches used by Schenker and his followers. As Joseph Kerman succinctly put it in his classic critique, "[t]he analyst's instinct is to reduce . . . ambiguities out of existence"; see "How We Got Into Analysis, and How Do We Get Out," *Critcial Inquiry* 7 (1980), reprinted in *Write All These Down* (Berkely: University of California Press, 1994), p. 25.

[3]Heinrich Schenker, *Tonwille* Vol. 10 (Vienna: A. Guttman Verlag, 1924), pp. 25-29.

Example 2. (a) Bars 5-7; (b) bars 7-10; (c) hypothetical example; (d) analysis of bars 6-7.

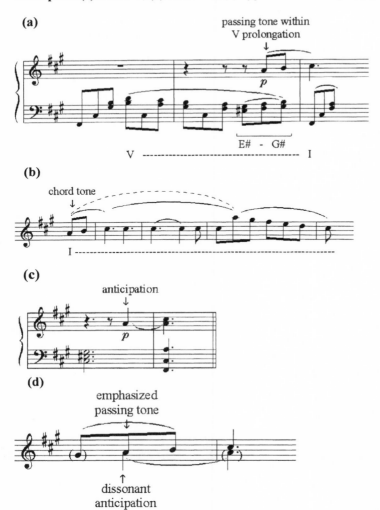

complicated (Example 2d.) Since the theme here begins on a passing tone, the passing tone is thereby emphasized. This emphasis in turn causes the passing tone to function additionally as an anticipation. As such, this dissonant passing tone acts also as a foreshadowed chord tone.

Furthermore, it may be argued that the melody exists not only as it appears within the music, but also within our memories (as when we recall the theme during motivic allusions to it). Out of context—as it would occur in memory—the opening note of the theme would indeed start with a chord tone. In this sense, too, the passing tone A of bar 6 may be regarded to function also as a chord tone, at least upon reflection.[4]

[4]In a personal communication, David Epstein has pointed out to further source of ambiguity here. Even though the piece is in 6/8 meter, it opens with accents occurring on every other beat (presumably in imitation of waves), so as to hint at a conflicting 3/4 meter. Within the notated 6/8 meter, the A of bar 6 comes on an offbeat, as more befits a passing tone. Within the conflicting "3/4 meter," on the other hand, the A comes on a downbeat, as more befits a chord tone.

In Mendelssohn's Op. 30, No. 6, conflicts that give rise to ambiguities take place on larger levels of structure as well. For instance, the metric layout of the main theme's opening phrase is contradicted by a counterstress in bar 9, forming a type of large cross rhythm against the underlying hypermeter (Example 3a and c). Note in particular how the leap in the melody in bar 9 demarcates the beginning of a tonic chord prolongation from bars 9-12, bars which are further grouped by the pedal in the piano. The resulting tension created by this large-scale rhythmic conflict is "corrected," so to speak, when the main theme returns in bar 37. At this point, the theme reappears within the middle of a larger progression; a new phrase starting on a tonic chord does not begin until two bars after the theme returns. This altered context creates a rhythmic reinterpretation of the theme, so that the emphasized measure, bar 39, now *does* occur at the beginning of a hypermeasure (Example 3b and d).[5]

This rhythmic reinterpretation creates a certain sense of resolution, as though it were "solving a problem" posed earlier in the composition. Problem solving serves as an important feature in many compositions; it can be thrilling when a previously tense musical idea returns so that a former source of conflict is removed. Yet such resolution is by no means mandatory, and it is not necessarily the purpose of analysis to describe how a composition solves the various problems established within it.

There are no necessities in a work of art; no predetermined goals that a composer must fulfill. As the philosopher R. G. Collingwood has argued, a work of art (as opposed to a work of craft) is distinguished by its *lack* of any predetermined function or aim.[6] For instance, analyses can and often do help us understand factors which lend a composition a sense of coherence, but it would be a mistake to regard musical coherence as a mandatory objective, as an end unto itself. A composition need not fulfill any specific goals; a composition cannot be judged merely on how completely it resolves conflicts, solves problems, expresses unity, or obtains closure. That a work has a sense of unity or closure is not in itself remarkable. What *is* interesting is to examine how and to what extent that unity or closure is achieved, and how this process colors the meaning of the composition.[7]

In the Mendelssohn piece, as is so many others, much of the poetic power derives from conflicts that are left *unresolved*. As an example, consider the register of the melodic line. In each phrase, the melody seems to reach up to and focus on a high A or a high G♯. It would be most natural for the melody ultimately to resolve to the tonic F♯ in this upper register, as

---

[5]The static nature of bars 33-36 promotes the notion that these measures include a rhythmic expansion. That bar 39 is a downbeat of a hypermeasure is supported not only by the resolution to the tonic in this measure, but also by the appearance of the high C♯ as a cover tone. For a different reading of the hypermetric structure of this passage, see William Rothstein, *Phrase Rhythm in Tonal Music* (New York: Schirmer, 1989), pp. 193-98.

[6]R. G. Collingwood, *The Principles of Art* (Oxford: Oxford University Press, 1938).

[7]See Fred Maus, "Concepts of Musical Unity," in *Rethinking Music,* edited by Nicholas Cook and Mark Everist (Oxford: Oxford University Press, 1999), pp. 171-92.

Example 3. (a) Bars 7-14; (b) bars 33-43; (c) strict counterpoint reduction of bars 7-14; (d) strict counterpoint reduction of bars 33-43.

in the hypothetical excerpt shown in Example 4a. However, although such an ending would have been most satisfactory, it would have expressed something quite different from what Mendelssohn evidently had in mind.

Within the actual melody, the melodic resolution to F♯ takes place in the lower octave (Example 4b). Note that an altered form of the "gondolier call" motive returns immediately before this resolution. The notes of the motive here are no longer disembodied, as they were in their initial presentation in bars 3-4, but rather are given chordal support and resolve immediately to the tonic. Ironically, this "embodied" version of the motive is underplayed in comparison to its earlier disembodied presentations, for the softer dynamics and foreshortened rhythm of the motive at this point creates a muted effect. The subdued sense here underlines the sudden melodic shift to the lower octave, a shift which leaves a noticeable gap in the melodic register. This in turn helps give the melody a sense of poignancy lacking in the hypothetical ending of Example 4a, where the removal of the register gap would create an inappropriately bold effect.[8]

[8]Heinrich Schenker discusses the unusual registral treatment of this work in Free Composition, ed. and trans. Ernst Oster (New York: Longman, 1979), § 238 and § 240.

To be sure, a high F♯ does appear in the coda, almost in the manner of an afterthought (Example 4c). The motion to the high F♯ compensates somewhat for the sudden registral dip at the end of the previous phrase. Significantly, however, a high G♯ is never allowed to resolve directly to the high F♯. This lack of resolution is highlighted by two frustrated returns of the "gondolier's call" in the coda. The high E♯'s of bars 46 and 50, which are emphasized by dynamics and a trill, clearly hearken back to the earlier, prominent gondolier calls of bars 3-4, 13-14, and 29-30. One surely expects the high E♯'s of bars 46 and 50 to be followed a G♯, thereby paralleling the earlier presentations of this motive. Such a continuation is thwarted, however, as the E♯ resolves almost directly to F♯.[9] As a result, the omission of the motion from a high G♯ to F♯ is keenly felt: though the fundamental line does resolve to scale-degree 1̂, the gondolier's call itself is left unresolved, as though fading out while the gondolier disappears around the bend. Even when the composition around it develops and resolves various conflicts, the gondolier's call remains unchanged, refusing to yield to the flow of time, as it were.

*   *   *   *   *

Some may find it odd that my discussion of species counterpoint should stray into hermeneutics. Yet I maintain that there is no contradiction here. A comparison of a musical artwork to a strict counterpoint exercise does not represent an attempt to simplify the composition, erase its ambiguities, or show its ability to perform assigned tasks. Rather, such a comparison—if properly applied—should help us gain increased sensitivity to the complexities, ambiguities, and poetic expressiveness of the masterworks of tonal music.

My attitude in this regard of course greatly bears the influence of my teacher, Carl Schachter. As he has shown his students many times, there is a continuum between the study of the technical facets of music and its poetic powers; one should not divorce its structural techniques from the expression that lies within the music. For Carl Schachter, the teaching of the fundamentals of species counterpoint and the investigation of musical meaning are part of the same process.

This is an attitude that has become a bit controversial in recent years. Nowadays, perhaps even more so than in Wordsworth's time, a number of scholars have been increasingly suspicious of a rationalistic approach to music. In extreme cases, some have even questioned whether rigorous voice-leading analyses are possibly motivated by an imperialistic urge, which tries to subjugate musical beauty by means of a Teutonic sense of logic.[10]

Following Carl Schachter, I would argue that this opposition of analytic rigor and musical expression is a false one. Strict counterpoint is not a tool of subjugation. Rather, it is a means that allows us to better understand the

---

[9]Although even this resolution is somewhat mollified by the interjection of an arpeggio between the E♯ and the tonic to which it resolves.

[10]See, for instance, Philip Brett, "Musicality, Essentialism, and the Closet," in Queering the Pitch (New York: Routledge, 1994), p. 14, and Robert Fink, "Going Flat: Post-Hierarchical Music Theory and the Musical Surface," in Rethinking Music (op. cit.), pp. 102-37.

Example 4. (a) Hypothetical version of bars 39-43 in which upper voice resolves to tonic in the upper register; (b) actual melody of bars 39-43; (c) analysis of registral treatment in bars 39-51 (after Schenker).

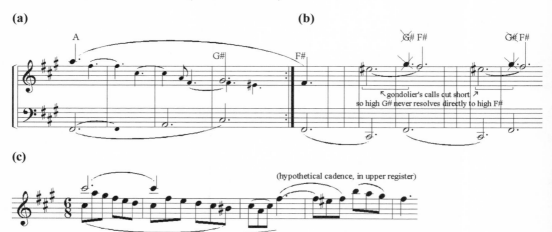

forces that underlie the interaction of pitches in tonal music. These interactions in turn help form a foundation for musical expression and meaning. When properly done, analysis does not give a sense of empowerment to the music analyst at the expense of the composition. On the contrary, a successful analysis should leave us humbled, as it allows us to discover previously unrecognized subtleties in an artwork. Indeed, the sense of awe and humility in approaching the works of the masters is perhaps the greatest lesson that Carl Schachter imparts to his students.

In concluding, I would like to recall a story told by Richard Feynman, the great physicist. Someone once argued with him that scientific reason blinds people to the beauty of things such as flowers. Feynman rebutted that, on the contrary, scientific understanding gives us greater admiration for the awe-inspiring magnificence of flowers, for it more fully reveals the fathomless complexities of their creation and construction. The more we learn through scientific knowledge, Feynman countered, the more we appreciate the subtle beauty of flowers.[11] And in a similar manner, as Carl Schachter has often shown us, the more we learn through rigorous, technical analysis of music, the better we are able to hear old Triton's wreathéd horn, or young Felix's haunting gondola song.

---

[11]Richard Feynman, *The Pleasure of Finding Things Out* (London: Penguin Books, 1999), p. 2. See also Richard Dawkins, *Unweaving the Rainbow: Science, Delusion and the Appetite for Wonder* (Boston : Houghton Mifflin Co., 1998), pp. 41-42.

III

THEORY

The Spirit and Technique of Schenker Pedagogy

Allen Cadwallader and David Gagné

Until fairly recently, the number of expert Schenkerian analysts was small. As a result, few people were qualified to teach the subject beyond the most basic level. Nevertheless, Schenkerian analysis was taught at many colleges, universities, and conservatories, frequently with unfortunate results. Misunderstandings abounded, and while most musicians had heard of Schenkerian analysis, few had any real idea what it is about. In fact, some impressions characterize his approach as involving a handful of very general premises that reduce compositions to simple structures resembling "Three Blind Mice."

Such misinformation has been countered by the series of excellent translations of Schenker's work, beginning with the English version of *Free Composition* in 1979.[1] The publication of Aldwell and Schachter's *Harmony and Voice Leading*, roughly contemporaneous with the translation of *Free Composition*, has also changed the field by presenting the principles of harmony in a Schenkerian context.[2] As a result concepts such as prolongation are now generally known and taught by many teachers throughout the country, and students who use *Harmony and Voice Leading* in music theory classes are well prepared for later studies in structural analysis.

As noted in the Preface to this volume, in the spring of 1999, musicians from around the world gathered at Queens College in New York City to celebrate the work of Carl Schachter, who had recently retired from Queens. One important reason (among many) why so many people attended and participated in this event is summarized by one word—influence. Carl's influence on the field of music theory is legendary. For over forty years his publications shaped our understanding of Schenker's work through clarification and amplification. His involvement in *Counterpoint in Composition* and *Harmony and Voice Leading* influenced and continues to influence the ways in which students and teachers teach and think about the fundamental characteristics of tonal music. His novel work in the field of rhythm, though based on incipient ideas by Schenker, ranks among the most profound and far-reaching theoretical notions developed in the second half of the twentieth century. His body of work is admired internationally for its musicality, depth, and originality.

---

[1]Heinrich Schenker, *Free Composition*, trans. and ed. Ernst Oster (New York: Longman, 1979).

[2]Edward Aldwell and Carl Schachter, *Harmony and Voice Leading* (San Diego: Harcourt Brace Jovanovich, 1978; 2nd ed., 1989; 3rd ed., 2002).

Another facet of Carl's influence may not be as immediately obvious to those who know of Carl primarily through his scholarly work. Also far-reaching is the inspiration of his *pedagogy*, his direct contact with students. Many became colleagues and continued in their own work the spirit and substance of his lifelong involvement with the work of Schenker. Some of these musicians were students in his undergraduate and graduate classes, and some were fortunate to have his guidance as a Ph.D. advisor. For others, Carl's tutelage and influence were manifest in private, one–on–one lessons. (This was a context that Schenker himself also favored; many of the details of Schenker's lessons were recorded in his "Lesson Books," which are discussed below). Still others were influenced as colleagues.

Although many of Carl's students have contributed ideas to the general body of Schenkerian thought, in the early 1990s we decided to continue the spirit of Carl's teaching by writing a book that would present in clear and logical form the foundation of Schenker's approach. In planning our project, we considered the historical development of Schenker's ideas, which we believe intrinsically suggests the basic premises of a sound pedagogical method.[3] In the following paragraphs we review some of the ideas that guided our work. Of course those ideas, like Carl's teaching and scholarship, involve a history that developed over a number of decades. We will, therefore, begin with several observations about the dissemination of Schenker's work.

*   *   *   *   *

Both before and after his death in 1935, Schenker's approach found a warm reception at the Mannes College of Music, and later at Queens College. One of Schenker's students, Hans Weisse, came to teach at Mannes in the 1930's, as did Felix Salzer, who arrived from Vienna in the 1940's. Salzer's book *Structural Hearing*, the first introduction to Schenkerian analysis, introduced Schenker's ideas to this country and also became well known abroad.[4] Though there were some differences between Salzer's and Schenker's approach, as well as that of some other students of Schenker, *Structural Hearing* embodied the deep musicality and refinement of the Viennese musical tradition.

Carl Schachter studied with Salzer while a student at Mannes and began to teach at the school immediately after his graduation. The two became close friends and colleagues, and later collaborated in writing the highly regarded book *Counterpoint in Composition*. Salzer also established *The Music Forum*, collaborating with William Mitchell and later with Carl Schachter. This beautifully produced series of collected articles in six volumes introduced a wide variety of excellent analytical and theoretical

[3]Allen Cadwallader and David Gagné, *Analysis of Tonal Music: A Schenkerian Approach* (Oxford and New York: Oxford University Press, 1998). In the Preface we dedicate our project to Carl, which reflects his spirit and inspiration.
[4]Felix Salzer, *Structural Hearing*, 2 vols. (New York: Dover, 1952).

articles, including many translations and studies of Schenkerian topics. The high standard it set has influenced a number of subsequent publications.

Saul Novack also studied with Felix Salzer in the late 1940's, and joined the Queens College music faculty several years later. A man of remarkable vision, he foresaw the possibility of making Queens College a center for Schenkerian studies. Felix Salzer eventually joined this endeavor and later the faculty of the City University Graduate Center when it was established. Charles Burkhart, who came to teach at Queens in the 1960's, also studied with Salzer. Carl Schachter came to teach at Queens and the Graduate Center in 1971, where he remained until his retirement in 1996.

The spirit of Carl's teaching has grown out of this lineage. Many of Carl's particular personal and professional qualities, that have inspired so much affection in his students, colleagues, and friends, are unique. But he is also part of an extraordinary tradition at Queens College, the Graduate Center, and the Mannes College of Music, that has been transmitted from Schenker through his students. It is that tradition that sets the backdrop for our work.

*　　*　　*　　*　　*

The cues we followed in developing our approach derive from the entire breadth of Schenker's work, both in published and unpublished form. Many of Schenker's papers and notes were posthumously collected by Ernest Oster, who in turn donated them to the New York Public Library. After the Oster Collection was opened to the public, it became apparent how vast were the unpublished materials not previously known to most scholars interested in Schenker's work. One such item of interest is the Brahms folder, which contains Schenker's unpublished analyses of Brahms's music. Also extremely revealing are his "Lesson Books," which resemble diaries and chronicle his teaching activities from approximately 1913–32. They comprise individually dated, detailed summaries of the lessons that he gave to various students, among them Anthony von Hoboken and Angi Elias. In these pages one marvels at the entries: the number of pieces discussed during the lesson times, the breadth and scope of Schenker's teaching. He guided his students through the existing literature on various compositions, and considered both theoretical and performance issues. One also finds comments on performances by famous artists; it is possible that he accompanied his students to concerts and later discussed the performances during the lesson times.

One fascinating aspect of the Lesson Books is that they often reflect Schenker's developing ideas. In the mid teens, the focus of lessons in analysis with his students includes form and harmonic and contrapuntal detail, precisely the kinds of topics explored in the critical studies of Beethoven's late piano sonatas published by Schenker during the years 1913–15.

Around 1920, the entries reveal a more sophisticated understanding of the compositional process. Schenker begins to discuss with his students the presence of *Urlinien*, not yet referring to the deepest structural line of a piece, but rather to multiple ascending and descending stepwise lines residing just beneath the surface of musical fabrics. From these ideas we derived the strategy of introducing the concept of "structural melody" early in the book, using, for example, themes from variations sets to illustrate how simpler, conceptually prior lines lie beneath elaborate figuration. Later entries in the Lesson Books continue to reflect the development of Schenker's ideas. In several situations, he mentions students by name, and evaluates the progress of their work. As before, the nature of the issues he mentions often reflects the ideas he was preparing for publication.

One of the first and most devoted students was Angi Elias, who in Schenker's later years served as his assistant and prepared numerous final copies of his fully developed analyses, perhaps for publication. We know that in October of 1926 Elias began to study Brahms's B minor Intermezzo with Schenker. The beautiful surviving sketch—resembling the graphs in the first and second volumes of *Meisterwerk*—is most likely the result of work done under Schenker's close supervision.[5]

What marvelous music lessons these must have been! Lessons in theory and analysis, to be sure, but critical analysis in the broadest possible sense. The Lesson Books offer an entirely different view of Schenker as a master teacher, one who diligently guided the training of those fortunate to study with him. The Lesson Books, of course, reflect the time-honored pedagogical tradition of the apprentice method, in which ideas are transmitted on a one–to–one basis from teacher to student. But they remind us of another facet of Schenker and his work, which can inform our teaching of his approach to tonal music. Schenker arrived at his broad theoretical postulates through the empirical analyses of countless compositions. We can describe this process as a series of insights, indeed of *revelations*; and it is clear from the many entries in his Lesson Books that his students were a privileged audience, accompanying him in his quest to elaborate the principles of tonal masterworks.

As Schenker's ideas have gained increasing prominence over the last two decades, a number of pedagogical approaches have emerged. Frequently the orientation is theoretical; many courses rely primarily on the reading of articles. But the essence of Schenker's method as conveyed to his students is that the theory grows out of the music, and always relates back to it. Therefore we believe that students should learn the principles of musical analysis from the study of actual compositions, rather than being presented with a theory as a series of facts or axioms that are then demonstrated in musical examples.

As mentioned above, it occurred to us that introducing students to linear analysis by tracing Schenker's own development of his procedures provides an excellent model for teaching. Thus it is possible to guide students through the same process of revelation that Schenker and his students experienced during the early part of this century, whether in the private studio or in the classroom. We shall now discuss some specific topics we believe are fundamental to an introductory course in Schenkerian analysis.

---

[5]For more on Angi Elias, see Allen Cadwallader and William Pastille, "Schenker's Unpublished Work on the Music of Johannes Brahms," *Schenker Studies 2*, ed. Carl Schachter and Hedi Siegel (Cambridge: Cambridge University Press, 1999), pp. 26–46. The Brahms sketch from the Oster collection is Kosovsky file 34/item 11.

Consider, for example, the notion of structural melody alluded to previously. In our view, this is an ideal point of departure from which to elaborate Schenker' ideas. The term "melody," of course, is used in a variety of different ways. We are referring to the upper part of an *Aussensatz*, or outer-voice structural framework. For Schenker, the study of melody in all its aspects was a central concern throughout his career. The vast treatise on counterpoint, the first volume of which appeared in 1910, is evidence for this observation, and the mature ideas of *Free Composition* reflect a lifelong interest in studying the principles of melody and counterpoint.

Those familiar with the development of his work may also recall that in the years before the second volume of Counterpoint, Schenker was applying the principles of *melodic fluency* to the study of compositions. As William Pastille has commented, Schenker viewed melodic fluency as a principle of "shaping melodic lines so that successions of large leaps are avoided."[6] In other words, melodic fluency refers to lines comprised essentially of steps, with skips carefully controlled. Pastille also notes that knowledge of the principles of melodic fluency provides: (1) the ability to uncover long-range melodic motions; and (2) the ability to discern underlying contrapuntal patterns. Indeed, Schenker did begin to reveal long-range motions in his analyses at this time. In his 1920 critical edition of Beethoven's Piano Sonata, Op. 101, Schenker uses the term *Urlinie*, not as in his later writings, but to designate ascending and descending lines that lie at the surface and foreground levels of musical fabrics. The logical next step for Schenker was the discovery of the *Urlinie* as we know it today.

This process of revelation provides an excellent model for teaching. After introducing the principles of bass-line prolongation and melodic fluency, the concept of the *Urlinie* can be effectively developed through the study of concise models such as a theme with one or more variations. Example 1, the first phrase of the theme and first variation from Beethoven's set on "God Save the King," serves to illustrate.

Example 1. Beethoven, Theme and Variation from "God Save the King."

[6]William Pastille, "The Development of the *Ursatz* in Schenker's Published Works," *Trends in Schenkerian Research*, ed. Allen Cadwallader (New York: Schirmer Books, 1990), pp. 71–85.

Notice first the character of the theme. The tune is melodically fluent and in many ways resembles the lines of strict counterpoint. We point out to our students the predominance of stepwise motion, with the two skips in the phrase—one preceding and one following the climax—serving to add variety and shape to the line as it rises and falls to the cadence. In the variation the theme recedes, as it were, into the musical fabric, becoming the underlying framework of the note–by–note surface line. The framework is embellished through elements of diminution studied progressively in strict counterpoint: passing and neighboring tones, and consonant skips. This introduces the concept that stepwise underlying associations exist between nonadjacent tones. It also foreshadows the notion of structural levels.

Like themes of variation sets, folk tunes are ideally suited for the beginning stages of analysis. In Example 2 we provide a partial "block chord" analysis of the traditional melody known as the "Ashgrove," a strategy we use to introduce the notion of polyphonic melody.

Example 2. "Ashgrove."

Notice in the example that the top voice of the chordal analysis reveals an embedded stepwise motion through a fifth, followed by another "attempt" at a fifth that is interrupted before the Da Capo. Considerable tension is accumulated at this formal juncture; the music awaits continuation and completion, which are achieved only at the end of the repetition of the first phrase. Indirectly, the technique of interruption is introduced, though not necessarily in a formal manner at this time. And we are only one step away from discovering the *Urlinie* of the complete composition. Thus the theoretical construct does not direct analysis as a given premise, but is discovered by students as they, like Schenker before them, delve beneath the surface of musical compositions.

The same process of revelation, with continued emphasis on diminution and melodic fluency, can lead students to discover some of the essential characteristics of harmonic structure, such as the distinction between chord and harmony. Example 3 shows two phrases from Bach's chorale, "Jesu, Jesu, du bist mein." After identifying consonant skips, passing and neighboring tones, most students can recognize that the same of elements of diminution that shape the upper voice also contribute to the "melody" of the bass, to successions of chords organized by broader harmonic principles. Some chords arise through neighbor motion, while others through passing tones or arpeggiations. In this manner students are led step by step to an awareness of Schenker's notion of harmonic *Stufen*.

Example 3. J.S. Bach, "Jesu, Jesu, du bist mein."

The previous topics are introductory and belong to the first part of a one-semester course in Schenkerian analysis. As students progress, we find that they become more interested in *theoretical* principles as they continue to analyze many pieces. We have found a strategy that is particularly useful in the final week or so of a one-semester course, one that fosters a deeper understanding of theoretical aspects of Schenker's work encountered during the semester.

The strategy involves the consideration of *alternative readings*. For experienced Schenkerians, the notion of the plausible alternative is familiar territory. Beginning students, however, can also benefit from considering various interpretations. One benefit is that they realize that analysis should not be thought of or approached as a hunt for some singular, fixed middleground pattern that lies beneath the surface, waiting to be "discovered" (and extracted) like some buried artifact. Schenker is flexible in the ways he applies his principles, a flexibility that arises because of the differing circumstances of different compositions. Students should be encouraged to adopt this perspective within reasonable boundaries. Furthermore, students are fond of comparisons, and often vigorously debate the merits of their interpretations as they consider the pros and cons of other readings in the class. And they are gratified to discover that they can participate with Schenker's own work.

This aspect of analysis can be introduced by using his analysis of the brief Aria by Handel that Brahms later used for his famous set of variations (Example 4a). We recommend that the students be informed of his reading only *after* they have completed their own, and have discussed it and other readings in class. In Example 4b we present an adaptation of Schenker's published graph, followed by an alternative reading in Example 4c.

Example 4. Handel's Aria in B♭.
   a) Music

   b) Schenker's analysis from $\hat{5}$ as the primary tone (adaptation)

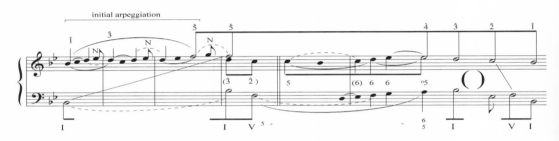

   c) Alternative analysis from $\hat{3}$ as the primary tone

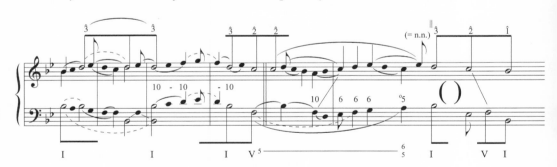

Experienced readers will immediately notice that the choice of the primary tone differs in these two interpretations. The strong emphasis and support of scale-degree 3 makes Example 4c the simplest and most intuitive interpretation, and the one that most students come to on their own in our experience. Nevertheless, eventually Schenker's uninterrupted 5-line interpretation is generally perceived as more subtle and elegant, with its long-range viewpoint and lesser degree of emphasis of scale-degree 3.[7]

[7]In teaching Schenkerian analysis, it is often best to present initially the most straightforward and intuitive representation, even though other (sometimes esoteric) readings might ultimately be preferred. Inexperienced students usually want to apply Schenker's principles in rigid and fixed ways, and can become frustrated if they feel (*cont.*)

On the other hand, Example 4c illustrates the many third motives (bars 1–4), which are significant in the diminution of the upper voice in both interpretations. After examining various interpretations, including Schenker's and ours, the students often raise certain theoretical issues; the one most likely to arise initially is the question of "5 versus 3," which every Schenkerian has considered.[8] Yet other more penetrating issues are illuminated in this comparison, which will promote a more comprehensive view of Schenker's approach as the course nears completion.

In Schenker's reading (Example 4b), the notion of the *unsupported stretch* $\hat{5}$–$\hat{4}$–$\hat{3}$ presents itself immediately. Several questions arise: What is the unsupported stretch and what did Schenker have to say about it in terms of its problematic character in the *Urlinie*? As a passing tone, how is $\hat{4}$ different from $\hat{2}$, and what harmonic possibilities does he suggest for the support of $\hat{4}$ at levels below the background? How does one justify Schenker's reading of a fleeting structural $\hat{4}$ that appears over the V6/5 chord at the end of the brief middle section? The instructor should take time to explain that the bass (bars 5–6) begins to move and unfold the dominant scale-step (from f to a) *before* structural $\hat{4}$ appears in the upper voice (as the goal of motion from an inner voice). In a middleground representation, $\hat{4}$ would appear over V, and thus exist as a dissonant passing tone in the *Urlinie*.[9] Consideration of questions such as these prepares the students not only for additional work in analysis, but also for the esoteric issues of *Free Composition*, sections of which can now be introduced.

In the analysis presented in Example 4c, the surface diminution must be interpreted somewhat differently, as least in terms of the level at which a tone or succession of tones resides. In particular, scale-degree 5 (f[2]) in the first section is not considered, in this analysis, as a tone of the *Urlinie*, but rather as a tone superposed from an inner voice and achieved through a third-progression. This interpretation illustrates the important point that brief lower-level lines frequently unfold *above* the tones of the *Urlinie*. One ramification in this case is that the primary tone of the *Urlinie* is achieved quickly in the first bar, as opposed to Schenker's reading of a relatively lengthy *initial arpeggiation* that establishes $\hat{5}$ in bar 3.

Instructors should also encourage students to discuss (in Schenker's analysis) the issue of the support of $\hat{5}$, appearing as it does over a I[6] and as the goal of a 10–10–10 surface motion. The tones of the *Urlinie* are often found in "weak" metrical and harmonic contexts at lower levels, yet arise

---

that a reading somehow departs from what they perceive as the "obvious." The flexibility they need to develop (as mentioned above) comes with experience; we believe a certain measure of consistency should be maintained for a period of time, unless it results in awkward and incorrect applications of Schenker's principles.

[8]In his unpublished work, for example, Schenker often inserts the designation "5 oder 3" in his graphs.

[9]Schenker does not show a V supporting $\hat{4}$ in Figure 16 of *Free Composition*. The V in the I–V–I support of $\hat{5}$–$\hat{4}$–$\hat{3}$, however, would disappear at the background level in favor of a prolonged tonic, yielding the formation shown in Figure 16,5 (the third pattern). In short, $\hat{5}$–$\hat{4}$–$\hat{3}$ unfolds over tonic harmony.

through normalization at deeper levels over root-position (and metrically strong) *Stufen*. One can easily make this point in this example, as well as the observation that the structural levels of a composition unfold simultaneously. Students rarely have difficulty accepting that structural $\hat{5}$ is "present" at deep levels from the very beginning of the piece, though at lower levels it is delayed as the harmonic bass develops through its own diminution.

Not to be found in Schenker's reading, but clearly present in Example 4c, is the common middleground pattern that underlies the brief middle section. Before the double bar, 3 moves to 2 over V, which is prolonged through the process V $^{5-7}$. The expansion of the first branch of an interruption is discussed in depth by Schenker and is for him a fundamental compositional technique. In *Free Composition* he explicitly attributes the development of form and tonal expansion to this procedure.[10] Hence, the main structural difference between the readings is that scale-degree 4 (E♭, bar 6) in the second graph does not belong to the *Urlinie*, but is the 7th of V^7, transferred from an inner voice above structural $\hat{2}$. This is an excellent example in which to discuss Schenker's "= n.n." designation, which he uses to indicate how an inner-voice passing tone, through transfer of register, acquires the appearance of a neighbor note to the primary tone of the first branch.[11] This "securing of the 7th" is often associated with the prolongation of the dominant and the development of formal sections.

On the basis of the pedagogical examples illustrated here, the reader can recognize many other issues for discussion. We do not advocate this approach merely to demonstrate how one arrives at a "correct" reading, when two (or perhaps even more) are plausible.[12] Instead, the point is that the comparison of two interpretations often highlights in specific pieces some of the more abstract analytical and theoretical issues associated with Schenker's work.

*   *   *   *   *

[10]At this point it is useful to discuss Figures 21 and 23 from *Free Composition*, and to review similar pieces studied during the course of the semester. As with Schenker's reading, the instructor will need to explain carefully the progression from the surface of the Aria to the deeper middleground levels, as shown in the two synoptic diagrams of Example 4c. One can mention (or review) that moving from one level to another involves the transformation processes of composing-out (*Auskomponierung*).

[11]This example of the n.n. involves additional explanation. Scale-degree 4 of this common middleground pattern (E♭ in this case) "resolves" to the primary tone $\hat{3}$ of the second branch (after the interruption) only in a limited sense. In general, the voice leading of the second branch, at deeper levels, does not grow out of that of the first branch. At the surface and foreground, however, scale-degree 4 does resolve down by step to $\hat{3}$ of the second branch, in effect serving as a kind of lower-level bridge. At the surface, therefore, the transferred seventh of the prolonged dominant sounds and functions as an upper neighbor to the reestablished primary tone $\hat{3}$.

[12]We inform our students that alternative readings are often possible, though one can usually arrive at a preferred reading (with this relatively simple example, both may be regarded as valid).

Carl Schachter's analytical view of a piece always began with an intense interest, even passion, for the work simply as music. His approach in this regard no doubt owes much to the inspiration of his teacher, Felix Salzer. This love of music awakens in his students new modes of understanding and appreciation. Like Salzer and Schachter, Queens faculty members Saul Novack and Charles Burkhart have conveyed this spirit in their teaching, a spirit that has guided us in our own approach to Schenker pedagogy.

These observations and examples express the spirit of our philosophy in the teaching of Schenker's ideas. We seek to guide our students in the process of revelation experienced by Schenker and his students almost 75 years ago. We would also suggest that Schenker's legacy compels us to consider that analysis is similar in spirit to performance. As William Benjamin has noted, "What Schenker asks us to do is to *compose* simple pieces which may intuitively be heard to underlie pieces from the tonal repertory. . . . His theory provides a rich array of techniques which allow for the rational reconstruction of the piece being 'analyzed.'"[13] We would argue that such a reconstruction by Schenker is a kind of performance. When we are successful in conveying this spirit in the techniques and strategies we use to teach Schenker's ideas, then our students can indeed experience the aural "flights of fancy" he attributed to the great composers.

---

[13]William E. Benjamin, "Schenker's Theory and the Future of Music," *Journal of Music Theory* 25/1 (Spring 1981), p. 159.

Prolongational and Hierarchical Structures in 18th-Century Theory

Joel Lester

History used to be simpler. You categorized historical issues according to contemporary perspectives of the preferred and denigrated positions, and you chronicled the events of a previous era in terms of the desired contemporary position.

Consider eighteenth-century theories of harmony and counterpoint. For much of the twentieth century, conventional wisdom held that the eighteenth century offered two basic approaches: theories of thoroughbass and counterpoint that taught voice leading in a manner leading to what might be called enlightened twentieth-century theory, and theories of harmony in which chords were isolated from their context, leading to nineteenth-century harmony texts and Riemannian theory. All this seemed obvious. Schenker himself pointed to Fuxian species counterpoint and thoroughbass as formulated by Carl Philipp Emanuel Bach as primary influences on his development, and he railed against Rameauian harmonic theories as the antithesis of his approach.[1]

As heartwarming as such perspectives may be to those who wish to align themselves with this or that historical figure, histories of this sort are inherently unreliable if their goal is to understand how eighteenth-century musicians conceived of harmonic and voice-leading structures. Viewing eighteenth-century theory through a twentieth-century lens anachronistically imposes twentieth-century theoretical polarizations onto eighteenth-century theory. Some parallels linking Schenkerian theory to Fuxian species counterpoint and some aspects of thoroughbass emerge overemphasized. And some even more striking parallels between Schenkerian thinking and a wide range of eighteenth-century theoretical traditions are ignored entirely.

Several factors make twentieth-century perspectives unequal to the task of understanding eighteenth-century antecedents to Schenkerian thinking. First, counterpoint, thoroughbass, and harmony are insufficient to describe the wealth of eighteenth-century theorizing about pitch structures. Each tradition

---

[1]Schenker argued this position most vociferously in "Rameau oder Beethoven: Erstarrung oder geistiges Leben in der Musik?" in *Das Meisterwerk in der Musik* 3 (Munich: Drei Masken Verlag, 1930), pp. 9–24; English translation by Ian Bent in *The Masterwork of Music* 3 (Cambridge: Cambridge University Press, 1997), pp. 1–9. William Mitchell penned a much more temperate presentation of this historical perspective position in "Chord and Context in Eighteenth-Century Theory," *Journal of the American Musicological Society* 16 (1963), pp. 221–39. Harald Krebs places this position in historical perspective in "Schenker's Changing View of Rameau: A Comparison of Remarks in *Harmony*, *Counterpoint*, and 'Rameau or Beethoven?'," *Theoria* 3 (1988), pp. 59–72.

was itself multifaceted. "Counterpoint" denoted species and fugue for Johann Joseph Fux (1660–1740), chord construction for Friderich Erhard Niedt (c.1674–1708), the study of intervals, voice leading, and harmony for Charles Masson (fl. late 17th century), Giovanni Maria Bononcini (1642–1678), and Johann Mattheson (1681–1764), activating a harmonic texture for Johann Philipp Kirnberger (1721–83), and a method of chordal harmonization for Heinrich Christoph Koch (1749–1816).[2] Notions of "thoroughbass" were just as diverse. Some thoroughbass writers taught harmonies by rote, others explained harmonies in terms of their voice leading, and still others applied the concepts of Rameauian harmony. Other approaches to composition— especially studies of *galant* melody by Joseph Riepel (1709–82)—sidestepped explicit discussions of counterpoint, thoroughbass, and harmony altogether, focusing instead on melodic articulation while assuming harmonic and voice-leading underpinnings that drew upon several traditions.

Second, points of agreement and disagreement among the theoretical traditions cut across any attempts to posit a School-of-Thoroughbass-and-Counterpoint-That-Teaches-Voice-Leading versus a School-of-Harmony-That-Teaches-Chords-Isolated-From-Context. For instance, while teaching species counterpoint, Fux explains triadic inversions, and he occasionally explains that a given chord belongs on a given solmization syllable, reflecting seventeenth-century harmonic theories.[3] Within harmonic theory, Jean-Philippe Rameau (1683–1764) drew upon knowledge common to earlier thoroughbass and contrapuntal theorists when he discussed chord inversions, chord roots, cadences as directed motion, evaded cadences as a source of continuity, placement of chords on specific scale degrees, and many other matters.[4]

Third, proponents of species counterpoint and thoroughbass disagreed on many basics. When Fux, in the prefatory remarks in *Gradus*, cautions students embarking on the study of species counterpoint about the long hard study ahead of them, he not only offers a platitudinous remonstrance about study habits—he also answers thoroughbass manuals whose title pages commonly promised mastery of composition in a few months.[5] Indeed, Fux's decision to

---

[2]More detailed discussions on these and other theorists and traditions appear in Joel Lester, *Compositional Theory in the Eighteenth Century* (Cambridge: Harvard University Press, 1992). This essay cites individual treatises and passages only in more specific discussions.

[3]Johann Joseph Fux, *Gradus ad parnassum* (Vienna: Johann Peter van Ghelen, 1725); facsimile editions in *Fux Sämtliche Werke*, ed. Alfred Mann (Kassel: Bärenreiter, 1967), vii/I, and (New York: Broude, 1974). German translation by Lorenz Mizler (Leipzig: Johann Heinrich Heinsius, 1742); facsimile edition (Hildesheim: Georg Olms, 1974). English translation of the portion on species counterpoint in Alfred Mann, *Steps to Parnassus* (New York: W. W. Norton, 1943), reissued with new preface and same pagination as *The Study of Counterpoint* (New York: W. W. Norton, 1965). All references below are to Mann's translations. Fux's discussion of triads appears at the beginning of the discussion of three-part counterpoint in first species, pp. 71ff. On pp. 73–74, Fux invokes a common seventeenth-century recommendation that a chord of the sixth should appear over *mi* in the bass (a rule that both prevents a diminished triad over the leading tone of a key and also urges I^6 instead of III over scale-degree $\hat{3}$ in major keys.

[4]Lester, *Compositional Theory in the Eighteenth Century*, Chapters 4 and 5. Thomas Christensen, *Rameau and Musical Thought in the Enlightenment* (Cambridge: Cambridge University Press, 1993).

[5] *The Study of Counterpoint*, p. 19.

publish *Gradus* may well have stemmed from his distaste for thoroughbass treatises. From the other side, Carl Philipp Emanuel Bach (1714–88), known as a theorist for his work on thoroughbass, stresses how his father "omitted all the dry species of counterpoint that are given in Fux and others. His [Johann Sebastian Bach's] pupils had to begin their studies by learning pure four-part thoroughbass."[6] In brief, Fux and C.P.E. Bach recognized no natural affinity between the bases of species counterpoint and thoroughbass.

Fourth, many (if not most) eighteenth-century musicians felt that their knowledge derived from many theoretical traditions, not just one. Leopold Mozart (1719–87) perhaps expressed it best in a June 11, 1778 letter to his son citing C.P.E. Bach, Jean le Rond d'Alembert (1717–83), Fux, Friedrich Wilhelm Marpurg (1718–95), Mattheson, Rameau, Riepel, Johann Adolphe Scheibe (1708–76), Meinrad Spiess (1683–1761), and Pier Francesco Tosi (c.1653–1732) as sources of "sound stuff."[7] Leopold's list sports an extraordinary range of approaches. Meinrad Spiess's *Tractatus musicus compositorio-practicus* supports retention of the old church modes (as does Fux's *Gradus*) for both ecclesiastical and secular music.[8] Fux presented species counterpoint and fugue. Marpurg espoused his own version of Rameau's harmonic theories.[9] Riepel espouses the teaching of composition in the latest style beginning with melodic articulation, not thoroughbass.[10]

Because eighteenth-century musicians viewed the theoretical traditions of their time differently than do theorists of the twentieth century, eighteenth-century precedents for modern theoretical notions may not always appear where we expect them if we view the traditions solely from twentieth-century perspectives. Although Schenker was strongly influenced by various aspects of eighteenth-century counterpoint and thoroughbass, looking solely at these approaches for precedents to his ideas overemphasizes the extent to which they reflected Schenkerian thought within the eighteenth century and overlooks significantly more important aspects of hierarchical and prolongational thinking elsewhere.

---

[6]From a letter by C.P.E. Bach to Nikolaus Forkel, English translation in Hans T. David and Arthur Mendel, *The Bach Reader* (New York: W. W. Norton, 1945, 1966), p. 111.

[7]English translation in Emily Anderson, *The Letters of Mozart and His Family*, 2nd ed. (New York: St. Martin's Press, 1966), pp. 548–49.

[8]Spiess, *Tractatus* (Augsburg: Johann Jacob Lotters seel. Erben, 1745; 1746). Fux argued vehemently with Mattheson in the 1710s in favor of the traditional modes over the major-minor keys in a letter exchange published by Mattheson in *Criticae musicae, 2* (Hamburg: Thomas von Wierings Erben, 1725); facsimile edition (Amsterdam: Frits Knuf, 1964); English translation in Joel Lester, "The Fux-Mattheson Correspondence: An Annotated Translation," *Current Musicology* 24 (1977), pp. 37–62.

[9]Marpurg also translated into German the popularization of some aspects of Rameau's theories published by the French mathematician D'Alembert in *Elemens de musique, théorique et pratique, suivant les principes de bar Rameau* (Paris: David l'aîné, Le Breton, Durand, 1752; later editions in 1759, 1762, 1766, 1772, 1779); German translation by Marpurg as *Systematische Einleitung in die musicalische Setzkunst, nach den Lehrsätzen des Herrn Rameau* (Leipzig: Breitkopf, 1757); facsimile ed. (Leipzig: Zentralantiquariat der DDR, 1980).

[10]Riepel, *Anfangsgründe zur musicalischen Setzkunst*, 5 vols. (Regensburg, Vienna, Augsburg, Frankfurt, Leipzig, 1752–68).

To us, species counterpoint inherently seems to contain notions of structural levels, prolongation of underlying sonorities, and diminutions. Passing tones and arpeggiations in second species, for instance, fill in a first-species frame. But there are good reasons to argue that this was not the way eighteenth-century musicians, including Fux himself, viewed species counterpoint. Some of these notions appeared more prominently in other theoretical traditions; others were barely present in *Gradus*.

Consider the notion of diminution. Fux does apply the notion of diminution, but only when he explains the origin of a few simple dissonance patterns. He does not build upon that insight in the actual composition of species counterpoint, and his formulation of that insight is in fact quite limited in relation to presentations by his contemporaries and predecessors. Specifically, Fux neither suggests nor implies that when composing a counterpoint exercise, students using those dissonance patterns should add them to a pre-existent frame. When composing a second-species exercises, for instance, he instructs the student to compose that second-species exercise, not to compose a first-species exercise and then fill it in with consonant and dissonant diminutions. In fact, Fux disparaged such a diminutional procedure as the bane of thoroughbass approaches to composition, where beginners learned just to add diminutions to simpler thoroughbass realizations (a process described most comprehensively by Niedt, as discussed below). For Fux, learning counterpoint meant applying voice-leading possibilities, not elaborating underlying structures.

In addition, Fux applies diminution solely to a few very simple patterns that had been explained in like manner for generations prior to the publication of *Gradus*. His application of diminution as an explanation for dissonances is also far more restrictive than what appears widely in the works of other theorists writing even before Fux was born. For instance, Fux describes second-species passing tones as diminutions "filling out the space between two notes that are a third distant from each other."[11] Such explanations were hardly new. Giovanni Maria Artusi (c.1540–1613) reduced much more complex dissonances to underlying patterns around 1600 while demonstrating what he deemed the faulty basis of Claudio Monteverdi's compositions in the new *seconda prattica*.[12] Likewise, Christoph Bernhard (1628–92), a proponent of the *seconda prattica* in the mid-seventeenth century, and Johann David Heinichen (1683–1729), in his explanations for the dissonances characterizing

[11]*The Study of Counterpoint,* p. 41.

[12]Artusi, *L'Artusi, ovvero Delle imperfettioni della moderna musica* (Venice: Giacomo Vincenti, 1600); facsimile ed. (Bologna: Forni, 1968); partial English translation by in Oliver Strunk, *Source Readings in Music History* (New York: W. W. Norton, 1950), pp. 393–404. A comprehensive discussion of Artusi's polemical battle with Claudio and Giulio Cesare Monteverdi (the composer and his brother) appears in Claude Palisca, "The Artusi-Monteverdi Controversy," in *The Monteverdi Companion*, ed. Denis Arnold and Nigel Fortune (London: Faber and Faber, 1968), pp. 133–66.

[13]Bernard, *Tractatus compositionis augmentatus,* ms. c. 1655; English translation in Walter Hilse, "The Treatises of Christoph Bernhard," *Music Forum* Vol. 3 (New York: Columbia University Press, 1973), pp. 1–197. Heinichen, *Der GeneralBass in der Composition (cont.)*

Example 1. Johann David Heinichen, *Der General-Bass in der Composition* (1728), pp. 615–16.

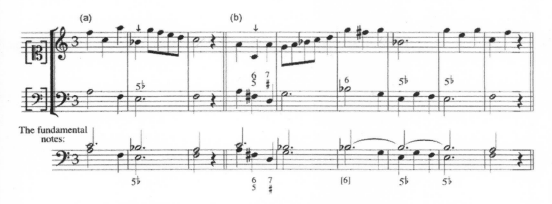

the latest "theatrical" music of his time, explained quite complex dissonances by demonstrating how they elaborated orderly underlying structures.[13]

Example 1 presents two of Heinichen's explanations of dissonances that are not treated according to the rules. In Example 1a, Heinichen shows how the dissonant B♭, approached and left by skip, passes from the linearly-adjacent C to an A only implied in the realization. In Example 1b, he shows how the dissonant C, also disjunct, is part of a dissonant harmony that remains unresolved until the next downbeat. For Heinichen, simple voice leading is the source of such jagged compositional surfaces.

These discussions far exceed Fux's use of diminution to explain complex voice leadings. Within the portion of *Gradus* that deals with species counterpoint, Fux uses such explanations solely to explain how passing tones, suspensions, and neighbors arise from consonant underlying structures. One might argue that Fux omits greater complexities from *Gradus* because more complex dissonances do not arise within the confines of species counterpoint. It is therefore instructive to turn to a later portion of *Gradus* that does not deal with the species approach. After teaching species counterpoint, the modes, and imitation and fugue—all at considerable length—Fux briefly discusses contemporaneous compositional styles, styles in which he himself composed operas and instrumental works.[14] In a manner similar in principle to Bernhard and Heinichen, Fux demonstrates how dissonances more complex than those of species counterpoint arise from *Figuren*. But whereas Bernhard and Heinichen introduced numerous quite complex dissonances in this manner,

(Dresden: the author, 1728); facsimile ed. (Hildesheim: Georg Olms, 1969). A discussion of Heinichen's treatment of theatrical dissonances (including an English translation of Heinichen's realization of the thoroughbass to an entire cantata by Alessandro Scarlatti) appears in George Buelow, *Thorough-Bass Accompaniment According to Johann David Heinichen* (Berkeley and Los Angeles: University of California Press, 1966); 2nd ed. (Ann Arbor: UMI Research Press, 1986).

[14]An English translation of this portion of *Gradus* appears in Joel Lester, *Between Modes and Keys: German Theory, 1592–1802* (Stuyvesant: Pendragon Press, 1989), Appendix 3. References below are to this translation.

Fux introduces only two relatively simple figures: *variation* (illustrated in Example 2) and *anticipation*. Concerning *variation* (in Example 2), he says that "variation departs from the common rules of counterpoint in that it proceeds from a consonance into a dissonance [marked with an asterisk in the example] and then from a dissonance into another dissonance [at the cross]." On the basis of these tepid dissonances, which he blames on singers who "were so little content with regular diminutions, and so fond of showing off the flexibility of their voice," Fux condemns singers for their "destruction of the harmony."[15]

Example 2. Fux, *Gradus ad parnassum* (1725), "variation."

That Fux avoided talking about the voice leading underlying complex dissonances is most apparent in his discussion of recitative. Instead of explaining how the dissonances in Example 3 might arise from underlying voice leading as Artusi, Bernhard, and Heinichen did in comparable situations, Fux tacitly admits his inability to explain these dissonances at all, noting that "the instrumental chords, which consist mostly of dissonances, depart from all the rules of counterpoint." They are "considered good according to the nature of recitative . . . In this style one should pay less attention to the harmonies than to the expression of the meaning of the words."[16] He simply teaches these dissonances by rote.

In brief, Fux applied diminutions so much more restrictively than earlier and contemporary theorists that it is unlikely eighteenth-century musicians turned to either *Gradus* or the species-counterpoint tradition it signally espoused for information on how complex motions arise within a voice-leading frame.[17] By contrast, when thoroughbass was used as an avenue to

[15]Ibid., p. 188.

[16]Ibid., pp. 204–9.

[17]William Clemmons, in "Johann Joseph Fux's *Gradus ad parnassum* and the Traditions of Seventeenth-Century Contrapuntal Pedagogy" (Ph.D. diss., CUNY, 2000), argues that Fux's major success in *Gradus* was to organize various long-standing strands of contrapuntal pedagogy with such success that species counterpoint effectively replaced those other traditions.

[18]Niedt's *Musicalische Handleitung* was published in three volumes: Vol. 1, *Handelt vom General-Bass* (Hamburg: Nicolaus Spieringk, 1700); 2nd ed. (Hamburg: Benjamin Schiller, 1710). Vol. 2, *Handleitung zur Variation, wie man den General-Bass und darüber gesetzte Zahlen variiren, artige Inventiones machen, und aus einen schlechten General-Bass Praeludia, Ciaconnen . . . leichtlich verfertigen können* (Hamburg: Benjamin Schiller, 1706); 2nd ed., ed. Johann Mattheson (Hamburg: Benjamin Schillers Wittwe & Johann Christoph Keller, 1721). Vol. 3, *Handlend vom Contra-Punct*, ed. Johann Mattheson (Hamburg: Benjamin Schillers Erben, 1717). The last edition of each volume appears in facsimile (Buren: Frits Knuf, 1976) and in English translation by Pamela Poulin and Irmgard Taylor as *The Musical Guide* (Oxford: Oxford University Press, 1988). All references here are to the last edition of each volume.

Example 3. Fux, *Gradus ad parnassum* (1725).

composition, diminution techniques lay at the core of the approach. The exemplary instance is the *Musicalische Handleitung* (1700–21) of Friderich Erhard Niedt.[18] Niedt first teaches how to realize a thoroughbass with no elaborations (Vol. 1). He then lists dozens of diminutions for every ascending and descending interval and applies these patterns to elaborate basses, melodies, multi-voice right-hand parts, and eventually full textures with repetitions and even varied dynamics (Vol. 2), as Example 4 illustrates.

Niedt then composes a seventeen-movement suite from a single thoroughbass. Example 5 shows the opening of the original bass and the beginnings of several derived movements. In addition to the diminution techniques he discusses earlier, other techniques are implicit, such as chordal arpeggiations (which imply that he recognized the functional equivalence of chordal inversions) and abbreviated or expanded progressions (which imply

Example 4. Niedt, *Musicalische Handleitung*, Vol. 2 (1721), Chapter 3, § 1 and 4, Chapter 6, § 8.

Example 5. Niedt, *Musicalische Handleitung*, Vol. 2 (1721), Chapter 12, § 1, 2, 9, 12.

that he regarded the chords and their progressions as potential structural frames for elaboration). The harmonic outline remains the same from dance to dance, but what we would call the passing chords are variable. Soprano lines are chosen from among the various voicing possibilities for the individual harmonies.

Niedt's approach to composition was far from new. In 1612, Johannes Lippius (1585–1612) had suggested composing by taking a series of root-position triads and elaborating it with what he called ornaments of pitch (including triadic inversions, running passages, additional voices, and the like), ornaments of duration (changing the rhythms), and ornaments of punctuation (or cadences), as well as repetition and imitation.[19]

Other aspects of the thoroughbass tradition provide further insights into the hierarchical status of harmonies. Although thoroughbass generally deals with the immediate succession of verticalities, there are occasional instances where thoroughbass writers treat larger contexts, showing that at least some thoroughbass theorists conceptualized the difference between fundamental harmonies and passing chords. Concerning Example 6, for instance, Heinichen shows how several harmonies can fulfill a single structural role. This passage appears in his demonstration of how to realize the unfigured bass to a secular cantata by Alessandro Scarlatti. In the illustrated progression, Heinichen first suggests using chords that commonly occur on given scale steps. He explains that C as tonic gets a triad, and B as leading tone gets a 6–chord. A, as scale-step 6̂, could (he says) support a triad. But, as Heinichen writes, "an experienced accompanist would prefer to give this A a major 6th, since the two bass notes C and B have preceded . . . In a major scale, if a bass descends stepwise by a fourth, the second bass note normally has a sixth and the third bass note has a major sixth. The reason is that *this progression forms a half cadence* with the fifth degree of the scale and requires the major sixth as leading tone [of the fifth degree] over the third note. Even though the half cadence in our example is broken off after the A, and in place of the final G an F♯ chord with a flat seventh is taken, this latter chord is only an inversion of the preceding chord whose resolution to G follows."[20] This remarkable passage straightforwardly explains that a four-bar prolongation with five consonant and dissonant chords is but an extended half cadence with diatonic and chromatic harmonies filling in the motion between the first and last chords,

[19]Lippius, *Synopsis musicae novae* (Strassburg: Karl Kieffer, 1612), fols. H1ʳ–H6ᵛ; English translation by Benito V. Rivera as *Synopsis of New Music* (Colorado Springs: Colorado College Music Press, 1977), pp. 48–53.
[20]Heinichen, *Der Generalbass*, 802–3; Buelow, *Thorough-bass Accompaniment According to Johann David Heinichen*, pp. 234–5.

Example 6. Heinichen, *Der General-Bass in der Composition* (1728), pp. 802–3.

Example 7. Rameau, *Generation harmonique* (1737), Example 28.

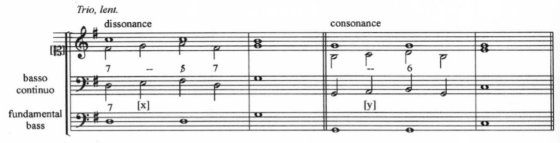

and with one of the harmonies prolonged by inversion. Heinichen's approach here—finding a simpler substructure—is similar to how he explains complex dissonances, confirming that such thinking was an integral part of his perspective on music.

Passages like this demonstrate that the notion of passing chords, whose origin has been attributed to the writings of Kirnberger in the 1770s, is actually quite widespread during the early part of the eighteenth century. In fact, Kirnberger's notion of passing chords is quite restricted. He speaks only of passing tones against sustained notes in the bass or melody, an instance of passing "harmonies" that was routinely explained in many thoroughbass and harmony treatises published decades earlier.[21] In 1737, for instance, Rameau illustrated the progression shown in Example 7—virtually identical to Kirnberger's illustration of passing chords.[22] Rameau explains that chord *X* is passing since it does not resolve the preceding seventh chord; chord *Y* is passing since its seventh (the top-voice A) is not resolved; these "foreign sounds never participate in the source of the harmony . . . [and] that other

[21]Kirnberger, *Die Kunst des reinen Satzes*, Vol. 1, rev. ed. (Berlin: Heinrich August Rottmann, 1776); facsimile ed. (Hildesheim: Georg Olms, 1968), pp. 50–51, p. 86. English translation by David Beach and Jürgen Thym as *The Art of Strict Musical Composition by Johann Philipp Kirnberger* (New Haven: Yale University Press, 1982), pp. 72–3, p. 104.

[22]Rameau, *Generation harmonique* (Paris: Prault fils, 1737), Example 28; facsimile ed. in *The Complete Theoretical Writings of Jean-Philippe Rameau*, ed. Erwin Jacobi (n.p.: American Institute of Musicology, 1967–72), Vol. 3.

[23]Rameau, *Generation harmonique*, pp. 185–6. "n'est qu'un moien d'en suspendre l'effet . . . & de le faire souhaiter avec plus d'ardeur; de sorte donc que ces Sons étrangers ne doivent jamais tenir au Corps de l'Harmonie . . . de sorte que cette autre Harmonie est competée pour rien . . . une pareille licence ne peut se pratiquer que dans une succession Diatonique entre toutes les parties."

Example 8. Levens, *Abregé des regles de l'harmonie* (1743), 46–7 (scored from tablature and a description of the chords in the text).

Example 9. Rameau, *Traité* (1722), Book 3, Chapter 41.

harmony counts for nothing . . . [S]uch license can only be practiced in a stepwise succession in all the parts."[23]

Charles Levens (1689–1764), a Rameau-influenced theorist in Bordeaux, approached the notion of passing chords from another perspective. He introduces the passage shown in Example 8 to show how notes that merely pass in a fast tempo can receive full chords if the tempo is sufficiently slow. He does not specify that the resulting harmonies are passing chords, but he strongly implies that the frame is more important than the passing chords.[24]

Rameau also occasionally treats local harmonic progressions within larger contexts. Concerning Example 9, for instance, he notes that "in the first and second bars in the fundamental bass, there are two identical progressions. I reserve the progression most closely related to the cadence [that is, the progression with the chords in root position] for the second bar, because a downbeat is where the cadence occurs normally."[25] Rameau believed that all harmonic progressions are basically cadences, and that to prevent bringing

[24]Charles Levens, *Abregé des regles de l'harmonie, pour apprendre la composition* (Bordeaux: Jean Chappuis, 1743), pp. 46–7.

[25]Rameau, *Traité de l'harmonie* (Paris: Ballard, 1722); facsimile eds. (New York: Broude, 1967) and in *The Complete Theoretical Writings of Jean-Philippe Rameau*, Vol. 1; English translation by Philip Gossett under the title *Theory of Harmony* (New York: Dover, 1971), Book 3, Chapter 41: "Dans la premiere & dans la seconde mesure de la Basse-fondamentale, j'apperçois deux progressions égales A, B; ainsi je reserve celle qui a le plus de rapport à la Cadence pour la seconde mesure; perçe que c'est le lieu où la Cadence se fait sentire ordinairement."

Example 10. Nichelmann, *Die Melodie* (1755), Examples 8 and 10.

[chords:]

[polyodic realization:]

[fundamental bass:]

harmonic motion to a halt, cadences are frequently evaded in midphrase. Here he uses this notion to explain how the root-position form of a progression can be structurally foreshadowed by its inversion. His thinking implies a relationship between local events and events of deeper structural significance.

Christoph Nichelmann (1717–62), who had studied composition in the Bach circle in Leipzig, applies Rameauian theory to harmonic prolongation in a different manner.[26] He argued that a good composer considers all the parts of a texture together when he writes an expressive piece. If one composes the melody first and adds harmonies later, as he says many modern composers do, the harmonies will be arbitrary and the piece unexpressive. Nichelmann argues his case by realizing chord progressions, as in Example 10. The harmonies in the original progression are prolonged by inversion in nearly every measure, by neighboring chords such as the C chord in bar 2 and the B♭ chord in bar 7, and by repetition such as the tonicizations of F in bars 4–8.

[26] Christoph Nichelmann, *Die Melodie nach ihrem Wesen sowohl, als nach ihren Eigenschaften* (Danzig: Johann Christian Schuster, 1755).

A pseudonymous pamphlet attacked Nichelmann's treatise, asking "what composer would write down a whole series of chords and from it extract a melody?"[27] The answer is clear. Whenever one begins with an underlying harmonic structure and rhythmicizes that structure, the result is what Nichelmann proposes. This was Niedt's method. And it was also Rameau's, both when he elaborates a progression (as shown in Example 9) and when he explains that experienced composers conceive the harmonic background along with a melody.[28]

The motivation of Nichelmann's critic appears in his next rhetorical question: "In a piece [composed by extracting the melody from a series of chords] could there ever be fire, spirit, and life?"[29] The emphasis on melody in the newer *galant* styles demanded a method of composition that considered melody primary.

Before turning to eighteenth-century *galant* theories of melody, however, a digression is in order concerning an issue not explicitly addressed in the diminutional theories surveyed here: namely, the techniques of motivic elaboration and interrelationship that are so essential to the creation of a coherent musical structure. Direct discussions of this issue do not appear in the eighteenth century. But the notion does arise in the context of other topics. One such context was permutation, under which rubric a theorist could show how basic motivic materials may be varied. Niedt's diminutional approach, for instance, implies that to achieve a single affect, the diminutions should be related to one another. Thus, patterns characteristic of his allemandes do not intrude in his minuets, and patterns from one minuet do not appear in another (even when both minuets are based on the same thoroughbass).

A more explicit discussion of coherence based on underlying voice-leading relations appears in *A Treatise of Musick* by Alexander Malcolm (1685–1763).[30] Example 11 shows a melody he harmonizes. He explains that the opening bass C is determined by the key, while the following G moves the bass to a lower register. Thereafter, he says "I chused to ascend gradually with the Bass, to preserve an Imitation that happens to be between the Parts, by the Bass ascending gradually to the 5th fundamental [that is, to scale-step $\hat{5}$] from the Beginning of the second Bar, as the treble does from the Beginning

---

[27]The pamphlet, *Gedanken eines Liebhabers der Tonkunst über Herrn Nichelmanns Tractat von der Melodie* (Nordhausen, 1755), was published under the pseudonym Dünkelfeind (Enemy of Darkness). The author may have been Carl Philipp Emanuel Bach. "Welcher componist würde sich wohl eine ganze Reihe Accorde hinschreiben und daraus hernach eine Melodie heraus ziehen?" (p. 14). A comprehensive summary of the dispute between Nichelmann and C.P.E. Bach appears in Thomas Christensen, "Nichelmann contra C. Ph. E. Bach: Harmonic Theory and Musical Politics at the Court of Frederick the Great," in *Carl Philipp Emanuel Bach und die europäische Musikkultur des mittleren 18. Jahrhunderts; Bericht über das Internationale Symposium der Joachim Jungius-Gesellschaft der Wissenschaften Hamburg 29. September – Oktober 1988*, ed. Hans Joachim Marx (Göttingen: Vandenhoeck & Ruprecht, 1990), pp. 189–220.

[28]E.g., Rameau, *Traité*, Book 3, Chapter 40.

[29]"Dünkelfeind," *Gedanken*, p. 14: "Und könte auch in einem solchen Stücke wohl Feuer, Geist und Leben seyn?"

[30] Malcolm, *A Treatise* (Edinburgh: for the author, 1721); later eds. through 1779; facsimile ed. of the 1721 edition (New York: Da Capo, 1970).

Example 11. Malcolm, *A Treatise of Musick* (1721), p. 29.

Example 12. Riepel, *Anfangsgründe*, Vol. 2, *Grundregeln zur Tonordnung insgemein* (1755), pp. 65–9.

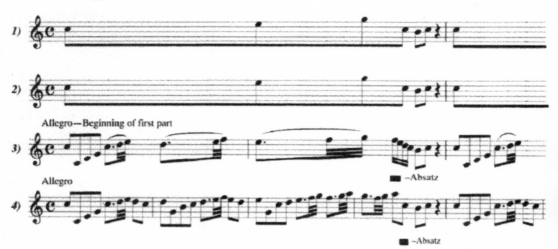

of the first Bar."[31] The rarity of such explicit mentions of hidden imitation in eighteenth-century theory does not necessarily imply that this sort of structure was not widely known. More likely, such structural matters did not regularly appear in print because they were not a prominent feature of any organized pedagogical method of the time.

After all, in 1722, Mattheson had lamented that even though "the melodic science is the first part of composition . . . the true basis of all the others," no composition method reflected this.[32] A composition method fully based on melody did not appear until Riepel began issuing the volumes of his *Anfangsgründe* in 1752. Riepel's approach is to teach composition through melodic articulation. He begins teaching how to write melodies right on page 1 of his first chapter, spurning thoroughbass, counterpoint, or harmony, "for without knowledge of melody nothing can be done with a bass."[33]

---

[31] Malcolm, *A Treatise*, p. 429.

[32] Mattheson, *Critica musica* (Hamburg: the author, 1722–23); facsimile ed. (Amsterdam: Frits Knuf, 1964), p. 261: "der Scientia melodica . . . den ersten Theil der Musicae poeticae . . . der wahre Grund aller andern sey."

[33] Riepel, *Anfangsgründe*, Vol. 5, *Unentbehrliche Anmerkungen zum Contrapunct* (Augsburg: Johann Jacob Lotter, and Regensburg: Jacob Christian Krippner, 1768), p. 1: "Dann ohne Kenntniss des Gesangs ist mit dem Bassse nichts auszurichten."

He reworks melodies via repetitions, extensions and abbreviations of phrases, insertions within phrases, and so on. Example 12 shows the very beginning of four versions of a symphonic allegro. Riepel begins with the version on staff 3. Staffs 2 and 1 contain successively briefer versions, and staff 4 offers an expanded version.

Each realization has its own integrity as a piece, with balanced phrases, related and contrasting motives, and so forth. In this sense, no version is an "analysis" of any other at a greater or lesser structural level, but simply a different realization. But Riepel knows that each realization projects a common substructure. He likens the shorter versions to painters' miniatures, which "present a life-size journey on a piece of paper only a hand's breadth wide . . . The miniature could be even smaller, namely only with letters, such as C–G–C"—where these letters indicate the main keys of the entire movement.[34]

Riepel's phrase expansions are thus akin to Niedt's diminutions or Levens's and Nichelmann's harmonic expansions. But by concentrating on melody, Riepel's approach is more directly applicable to the surfaces of actual musical compositions. He does not transform abstract progressions, but musical units with specific roles: phrase beginnings, middles, or ends; phrases ending on the tonic, the dominant, or the dominant of the dominant; phrases that open an allegro, occur in a new key, and so forth.

Riepel also works with the motivic implications of his materials as well as with the harmonic and voice-leading implications. For instance, consider his expansion in Example 12 of the opening bars of staff 3 into double that length to create the version on staff 4. To accomplish this expansion, Riepel employs varied sequences of the motive of the first measure on staff 3 to expand a two-beat melodic span from C–E into a three-measure span. He retains the rhythm of the C–E span (the dotted eighth and two thirty seconds) within that expanded version, allowing the first such rhythmic unit in bar 1 to be a foreshadowing diminution of the overall melodic progression (in both the shorter and longer versions). Since the longer version allows greater scope to the melodic development, he then uses the last such rhythmic unit in the third measure (the E–F–G on the third beat) to foreshadow an upward expansion of the melodic motion (akin to the motion in bars 1–2 in the shorter version, which foreshadows and then moves through C–D–E). These sorts of expansive processes affecting voice leading and rhythm as well as phrasing characterize other aspects of this set of examples (as well as numerous other examples in Riepel's chapters).

The only eighteenth-century theorist who pursued Riepel's approach was Koch in his *Versuch einer Anleitung zur Composition*, published in three volumes between 1782 and 1793.[35] Koch delves into the issues more deeply

---

[34] Riepel, *Anfangsgründe*, Vol. 2, *Grundregeln zur Tonordnung* (1755), p. 65: " . . . just wie die Mahler, mit sogenannter Miniatur, nur auf einem handbreiten Papier einen Reisen in Lebensgrösse vorstellen . . . die Miniatur noch kleiner, nämlich nur mit Buchstaben, z. Ex. C–G–C."

[35] Koch, *Versuch* (Rudolstadt and Leipzig: Adam Friedrich Böhme, 1782–93); facsimile ed. (Hildesheim: Georg Olms, 1969). Partial English translation by Nancy Baker as *Introductory Essay on Composition* (New Haven: Yale University Press, 1983).

Example 13. Koch, *Versuch*, Vol. 3, pp. 226–30.

than Riepel, partly because of the better organization of his treatises, but more significantly because he postpones his discussion of melody until after he has presented his views on harmony. For Koch, "the highest degree of perfection of the creative spirit among composers is nothing other than the ability to conceive of melody harmonically; that is, to invent it so that one is capable of bringing forth simultaneously the main features of its harmonic accompaniment.[36] As a result, when Koch presents examples like Riepel's, his examples carry their explicitly implied harmonic support.

Scholars studying Koch's examples have generally regarded them as manipulations of motives, cadences, phrase patterns, and the like. But since his melodies are "harmonically conceived," they are in effect harmonies and voice leading writ large. By considering melodies as implicit expressions of harmonies and voice leading, Koch in effect found a systematic way to discuss large-scale structures as pitch processes despite the fact that the pitch-syntax theories of his time (including his own such theories) dealt almost exclusively with note-to-note connections. For him, point-to-point harmonic connections (and their associated voice leadings) support melodies, melodies are the basis of phrases that articulate harmonic structures, and larger musical constructions expand phrases.

All this is clear in the capstone example to his discussion of melodic means of extension, the expansion of an eight-measure period into the 32-measure first reprise of a sonata-type allegro. Example 13 presents this example, lining up corresponding parts of the simpler and more complex realizations that Koch presents seriatim.

Koch's explanations of the prolongational techniques refer to motivic effects. But because he has established melody as harmony writ large, Koch is working with harmonic units as well as melodic procedures. Bars 1–3, for instance, compose out the melodic third G–B, an interval stated on beat 2 of bar 1 and also the frame for the first phrase (bars 1–2 of the initial version; bars 1–4 or 1–5 of the expanded version). Just as Levens had suggested four decades earlier, the rapid passing tone A (m. 1, beat 2, second sixteenth of the initial version) is simply a passing dissonance; but when played slower (as a full measure of A prolonged in bar 2 of the expanded version), it would no doubt receive a fuller harmony (some sort of dominant here). Likewise, just as Rameau showed over 60 years earlier how a local motion can present a less fundamental form of a progression that appears nearby in a more appropriate location, the progression of bars 1–4 (or bars 1–2 of the initial version) is encapsulated by the "appendix" to the phrase in bar 5. This is the type of phrase-appendix whose role Koch explains as "more precisely defining the content of the phrase."[37] Quite likely, Koch intended a clear-cut quarter-note bass line G–C–D–G from the end of bar 4 through bar 5 (as shown in

---

[36]Koch, *Versuch*, Vol. 2, p. 81: "die Vollkommenheit des erfindenden Geistes des Tonsetzers in ihrem höchsten . . . ist nichts anders als die Fertigkeit die Melodie harmonisch zu denken, das heißt, die so zu erfinden, daß man auch zugleich vermögend ist, die Hauptzüge ihrer harmonischen Begleitung sich dabey vorzustellen."

[37]Koch, *Versuch*, Vol. 3, p. 193: "der Inhalt des Satzes durch den Anhang genauer bestimmt werden."

Example 14). This bass line summarizes the harmonic content of bars 1–4 just as the melody summarizes their melodic scope. Such melodic and harmonic complementation occurs throughout the transformation of the initial version to the expanded version.

It is because of his command over so many of the compositional resources of his age that Koch is of such interest today. Other theorists had offered individual ideas. But Koch alone was able to apply these notions to the primary musical-structural issue of the Classical era—the creation of articulated musical surfaces. In doing so, he provides a coherent and comprehensive approach to the music of his time. The hierarchical and prolongational perspectives he uses in these discussions are not the property of any one theoretical tradition, or even of the theoretical tradition in which one might most expect to find such insights according to twentieth-century theoretical ideologies. Rather, these insights were the common property of perceptive musicians in all eighteenth-century theoretical traditions.

Example 14. Koch, *Versuch*, same passage as in expanded version in Example 13, with added hypothetical bass.

Thoughts on Schenker's Treatment of Diminution and Repetition in Part III of *Free Composition*, and its Implications for Analysis

Wayne C. Petty

In his preface to Schenker's *Free Composition*, Ernst Oster gives the following advice to readers who might be approaching this book for the first time:

> A very practical suggestion to the uninitiated reader might be that he adopt a somewhat unusual procedure and not begin at the beginning. The opening part, "The Background," assumes a more than superficial knowledge of the whole of Schenker's system; without this knowledge this part would probably remain largely meaningless. The reader should instead begin with the section on diminution (§§251 ff.), a very good introduction to Schenker's way of thinking, and continue through the next three sections (up to §275). Next, he should study part III, "The Foreground," in its entirety, skipping, however, the difficult section on linear progressions (§§203 to 229). At this point, he will be ready to tackle the opening part—"The Background."[1]

When Oster wrote these words in 1977, he could hardly have foreseen all the changes that the next twenty-five years would bring to Schenker studies. Translations of Schenker's other writings have made his works more accessible; new essays, monographs, and textbooks have explored and extended Schenker's ideas; postmodern studies have launched a new phase of criticism in which Schenker's beliefs are often challenged. All these factors, and others, are sure to affect many of the first-time readers for whom Oster was writing. But despite the new climate in which we read Schenker, Oster's advice remains sound. There are many good reasons to begin *Free Composition* not with the opening chapter on the background, but with the section on diminution. Even a quick glance through the examples to this section, Figures 116–125, shows this to be one of the most richly illustrated passages in the entire book; working through these examples alone can be revelatory, as we witness Schenker's extraordinary ear for tonal relationships of all kinds. Further reasons might be mentioned as well. For a grasp of Schenker's theory as a whole, an understanding of his views on diminution is absolutely crucial. To understand the key concept of

---

[1]Preface to the English Edition, in Heinrich Schenker, *Free Composition (Der freie Satz)*, trans. and ed. Ernst Oster (New York: Longman, 1979), xiii. Subsequent page references to *Free Composition* will be given in the text.

composing-out, for instance, one must first have a sense of the importance that Schenker attaches to diminution and of the way he conceives it as a fundamental and dynamic musical process. From the standpoint of Schenker's history, these pages of *Free Composition* can also provide some important context. For it is here that Schenker points to his antecedents (such as C. P. E. Bach) who had already suggested viewing tonal organization as layered. Here the reader can glimpse, if only partially, the author's complex relationship to earlier thinking about music. But perhaps most importantly, this section of *Free Composition* may suggest as well as any other the ambitious scope of Schenker's project and the sheer breadth of his thought. Here Schenker has written what amounts to a short history of music, a story in which diminution, originating in the human voice, is gradually emancipated from the word, achieving organic life in the hands of a few master composers through whom music realized its destiny, "to culminate in the likeness of itself" (93). In the provocative telling of this story, Schenker touches on a wide range of issues in music theory, analysis, composition, and performance, revealing an integrative tendency in his thought, a drive toward synthesis, which fuels his entire project. This was perhaps what led Oster to regard this section as not merely about diminution, but much more: "a very good introduction to Schenker's way of thinking."

One issue of central importance that Schenker addresses throughout this section, making it like a miniature introduction to his approach, is *repetition.* (§254 and Figure 119 are key passages here.) The restatement of a diminution constitutes for Schenker the most vivid and direct manner for a composer to establish, and for a listener to recognize, the relatedness of one part to another. When we hear two parts as statement and repetition, the relation of *similarity* alone causes us to perceive a connection between them. Connections among parts then promote the formation of parts into a whole, which is synthesis. Schenker thus finds great significance in repetition. He offers in Figure 119 a large number of examples—some belonging clearly to the foreground, others to the middleground—that greatly extend what counts as a restatement, insisting that we should "learn to recognize such repetitions as the prime carriers of synthesis" (100). But not every whole that might form through such relations of similarity counts for Schenker as an organically unified whole. The parts must enjoy the further, and more fundamental, relation of *continuity* provided by the voice-leading layers. Those layers bind the parts into a temporal order—that provided ultimately by the tonal progression of the background.[2] This is why, on one hand, Schenker does not insist that parts relate by similarity, only that they relate to the whole through the voice-leading layers (§253: "The achievement of organic relationship in genuine diminution through the whole"); and why, on the other hand, he does not allow parts to form unities between different pieces (§262: "Rejection of so-called 'wandering melodies'"). This attitude informs not only *Free Composition* but all of Schenker's late work. It helps explain his consistent rejection of thematically based approaches that insist on similarity for unity, and of naïve historicizing, which tends to form

---

[2]See Kevin Korsyn, "Schenker and Kantian Epistemology," *Theoria* 3 (1988), pp.1–58.

unities (say, of style or influence) from parts of different pieces. We might resist Schenker on some of these points; we might try to configure part/ part or part/whole relations in some other way; we might focus on the ideological work performed by any theory of unity in art; but whatever our response, we should acknowledge, at the very least, that Schenker has taken principled positions toward some fundamental artistic problems and argued them with tremendous vigor.

The view of diminution and repetition that Schenker presents in *Free Composition* will always have heuristic value for many musicians, I think, for it can allow us to discover a wealth of relationships in a piece, to ground those relationships in harmony and voice leading, and to connect them to the whole. But it also presents some risks. The allure of all these hidden treasures can tempt us to make a fetish of repetitions, especially the concealed ones. Analyses can result which may abound in motivic parallelisms without ever transcending the merely "correct" or plausible. I do not see an easy solution to this problem. To discern the beautiful analysis from the ordinary requires so many things—a passion for discovering the compositional ideas behind a piece, practice and experience with many different pieces, relentless criticism of one's own work, the intangibles of musical taste and judgment—that to explore these issues fully would probably require nothing short of an ethics of music analysis. I do find, however, one kind of situation where hearing a concealed repetition is often persuasive, where it does seem to capture the idea behind a passage. That is when I hear a foreground pattern enlarged but some additional musical factor associates the concealed repetition with the foreground pattern. A good example of this occurs in the opening section, bars 1–18, of the Two-Part Invention in D minor, BWV 775, by J. S. Bach.[3]

Perhaps a good place to begin is with the subject of the Invention, given in Example 1a. The subject's compound melody implies a two-voice pattern, shown in Example 1b, in which a 5–6 shift in the opening bar prepares the diminished seventh bb^1 over $c\sharp^1$ on the downbeat of the second bar. At this point it would certainly be possible to hear the diminished seventh as a suspension that resolves to the a^1 on the second beat of bar 2; but the wider context implies that the a^1 passes between two members of a diminished-seventh chord on $c\sharp$, filling out a third from bb^1 to g^1, with this g^1 in turn functioning as a passing tone within a third-progression that spans the subject as a whole (Example 1c). Since the bb^1 has not really resolved, a three-voice setting like the one in Example 1d would be implied; it is still possible, nevertheless, to imagine the five-note pattern a^1–bb^1–a^1–g^1–f^1 of Example 1c as a basic reading for the subject. Not every subsequent statement of the subject should be read this way, but this reading seems best to capture the subject's overall shape on its first appearance.

We know that repetition will be a prime feature of the D-minor Invention because of the way the piece opens with a three-fold statement of the

---

[3] Allen Forte has also suggested a motivic enlargement in this passage; see his *Tonal Harmony in Concept and Practice*, 3rd edition (New York: Holt, Rinehart and Winston, 1979), pp. 436–38.

subject. Indeed, we soon realize that Bach's design will involve presenting the subject almost continuously in one of the voices, making subtle adjustments to its first and last melodic intervals, as well as to its contrapuntal setting, to allow the subject the mobility it needs to carry the piece forward. Once we begin interpreting the middleground, however, we may start to recognize other repetitions as well. Example 2 shows a possible reading of two motivic enlargements (concealed repetitions) in the opening section of the piece; these trace out the melodic pattern of the subject given earlier in Example 1b.

Example 1. J. S. Bach, Invention in D minor, BWV 775, analysis of the subject.

The first of these enlargements occurs in the *Fortspinnung*, the passage that continues the subject sequentially in bars 7–14. In this passage overlapping forms of the subject appear first in the upper voice then in the lower, with a harmonic sequence of descending fifths and a 10–7 linear intervallic pattern binding these into a single progression. Here the inner voice traces out the pattern b♭¹–a¹–g¹–f¹, which we can imagine linking back to the opening a¹ to enlarge the melodic pattern of the subject. As the descending-fifths sequence completes itself with the return to the root D in bar 14, so the motivic enlargement also finishes. This enlargement is rather easy to hear, and to bring out in performance, because many of the notes fall on downbeats.

The second enlargement appears in the closing phrase that confirms a modulation to the mediant at bars 14–18. Here the melodic progression b♭¹–a¹–g¹–f¹ is more heavily concealed by the diminution and reharmonized as a cadential progression in F major ($\hat{4}$–$\hat{3}$–$\hat{2}$–$\hat{1}$). But it is not so difficult to discern if, again, we retain the opening a¹ in memory, then we follow the counterpoint. To begin with, Bach has left a suspended 7, c², implied in the top voice at bar 14. A change of design then brings the resolution to b♭¹ (7–6) within the bar. (The preceding 7s had lasted an entire bar.) This b♭¹ in turn prepares a diminished fifth as the bass rises to e in bar 15, giving a key-defining interval for F major. If we then follow the contraction of that diminished fifth to a¹–over–f in bar 16, plus the ensuing fall to the cadence in the upper voice, we can discern the second enlargement of the subject's melodic pattern. Hearing this enlargement, we can sense the subject guiding the counterpoint of the entire opening section—that is, all of bars 1–18. We can imagine the initial 5–6 shift in the subject giving rise to a larger 5–6 motion in bars 1–14, yielding the 6/3 over D that leads to the key-defining progression in F major, with the remainder of the subject reharmonized to confirm the new key.

Example 2. J. S. Bach, Invention in D minor, BWV 775, analysis of bars 1-18.

Opening phrase   *Fortspinnung*   **Closing phrase**

What makes this reading of concealed repetition convincing to me is the way in which bars 14–15 associate with the original subject. At bar 14 the completion of the descending-fifths progression encourages hearing bar 14 as a continuation of the tonic pitch that began the piece. At this point, the upper voice presents a new idea that follows the outline of the subject, thereby associating the 6/3 in bar 14 with the original 5–6 shift in bar 1. (Compare the points marked with an asterisk in Example 2.) As the long-range 5–6 shift completes itself in bars 1–14, therefore, the upper voice recalls the outline of the subject, so that the end of bar 14 directs the ear back to the end of bar 1.

That brings the concealed repetition to the fore. I find that this produces what might be called a kind of "triangulation" that supports the analysis: the repetitions in themselves suggest a potentially significant relationship between foreground and middleground, then a third term, the added association, helps confirm that relationship, in this case the one between bars 1–2 and bars 14–15 (and all that follows from that). When I find such a network of internal relations, I usually feel reasonably sure that the repetition forms the guiding idea for the passage.

What I have illustrated here, briefly and partially, is an attitude toward diminution and repetition that accepts, on one hand, the possible significance of concealed repetitions, while asking, on the other hand, how additional features of the piece might support that reading—how, in other words, the piece might offer clues to discovering its own hidden treasures. In the Bach Invention it was a change of design that brought back a tone-succession implied by the subject, as if to relate the enlargement back to the original pattern. In another piece it might be something else—a telltale ornament, for instance, or a striking change of texture. A sensitivity to such factors can often help us develop the kind of reading which, in the words of this volume's honoree, "will encompass all the important aspects of the piece in a satisfactory way," one that transcends "mere correctness or plausibility."[4]

[4]Carl Schachter, "A Dialogue Between Author and Editor," in *Unfoldings*, ed. Joseph N. Straus (New York and Oxford: Oxford University Press, 1999), p. 12.

Looking at the *Urlinie*

Hedi Siegel

In 1925, the Viennese artist Victor Hammer completed a mezzotint portrait of Heinrich Schenker.[1] This portrait, which shows Schenker in his late fifties (see Plate 1), provides a link to a somewhat surprising side of Schenker's ideas—the elements of his thought that relate to the visual arts and art theory. Some of these ideas may be traced to the correspondence between Schenker and Hammer, which took place between 1913 and 1931. The letters (held by the New York Public Library and the University of California at Riverside)[2] document what appears to be Schenker's only friendship with a practicing painter; they record an exchange of ideas that centered on the *Urlinie*, a concept that had emerged from Schenker's ongoing work on the theory of free composition just at the time he and Hammer began their friendship. Schenker explained his *Urlinie* to Hammer; Hammer recognized it as a construct that existed in pictures, and he in turn explained this to Schenker.

---

[1]The portrait has been widely reproduced. Its first appearance in a publication was as the frontispiece for Otto Vrieslander's article "Heinrich Schenker," *Die Musik*, Vol. 19, No. 1 (October 1926), pp. 33–38. It has been exhibited in museums and galleries; in the year of its completion a print was acquired by the Albertina museum in Vienna. It was included in the major exhibitions of Hammer's work, e.g., at the Grolier Club in New York City (1995), at the North Carolina Museum of Art in Raleigh (1965), and at the University of Chicago (1948). A print is held by the Library of the University of California at Riverside, Special Collections Department; see Robert Lang and Joan Kunselman, *Heinrich Schenker, Oswald Jonas, Moriz Violin: A Checklist of Manuscripts and Other Papers in the Oswald Jonas Memorial Collection* (Berkeley: University of California Press, 1994), p. 195 (the entry for box 72, folder 14, item 7).

Through the kindness of the late Carolyn Reading Hammer (an American printer and book maker who became Victor Hammer's second wife in 1955), both Carl Schachter and I now own a print of the portrait, so we share a particular interest in the circumstances surrounding its creation. Carl encouraged me to use the portrait as the point of departure for the first version of this essay, which was given as the keynote address at the annual meeting of the Music Theory Society of New York State (Hunter College, 1998). I am more grateful than I can express for his inspiration, help, and advice during its preparation. A revised version of the address was read at the Third International Schenker Symposium (Mannes College of Music, 1999). The present version incorporates further revisions.

[2]Schenker's letters to Victor Hammer were donated to the New York Public Library by Carolyn Hammer. I am grateful to Robert Kosovsky of the Music Division for making them available to me. The letters Hammer wrote to Schenker may be found in the Oswald Jonas Memorial Collection, University of California at Riverside, box 11, folder 36. (Photocopies of Schenker's letters to Hammer are located in box 5, folder 15a.) For their kind assistance at the University's Rivera Library, I am indebted to Robert Lang, Gladys Murphy, and Sidney Berger (Head of Special Collections in 1994, when I consulted the materials in the Jonas Collection). Robert Lang sadly did not live to complete his work on the Hammer–Schenker relationship—he had planned to publish a comprehensive study. (*cont.*)

Plate 1. Hammer's mezzotint portrait of Schenker.

Portions of the letters and their enclosures are reproduced in this article by courtesy of the Music Division of the New York Public Library, Astor, Lenox, and Tilden Foundations, and the Special Collections Department, Rivera Library, University of California at Riverside.

Victor Hammer, who seems to have been Schenker's main conduit to the sphere of the visual arts, was born in Vienna in 1882 (he was fourteen years younger than Schenker). The mezzotint technique he used for Schenker's portrait was one he particularly favored. He used it for a self-portrait that dates from 1925, the same year he completed his portrait of Schenker (see Plate 2). This technique had been used quite extensively in the eighteenth and nineteenth centuries; Hammer revived it partly because it enabled him to create dramatic contrast as well as delicate shading. Hammer's output consists largely of portraits—paintings, sculpture, drawings, woodcuts, and engravings as well as mezzotints. A number of his major paintings

Plate 2. Hammer's mezzotint self-portrait.

are of Biblical and mythological subjects; he also drew up the architectural plans for a chapel and supervised its construction. He is widely known today for his unique contribution to typography and the book arts. In addition to his work as an artist and craftsman, he wrote essays on the philosophy of art, most of which were published after his emigration to America in 1939.[3]

Hammer had a great interest in music, and even before he met Schenker he had read some of his early writings.[4] He spent a good deal of time making music, playing the clavichord, lute, and clarinet.[5] He knew some of

[3]See John Rothenstein, *Victor Hammer: Artist and Craftsman* (Boston: David R. Goodine, 1978); *Victor Hammer: Artist and Printer*, compiled by Carolyn R. Hammer (Lexington, Kentucky: The Anvil Press, 1981); and *Victor Hammer: An Artist's Testament*, compiled by Carolyn R. Hammer (Lexington, Kentucky: The Anvil Press, 1988). This comprehensive three-volume series includes illustrated essays on Victor Hammer's life and work, an extensive bibliography, and substantial extracts from Hammer's own writings. Concerning Hammer's mezzotint technique, see Ulrich Middeldorf's essay and illustrated catalogue, "Mezzotints," in *Victor Hammer: Artist and Printer*, pp. 11–53; a detailed description of Hammer's mezzotint portrait of Schenker (reproduced in the volume as Plates 6a and 6b) is given on p. 22. Victor Hammer's self-portrait of 1925 is reproduced on p. 33 of the volume as Plate 4.

[4]In his early letters to Schenker, Hammer mentions that he had read the preface and some parts of Schenker's monograph on Beethoven's Ninth Symphony (letter of September 12, 1913), and was familiar with the *Ornamentik* (letter of September 26, 1913). See Schenker, *Beethovens neunte Sinfonie* (Vienna: Universal Edition, 1912); *Beethoven's Ninth Symphony*, trans. John Rothgeb (New Haven: Yale University Press, 1992) and *Ein Beitrag zur Ornamentik* (Vienna: Universal Edition, 1904, revised 1908); "A Contribution to the Study of Ornamentation," trans. Hedi Siegel in *The Music Forum*, Vol. 4 (1976), pp. 1–139.

[5]See Rothenstein, *Victor Hammer: Artist and Craftsman*, pp. 26–27 and Plate X (showing a self-portrait Hammer painted in the 1920s, in which a clavichord and lute form part of the composition). Hammer built several clavichords and, as he told Schenker in his letter of September 17, 1913, owned an old clavichord as well as two early pianos (including one built by André Stein in 1820). In his letter to Schenker of March 23, 1922, Hammer discusses some of the fingerings in Schenker's critical edition of Bach's Chromatic Fantasy and Fugue and suggests alternatives more suited to performance on the clavichord. See Schenker, *J. S. Bach, Chromatische Phantasie und Fuge: Kritische Ausgabe* [*cont.*]

the musicians in Schenker's circle and was a particular friend of Hans Weisse, one of Schenker's leading students. Weisse dedicated several of his compositions to Victor Hammer and his wife, for performance during the Hammers' frequent family chamber music sessions. Hammer's wife, Rosl, sang and played the piano; in his first letter to Schenker (September 12, 1913), Hammer asked if he would consider teaching her. Schenker declined, but around 1921 the two men met and developed a close friendship, conversing and corresponding often. Although Hammer's main residence was in Florence, he traveled a great deal, frequently returning to Austria. He maintained a studio in Vienna, where Schenker sat for the portrait.

Both men welcomed the opportunity for discussion provided by the sittings. In January of 1924, when Hammer wrote to Schenker from Florence to ask him if he would consider sitting for a portrait, he added:

> I am already looking forward to it and . . . it will also benefit me; I intend to ask you many questions during the sittings.[6]

Schenker replied:

> Shall I tell you how pleased I am about your proposal? I'll be brief: only your paintbrush, only your pencil, will speak the truth about me, so highly do I value your truthfulness and artistry. . . . I, too, am looking forward to the sittings, because I still have much to discuss. . . . [7]

Hammer learned about the *Urlinie* from his conversations with Schenker, and also from his letters and published writings. We know that Schenker "showed" it to him: in 1922 he sent Hammer and his wife a sketch of the *Urlinie* of Mendelssohn's "Altdeutsches Lied" that Rosl Hammer had been singing and had found difficult to understand (see Example 1). Hammer had written to Schenker that she was floundering around—he used the phrase "sie schwimmt" ("she swims")—and he had appealed to Schenker for help.[8]

Schenker had intended to clarify the Mendelssohn song for the Hammers during their next visit, but they had to cancel their plans. So instead he sent them a letter and enclosed a sketch of the song (see Plates 3 and 4), dated May 1922 and inscribed "to the still floundering Hammer couple!" ("den noch schwimmenden Ehepaar Hammer!"). The letter begins:

(Vienna: Universal Edition, 1910; revised by Oswald Jonas, 1969); *J. S. Bach's Chromatic Fantasy and Fugue: Critical Edition with Commentary*, trans. Hedi Siegel (New York: Longman, 1984).

[6]From Hammer's letter of January 5, 1924 (misdated 1923): "Ich freu mich schon drauf und . . . nicht ohne Eigennutz, ich werde Sie sehr vieles fragen während der Sitzungen." (The translations in this essay are mine unless otherwise indicated. I am grateful to Suzanne Osborne for her suggestions regarding the translations and transcriptions.)

[7]From Schenker's letter of January 13, 1924: "Soll ich Ihnen sagen, welche Freude Sie mir mit Ihrer Absicht machen? Ich fasse mich kurz: Ihr Pinsel allein; Ihr Stift allein wird die Wahrheit über mich sagen, so hoch schätze ich Ihr Wahrheits- und Kunstkönnen ein. . . . Auch ich freue mich auf die Sitzungen, weil ich noch viel auszutragen habe." Several letters written in 1925 show that Schenker was very pleased with the finished portrait.

[8]Hammer's letter of March 23, 1922.

Example 1. Mendelssohn, "Altdeutsches Lied," Op. 57, No. 1 (transposed down to D major from the original key of E major, as in Schenker's sketch).

Esteemed and dear Mr. Hammer!

Do you realize that you didn't come to see us after all, in spite of what you promised? So now I have no choice but to send you and your "floundering" wife the small *Urlinie* of Mendelssohn's "Altdeutsches Lied" by mail.

Schenker describes this *Urlinie*:

The 5̂ etc. [the 5̂ and the succeeding numbers marked with carets in the sketch] represent the notes of the D major diatony.

He then writes out the letter names of the diatonic pitches d e f♯ g a b c♯ d and numbers them 1 through 8. He continues:

They are the recipients of all melodic individuality, and I have also shown how they are served by the harmonic degrees (*Stufen*). All the remaining numbers belong to figured-bass notation. *Urlinie* and *Stufen* then make up the tonality, expressed horizontally and vertically. Isn't it wonderful how the line dives headlong from 8 (8 to 1)! What breadth! May this little picture (*Bildchen*) render some kind of service.[9]

[9]From Schenker's letter of May 25, 1922: "Verehrter und lieber Herr Hammer! Wissen Sie davon, daß Sie—entgegen Ihrer Jasage—bei uns nicht gewesen sind? So bleibt mir nur übrig, die kleine 'Urlinie' zu Mendelssohns 'Altdeutschem Lied' Ihnen und Ihrer 'schwimmenden' Frau durch die Post zu übersenden. Die 5̂ u.s.w. stellen die Töne der D dur Diatonie [*cont.*]

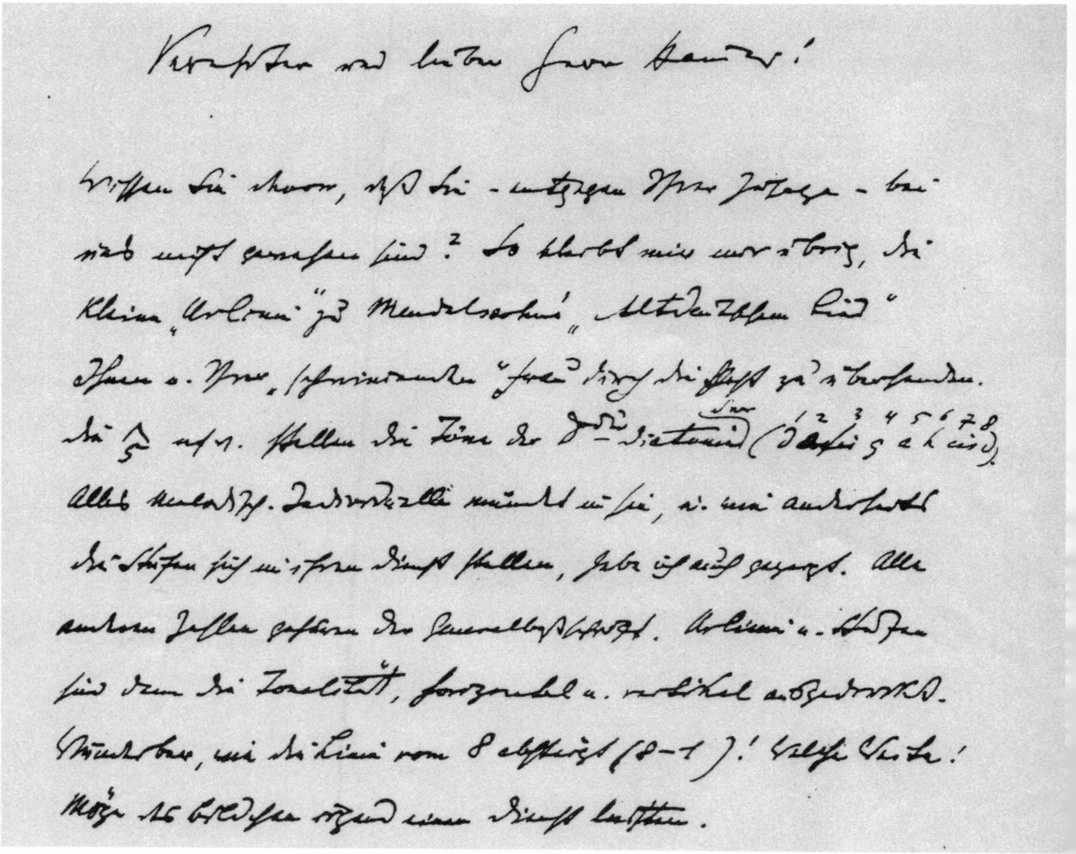

Plate 3. From Schenker's letter to Hammer, May 25, 1922, page 1.

In 1920—just two years before he wrote this letter—Schenker had introduced the *Urlinie* in his *Erläuterungsausgabe* of Beethoven's Op. 101; he had taken it up again in 1921, in the first issue of *Der Tonwille*.[10] Schenker's *Urlinie* of the Mendelssohn song resembles those in the early *Tonwille* issues (where he had begun to call some of his graphs *Urlinie-Tafeln*).[11] It shows the underlying stepwise melodic motion, but stays very

---

dar. . . . Alles melodisch Individuelle mündet in sie, und wie anderseits die Stufen sich in ihren Dienst stellen, habe ich auch gezeigt. Alle anderen Zahlen gehören der Generalbaßschrift. Urlinie und Stufen sind dann die Tonalität, horizontal und vertikal ausgedrückt. Wunderbar, wie die Linie vom 8 abstürzt (8–1)! Welche Weite! Möge das Bildchen irgend einen Dienst leisten."

[10]See Schenker, *Die letzten fünf Sonaten von Beethoven, Sonate A Dur Op. 101, Erläuterungsausgabe* (Vienna: Universal Edition, 1920), p. 22 ff.; revised edition by Oswald Jonas (Vienna: Universal Edition, 1972), p. 7 ff; and "Die Urlinie: Eine Vorbemerkung," *Der Tonwille*, Heft 1 (1921), p. 22 ff. For this and subsequent references to *Der Tonwille*, see also the complete English translation, ed. William Drabkin (Oxford: Oxford University Press, 2004-5), which appeared when the present book was in press.

[11]The first *Urlinie-Tafeln* appear in *Der Tonwille*, Heft 2 (1922), as supplements to the essays on Mozart's Sonata in A minor, K. 310, and Beethoven's Sonata Op. 2, No. 1.

close to the actual melody of the song (see Plate 4 and Example 1). One unusual feature not yet found in *Der Tonwille* is the symbol that would later become the interruption sign (between the staves, after the opening $\hat{5}$–$\hat{4}$–$\hat{3}$–$\hat{2}$). Its use here differs from Schenker's mature graphs: it is followed by a new descent from $\hat{8}$. The faint note-heads near the bottom of the page of the sketch were most likely added at some later time; perhaps Hammer brought the page with him on one of his next visits. Schenker probably first showed him that the *Urlinie* both begins and ends with a four-note descent: he drew a large bracket around the note-heads A–G–F♯–E (the $\hat{5}$–$\hat{4}$–$\hat{3}$–$\hat{2}$ at the beginning of the song) followed by G–F♯–E–D (the $\hat{4}$–$\hat{3}$–$\hat{2}$–$\hat{1}$ at the end). Then he wrote out the D major scale going up to $\hat{8}$, marking off the important $\hat{5}$. He may have drawn the arrow moving backwards from right to left to show Hammer how the piece itself proceeds down from $\hat{8}$. And perhaps the E–B–E sketched at the end of the line shows the $\hat{1}$–$\hat{5}$–$\hat{8}$ in the original key of E major.

But even before he had received Schenker's analysis of the Mendelssohn song, Hammer had grasped the basic principles of Schenker's *Urlinie* idea (perhaps from the first issue of *Der Tonwille* that Schenker had sent him) and had realized that it and some related concepts were very close to ideas he had encountered in the theory of art. He expressed this to Schenker in a letter written in 1921, in the early days of their friendship. In a passage that appears to follow up on a recent conversation he writes (see Plate 5):

> I am so pleased with your "Tonwille," and you are quite right, there are striking and convincing parallels with the visual arts. The *Urlinie* is evident in every good picture, but the creator of the work can never "invent" it; it has always been present and can at most be purified, clarified, and elucidated. It remains hidden to the ordinary viewer, who nevertheless is sure to feel its effect.

Near the end of the letter he writes:

> I am looking forward to seeing you and speaking with you again; perhaps I won't be completely useless to you. In any case, I thank you, dear Herr Doktor; you understand simplicity, something very few can grasp.

Hammer adds a postscript:

> You should read Fiedler, *Schriften über Kunst* and Hildebrand, *Das Problem der Form in der bildenden Kunst.*[12]

---

[12]From Hammer's letter of December 9, 1921:"Ich freue mich so mit Ihrem 'Tonwillen,' und Sie haben ganz recht, es sind so auffallende und überzeugende Parallelen mit der bildenden Kunst. Die Urlinie ist in jedem guten Bild nachweisbar, man kann sie (wenn man selber schafft) aber niemals 'erfinden' sie ist von Anfang an da, kann höchstens gereinigt, geläutert und geklärt werden, dem gewöhnlichen Beschauer bleibt sie verborgen aber ihre Wirkung spürt er unfehlbar. . . . Ich freue mich sehr Sie wieder zu sehen und zu sprechen, vielleicht kann auch ich Ihnen nicht ganz unnütz sein. Jedenfalls danke ich Ihnen sehr lieber Herr Doktor, sie verstehen das Einfache, gerade das fassen die Wenigsten. . . . Lesen Sie: Konrad Fiedler, Schriften über Kunst, R. Piper, München [und] Hildebrand, Das Problem der Form in der bildenden Kunst." The edition of Fiedler's collected writings referred to by Hammer, Conrad Fiedler, *Schriften zur Kunst,* edited by Hermann Konnerth (Munich: Piper, 1913–14), has been reprinted in an expanded edition by Gottfried Boehm (Munich: Wilhelm [cont.]

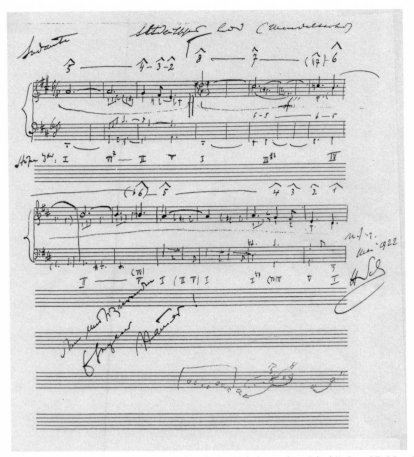

Plate 4. Schenker's sketch of Mendelssohn's "Altdeutsches Lied," Op. 57, No. 1.

These books that Hammer recommended to Schenker, the writings of Adolph von Hildebrand, an important neo-classic sculptor, and Conrad Fiedler, a late nineteenth-century art theorist who was a member of Hildebrand's circle, had profoundly influenced Hammer's own work and thought. The extent of Hildebrand's influence can be grasped if we look ahead to an essay published in 1967, the year of Hammer's death. Hammer recalls the time he actually met Hildebrand in person and reveals that Hildebrand's book on form was his source for the artistic concept that "is evident in every good picture":

Fink, 1971). Adolph von Hildebrand's *Das Problem der Form in der bildenden Kunst* was first published in Strasbourg in 1893. It was reissued in several editions and translations: e.g., *The Problem of Form in Painting and Sculpture*, trans. Max Meyer and Robert Morris Ogden (2nd ed., Leipzig: Stechert, 1932; reprinted, New York: Garland, 1978).

In his reply of December 19, 1921, Schenker writes that he intends to buy these books. Writing the following spring (May 25, 1922), he tells Hammer he hopes to read them over the summer. In his letter of January 13, 1924, however, he indicates that he has not yet bought the Fiedler volumes, though he does have Hildebrand's book.

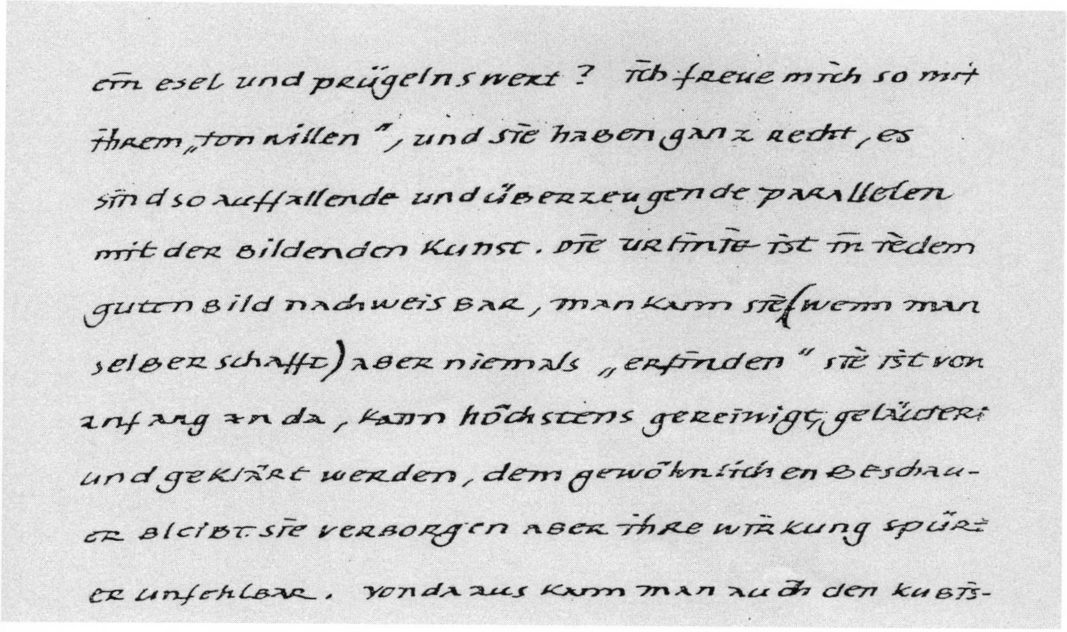
ein esel und prügelnswert? ich freue mich so mit
ihrem „ton willen", und sie haben ganz recht, es
sind so auffallende und überzeugende parallelen
mit der bildenden kunst. die urlinie ist in jedem
guten bild nachweisbar, man kann sie (wenn man
selber schafft) aber niemals „erfinden" sie ist von
anfang an da, kann höchstens gereinigt, geläutert
und geklärt werden, dem gewöhnlichen beschauer bleibt sie verborgen aber ihre wirkung spürt
er unfehlbar. von da aus kann man auch den kubis-

Plate 5. From Hammer's letter to Schenker, December 9, 1921, page 2.

> In 1910 or 1911 I had an interview with Adolph von Hildebrand. His book, "The Problem of Form," had fascinated me but I felt that I did not understand it and hoped that he would explain part of it to me.

Hammer then summarizes what he came to understand as Hildebrand's basic message:

> The foremost task of the artist is to present to the eye a purely visual structure which the beholder—though he cannot see it—he can apprehend it.

Hammer gives an example; a portrait commissioned in 1943 by a patron, Parmenia Ekstrom (see Plate 6):

> I have painted a portrait of Parmenia. She wears a black dress, the hands holding a string of red beads are clearly drawn, the background is uniformly green, the likeness is good. The beholder sees these things—one might say, passively sees them. However, the artist's chief concern is with that which the beholder will not see, but will apprehend: the underlying structure of the portrait. On the following page are the concealed facts (forms) of this portrait [Plate 7]; the frame encloses them (and sets them apart from all else).
>
> It is such a formal structure that sustains the artist while he works, and bears witness to his work as an artist.[13]

[13]Hammer, "Parmenia's Portrait," fragment no. xliii in *Some Fragments for C.R.H.: Pieces for an Artist's Testament (1966–1967)* (Lexington, Kentucky: The Stamperia del Santuccio, 1967), pp. 78–81. (The diagram shown here as Plate 7 appears on p. 80.) This book of (*cont.*)

Plate 6. "Parmenia," Hammer's portrait of Parmenia Ekstrom.

Plate 7. Hammer's diagram of "Parmenia."

Though this was written long after Hammer's contact with Schenker, it suggests that Schenker's *Urlinie* must have reminded Hammer of what he had learned from Hildebrand;[14] he equated it with the "underlying structure" of a painting and the "purely visual structure" that is not seen but is apprehended.

One of the topics Schenker and Hammer must have talked about during the sittings for the portrait was Schenker's choice of the word *Urlinie*. Hammer focused on the word *Urlinie* rather than *Ursatz*, the term Schenker had introduced in 1923 to designate the fundamental structure.[15] As we shall see, Schenker did write to him about the *Ursatz*, but it was the *Urlinie*—a line drawn in music—that captured Hammer's imagination. In the letters that seem to continue their conversations, they discussed the applicability of the term to both their disciplines, and Hammer showed

---

short pieces for Carolyn Reading Hammer is reprinted in *Victor Hammer: An Artist's Testament*, pp. 255–96; for "Parmenia's Portrait," see pp. 290–91. (The diagram, along with the sentence describing it, are omitted from the reprint.) Hammer's portrait, "Parmenia," (shown here as Plate 6) appears as a color print in Rothenstein, *Victor Hammer: Artist and Craftsman*, Plate III.

[14]In a letter dated March 23, 1922, Hammer wrote (in regard to Schenker's theories): "Some parts appear to me as disguised laws of my own art that I learned long ago." ("Somanches tritt mir als Verkleidung längst bekannter Gesetze meiner Kunst entgegen.")

[15]See "Urlinie und Stimmführung," *Der Tonwille*, Heft 5 (1923), p. 45.

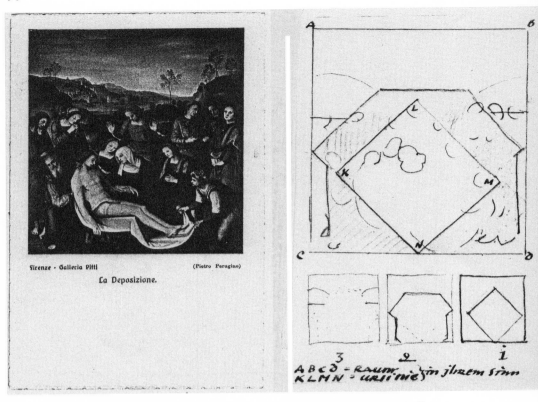

Plate 8. Pietro Perugino's "La Deposizione" with Hammer's diagram.

Schenker how it could represent the hidden structure of a painting. Early in 1926, he wrote a long letter from Florence and enclosed several picture postcard reproductions of paintings in the Pitti Gallery. To each reproduction he attached a transparent overlay containing his drawing of the painting's underlying structure. One of them showed Pietro Perugino's "La Deposizione" (see Plate 8). The legend below the drawing indicates that that the rectangle labeled A, B, C, D is the *Raum*, or space; the shape labeled K, L, M, N represents the *Urlinie*, with both words used "in Ihrem Sinn," that is, in Schenker's sense. Beneath the diagram of the painting Hammer drew the shapes numbered 1, 2, and 3 from right to left. On the back of the postcard Hammer wrote that these represent the three principal shapes found in the painting; they can be viewed as being placed over each other, with the first and simplest form in front, the second behind it, and the third very far back. The *Urlinie* (in Schenker's sense of the word) is the shape in the front—the diamond shape K, L, M, N; it is the same as the simplest shape drawn below the painting on the right, shape No. 1.[16]

The three shapes Hammer drew below the painting might call to mind Schenker's foreground, middleground, and background. Schenker's idea of structural levels arose around the time he and Hammer began to exchange ideas; the terms *Vordergrund* and *Hintergrund* appear in the first issue of

---

[16]Hammer's letter of January 22, 1926. The accompanying postcards and overlays are found in box 11, folder 37, of the Jonas Collection.

Plate 9. From Schenker's letter to Hammer, November 22, 1925, page 1.

Der Tonwille.[17] It is significant that he was looking at this diagram and others like it at the time he was developing and refining his multi-level, layered representations. While Hammer had some reservations about Schenker's choice of the word *Urlinie*, he praised his adoption of terminology derived from that of the visual arts. He told Schenker that his choice of the words, *Tonraum*, *Vordergrund*, and *Hintergrund* to designate elements that create form in music was "wise and precise."[18]

In questioning Schenker's use of the word *Urlinie*, Hammer wrote to him in great detail about the relationship he saw between *Urlinie* and *Raum*, the space or frame of a painting.[19] Schenker replied in a letter dated November 22, 1925, writing to Hammer about this relationship in music.

The example on the first page of the letter (see Plate 9) recalls the illustration of the 1–3–5–8 *Tonraum* presented in the "Elucidations" that were first published in 1924, in Issue 8/9 of *Der Tonwille*. There, Schenker described it as "the shortened form of the sonority of Nature, which when sounded successively defines tonal space."[20] In the letter shown in Plate 9, Schenker writes of the 1–3–5–8 *Natur-Raum* (see the words immediately

[17]See, for example, "Die Urlinie: Eine Vorbemerkung," *Der Tonwille*, Heft 1 (1921), p. 22, where Schenker writes about repetition in relation to the foreground and background.

[18]From Hammer's letter of October 31, 1925: "Die Tonräume, Vordergrund, Hintergrund…, das alles sind sehr klug und scharf gewählte Ausdrücke für das was Sie uns im musikalischen Kunstwerk als formbildend aufzeigen."

[19]Hammer's letter of October 31, 1925.

[20]*Der Tonwille*, Heft 8/9 (April–September 1924), p. 49. The "Erläuterungen" appeared on pp. 49–51 of that issue; they were republished in Heft 10 (October 1924), pp. 40–42. They were also reissued in the first two yearbooks of *Das Meisterwerk in der Musik*, Vol. 1 (Munich: Drei Masken Verlag, 1925), pp. 203–205 and Vol. 2 (Munich: Drei Masken Verlag, 1926), pp. 195–97. The translation given here is by Ian Bent, in *The Masterwork in Music* (Cambridge: Cambridge University Press, 1994–97), Vol. 1, p. 112, and Vol. 2, p. 118.

above the example): "The musician's space, given to him by Nature, is very limited . . . ." He continues (below the example), "but even the smallest space is large enough to contain a world of creation, so he can fulfill, or fill the space:"[21]

On the next page of the letter (see Plate 10), Schenker continues with examples of the *Raum-Begriffe* (spatial concepts) that fill this space: a *Quint-Raum* (space of a fifth), a *Terz-Raum* (space of a third). His examples of $\hat{5}-\hat{1}$ and $\hat{3}-\hat{1}$ descents are all drawn from pieces Schenker discusses in the first two yearbooks of *Meisterwerk*, which date from this same time.[22] Then Schenker tells Hammer that these musical spaces of a fifth or a third are filled by the unfolding *Urlinie* (see Plate 11):[23]

> But I make a very clear distinction between the "space" itself and what takes place within that space. And the primary unfurling of a living musical work within a space, the very first and most concise conception, the first composing-out, the initial outline, is the "*Urlinie*." It thus implies a space, but is itself already the work, its being, its content, albeit at the most remote background stage.

On the third page of the letter (see Plate 12 on page 98), Schenker provides more detailed examples of the *Urlinie* as it unfolds within a space. At the top of the page is a sketch of the Bach C minor Fugue.[24] Then he depicts

[21]From Schenker's letter of November 22, 1925, page 1: "Des Musikers Natur-Raum ist sehr begrenzt . . . . aber selbst der kleinste Raum reicht hin, eine Welt von Schöpfung zu beherbergen, so weiß er den Raum zu erfüllen, zu füllen:" (In this and subsequent quotations from Schenker's letters, the translations omit the underlining and double underlining found in the German original and reproduced in the transcriptions.)

[22]The text above the examples in Schenker's letter of November 22, 1925, page 2, reads: "Nachstehendes ist blos als 'Raum'-Begriff notiert, als Quint-, Terz-Raum." ("What follows is notated only as a spatial concept, as a space of a fifth, space of a third.") The five examples (and the corresponding *Meisterwerk* essays) are:

a) Bach, Fugue in C minor, Well-Tempered Clavier, Book I; discussed in "Das Organische der Fuge," *Meisterwerk*, Vol. 2, pp. 57–95; "The Organic Nature of Fugue," *Masterwork*, Vol. 2, pp. 31–54.

b) Mozart, Symphony in G minor, K. 550, first movement; discussed in *Meisterwerk*, Vol. 2, pp. 107–157; *Masterwork*, Vol. 2, pp. 59–96.

c) Mozart, Sonata in F major, K. 332, first movement; discussed in "Fortsetzung der Urlinie-Betrachtungen," *Meisterwerk*, Vol. 1, pp. 187–200; "Further Considerations of the Urlinie: I," *Masterwork*, Vol. 1, pp. 104–111 (Fig. 3).

d) Chopin, Nocturne in F♯ major, Op. 15, No. 2; discussed in "Fortsetzung der Urlinie-Betrachtungen," *Meisterwerk*, Vol. 2, pp. 11–42; "Further Considerations of the Urlinie: II," *Masterwork*, Vol. 2, pp. 1–19 (Fig. 32).

e) Chopin, Etude in G♭ major, Op. 10, No. 5; discussed in *Meisterwerk*, Vol. 1, pp. 163–73; *Masterwork*, Vol. 1, pp. 90–98.

[23]From Schenker's letter of November 22, 1925, page 2, the paragraph numbered "2": "Aber vom 'Raum' an sich unterscheide ich sehr deutlich das, was im Raume vor sich geht. Und die allererste Aufrollung des lebendigen Kunstwerkes im Raume, die allererste kürzeste Fassung, erste Auskomponierung, erster Aufriß, das ist die 'Urlinie.' Diese sagt also einen Raum bereits voraus, ist selbst aber schon das Werk, sein Geschehen, sein Inhalt, wenn auch erst im äußerster Hintergrund-Fassung."

[24]Cf. "Das Organische der Fuge," Fig. 1. In Schenker's letter of November 22, 1925, page 3, the text surrounding the first example reads: "d. h. den Raum 5–1 läuft die Urlinie (*cont.*)

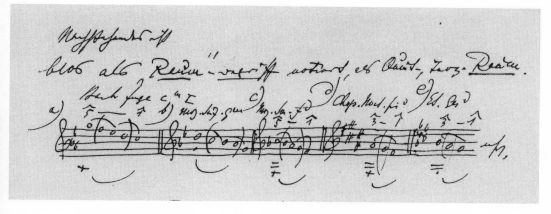

Plate 10. From Schenker's letter to Hammer, November 22, 1925, page 2.

the intervallic space (*Raum*) of the variation theme of Mozart's Sonata in A major, K. 331, as the vertical fifth A–E and shows its *Urlinie*, supported by the scale degrees I and V:[25]

> The *Urlinie* is such a definitive representation of the work (within a space) that it also serves to lead the *Ursatz*—the very first counterpoint—which clearly determines the decisive succession of scale degrees [and], above all, the form![26]

This is the crux of what Schenker wrote to Hammer about musical space: he relates it to musical form. By 1925, Schenker saw the form of a work as coming from the *Ursatz*, in which the *Urlinie*'s linear representation of intervallic space is combined with harmonic degrees.

It is not surprising that Schenker's letter to Hammer sometimes rephrases what had or was about to appear in *Tonwille* or *Meisterwerk*. Hammer attempted to keep up with all of Schenker's latest publications, and Schenker may have been trying to help him understand them. Perhaps more important, however, is the reflection of their discussions in these publications. There are some passages, especially in the second yearbook of *Meisterwerk*, published in 1926, which seem to show traces of the new ideas Hammer was conveying to Schenker.

In the "Further Consideration of the Urlinie" that begins the second *Meisterwerk* volume, Schenker directly compares the visual arts and music when writing about the concept of space. He writes that since Nature provides the painter with infinite space, it is the task of the painter to provide

---

zweimal abwärts und der Rest bleibt eigentlich stehen, denn eine Oktavauskomponierung wie diese belegt nur einen Ton." ("i.e., the *Urlinie* twice descends through the space 5–1 and then remains stationary, since a composing-out of an octave such as this covers only one tone.")
[25]Cf. "Fortsetzung der Urlinie-Betrachtungen," *Meisterwerk*, Vol. 1, p. 189; *Masterwork*, Vol. 1, p. 105, Fig. 1.
[26]From Schenker's letter of November 22, 1925, page 3, the paragraph following the musical examples: "Die Urlinie ist so <u>sehr schon das Kunstwerk</u> (<u>im Raume</u>), daß sie auch den <u>Ursatz</u> führt, also den allerersten Kontrapunkt, der deutlich die entscheidende Stufenfolge, vor allem die <u>Form festlegt</u>!"

a boundary for the space he will represent in his painting. It is possible that Schenker might have been thinking of the rectangular space marked A, B, C, D in Hammer's diagram of the Perugino painting (see Plate 8)— the rectangle that represented its frame or boundary:

> By nature infinite, the space available for visual works of art must be bounded by the painter and, in the setting of boundaries, created anew. The eye of the painter, and of the viewer, demands not merely selectivity in art, but also boundary.

He goes on to say that the opposite is true in music: since Nature provides the composer with the small, finite spaces of the intervals in the overtone series, it is task of the musician to fill a space that already has a boundary. (This recalls what he had said in the first page of his letter of November 22, 1925, Plate 9 above.)

> With music, things are different: here the spaces available to melodic motion are the spaces of the octave, fifth and third offered by Nature. Larger spaces, more distant boundaries, do not exist; the musician's only task is to fill these spaces. The spaces of tonal movement are therefore finite and small; but the possibilities for filling them are infinite.[27]

Schenker of course continued to refer to the concept of space throughout the *Meisterwerk* yearbooks and in *Der freie Satz*. There, he refined the concept of *Urlinie-Raum*—the space occupied by the *Urlinie*.[28] This goes beyond the scope of the present study, which focuses on the period of *Tonwille* and *Meisterwerk*, the time of the Schenker–Hammer correspondence.

The *Meisterwerk* essays seem to show further signs of Hammer's influence. A well-known passage in the second yearbook may reflect an idea derived from the nineteenth-century philosopher Conrad Fiedler, the other writer on art that Hammer recommended to Schenker along with Hildebrand. There is direct evidence that Schenker read Fiedler's and Hildebrand's writings. Part of a letter from Hildebrand to Fiedler is quoted in Issue 7 of *Tonwille*, and two of Fiedler's aphorisms are included in the second book of *Meisterwerk*.[29]

The impact of Fiedler's theory of art on Hammer's philosophy can only be hinted at here. Hammer is largely responsible for making Fiedler's works available in America; he issued three books of his writings in translation (two were printed in American Uncial type, a typeface of Hammer's own design).[30]

[27]"Fortsetzung der Urlinie-Betrachtungen," *Meisterwerk*, Vol. 2, pp. 22–23. The translation given here is by John Rothgeb, in "Further Considerations of the Urlinie: II," *Masterwork*, Vol. 2, p. 8.
[28]See, for example, §§5, 13, and 25 in Schenker, *Der freie Satz*, edited and revised by Oswald Jonas (Vienna: Universal Edition, 1956); *Free Composition*, trans. and ed. Ernst Oster (New York: Longman, 1979). The conceptual space depicted by Schenker and the visual imagery of *Free Composition* were discussed by Brian Hyer in "Picturing Music," a paper read in 1994 at the annual meeting of the Society for Music Theory.
[29]For Schenker's quotation from Hildebrand's letter, see "Vermischtes," in *Der Tonwille*, Heft 7 (January–March 1924), p. 42. On January 13, 1924, Schenker wrote to Hammer about having discovered it in a collection published by Piper in Munich; he particularly *(cont.)*

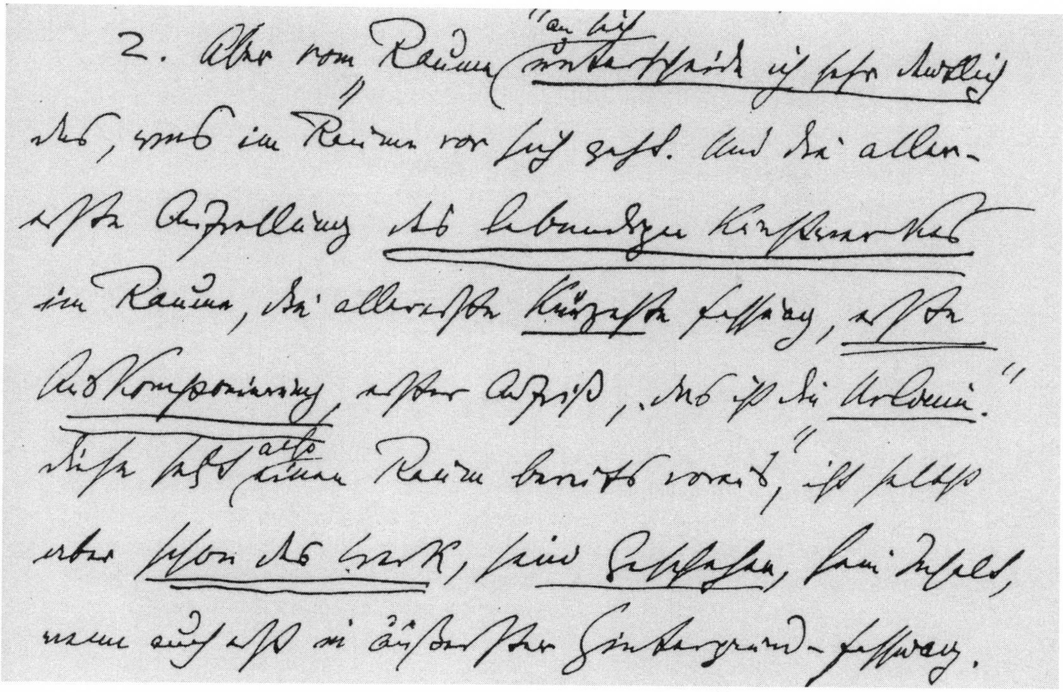

Plate 11. From Schenker's letter to Hammer, November 22, 1925, page 2.

Fiedler postulated that the laws of the visual arts differ from the laws of nature; artistic laws derive from what the eye sees and organizes into a formal structure. He believed that this formal structure is somehow pre-existent. He writes in his book *On Judging Works of Visual Art*:

> The content of a work of art . . . does not owe its existence to the essential creative powers of the artist. It already existed before it found expression in the artwork; the artist does not create it, he only finds it *(der Künstler schafft ihn nicht, er findet ihn nur)*. . . .[31]

---

liked the way Hildebrand described the relationship of the individual parts of a human form to the whole. For Schenker's quotation of Fiedler's two aphorisms, see "Vermischtes: Gedanken über die Kunst und ihre Zusammenhänge im Allgemeinen," *Meisterwerk*, Vol. 2, pp. 212–13, trans. Ian Bent in "Miscellanea: thoughts on art and its relationships to the general scheme of things," *Masterwork*, Vol. 2, pp. 128–129. The two aphorisms may be found in Fiedler, *Schriften zur Kunst*, Vol. 2, p. 100 (aphorism no. 156) and p. 111 (aphorism no. 179).

[30]Fiedler, *Nine Aphorisms from the Notebooks of Konrad Fiedler*, selected by Victor Hammer, trans.George Kreye (Aurora, New York: The Wells College Press, 1941); *Three Fragments from the Postumous Papers of Conrad Fiedler*, trans. Thornton Sinclair and Victor Hammer (Lexington, Kentucky: Stamperia del Santuccio, 1951); *On the Nature and History of Architecture*, trans. Alvina Brower, Victor Hammer, and Edgar Kaufmann, Jr. (Lexington, Kentucky: [The Press of Carolyn Reading], 1954). The introductory essays on Fiedler that Hammer wrote for these publications are reprinted in *Victor Hammer: An Artist's Testament*, pp. 99–104 and 107–109; see also pp. 237–39 ("The Theory of 'Pure' Visibility"), and pp. 249–251 ("Marées, Hildebrand and Fiedler"), reprinted from Hammer's *Concern for the Art of Civilized Man* (Lexington, Kentucky: Stamperia del Santuccio, 1963).

[31]In the German original, the beginning of the passage reads as follows: "Der Inhalt des Kunstwerkes . . . ist nicht der, der sein Dasein der wesentlich künstlerischen Kraft *(cont.)*

This is one of Fiedler's ideas that found its way into Hammer's philosophy of art: he equated Fiedler's "content of a work of art" with Hildebrand's "underlying structure of a painting." Thus he believed that the structure of a painting was already there, waiting to be found. It is this thought that he transmitted to Schenker in his letter of December 9, 1921, cited above, where, after noting that "the *Urlinie* is evident in every good picture," he continued: "but the creator of the work can never 'invent' it (*man kann sie . . . aber niemals 'erfinden'*); it has always been present and can at most be purified, clarified, and elucidated." Schenker may have been recalling these words when he wrote, in the second book of *Meisterwerk*, "Ich habe die Urlinie erschaut, nicht errechnet!"[32] This echo of Fiedler in Schenker's wording has been pointed out by Timothy Jackson;[33] we can now postulate that Hammer served as the link between Fiedler and Schenker. Schenker's use of the word *erschauen* has been traced by William Pastille to Goethe's concept of *Anschauung* and the "flash of insight that is its ultimate result."[34] It is significant that *erschauen*, like *Anschauung*, comes from *schauen*, meaning "to behold" or "to see." Here again we have language derived from the visual process; Schenker is speaking of a kind of inner vision. In any case, it is likely that both Goethe and Fiedler served as antecedents for Schenker's wording.[35]

I will cite one further passage from the second *Meisterwerk* yearbook which brings together eye and ear—a passage which may well have arisen from Schenker's conversations with Hammer. The essay on the Sarabande of Bach's Suite No. 3 for solo cello begins:

---

des Urhebers verdankt; er ist vorhanden, bevor er sich dem Ausdrucke im Kunstwerke anbequemt hat; . . . ." See Fiedler, *Über die Beurteilung von Werken der bildenden Kunst* (1876), reprinted in *Schriften zur Kunst*, Vol. 1, pp. 13–14. See also the translation given in Fiedler, *On Judging Works of Visual Art*, trans. Henry Schaefer-Simmern and Fulmer Mood (Berkeley: University of California Press, 1949), p. 11.

[32] *Meisterwerk*, Vol. 2, p. 41, trans. by John Rothgeb as "I *apprehended* the Urlinie, I did not *calculate* it!" in "Further Considerations of the Urlinie: II," *Masterwork*, Vol. 2, p. 19; and by William Pastille as "I saw through to the Urlinie, I did not figure it out!" in his article, "Music and Morphology: Goethe's Influence on Schenker's Thought," *Schenker Studies*, edited by Hedi Siegel (Cambridge: Cambridge University Press, 1990), p. 37.

[33] See Timothy Jackson's review of *Schenker Studies* and of *Trends in Schenkerian Research*, ed. Allen Cadwallader (New York: Schirmer Books, 1990): "Current Issues in Schenkerian Analysis," *The Musical Quarterly*, Vol. 76, No. 2 (1992), pp. 247–48. My discussion of the connection between Fiedler and Schenker is much indebted to Jackson's work.

[34] Pastille, "Music and Morphology," p. 37.

[35] The writings of Goethe were of course also an important influence on Schenker's ideas on the visual arts. In *Der Tonwille*, Schenker presents extracts from Goethe's writings on painting, sculpture, and the other art forms and praises his perceptive insights (while deploring what he saw as a lack of technical musical understanding and failure to recognize the great musicians of his time). See "Vermischtes: Deutsche Form" in *Der Tonwille*, Heft 5 (1923), pp. 46–48. Ian Bent, in "Heinrich Schenker e la missione del genio germanico," *Rivista Italiana di Musicologia*, Vol. 26, No. 1 (1991), pp. 9–10, points this out, and writes about the task that he believes Schenker set for himself: in part, it was to do for music what Goethe had done for the other arts.

The eye can follow and encompass the lines of a painting or architectural structure in all their directions, breadth and relationships; if only the ear could hear the background of the Ursatz and the continuous musical motion of the foreground as profoundly and as extensively! Then the twenty-four bars of this sarabande would be perceived as a gigantic structure, whose many broad and striking events, while seeming to have a private, autonomous existence, all bear a profound and exacting relation to the whole.[36]

We have seen that there are some passages in Schenker's writings that may bear the mark of Hammer's influence. In Hammer's writings, there is one passage that is unmistakably derived from Schenker's thought. In 1936, one year after Schenker's death, Hammer paid him a direct tribute. Writing in an autobiographical essay, he describes the procedure of preparing a portrait:

The characteristics of the live image (meaning you, dear model) are carefully explored in the many preparatory studies; his individuality is the starting point of the construction. But the construction is always the same; we always seek to create the same work of art according to the same law; and each time only its outward appearance varies. *Semper idem, sed non eodem modo* (always the same, but not in the same way), invoking the memory of Heinrich Schenker. . . . [37]

Here Hammer is quoting the motto Schenker coined for himself, the motto he would have remembered from his conversations with Schenker, or perhaps from the title pages of Schenker's publications.

Hammer also seems to be invoking Schenker's memory in a passage found in his *Theory of Architecture*. Setting forth the "requisites of classical art," he focuses on the concept of structural levels or planes (an idea touched on in his correspondence with Schenker, as we have seen):

Standing out against a background, however infinite, but determined by the frame, all forms in the middle plane fall into definite places within the confines of foreground and background, since they now rest on a ground plan. . . . The fact that all this happens within the framework of foreground and background and on a definite ground plan—this is the sole content of a classic work of art. To shape these events with his hands is to the true artist an ever novel, never repeated, and always the same, pure task.[38]

Expanding on this subject in his essay, *On Classic Art*, Hammer again demonstrates a close affinity to Schenker's thinking. He describes how an artist views a painting:

[36]*Meisterwerk,* Vol. 2, p. 99, trans. Hedi Siegel in *Masterwork*, Vol. 2, p. 55. An earlier version of this translation appeared in *The Music Forum*, Vol. 2 (1970), p. 274.
[37]Hammer, "Past, Present, and Objectives," excerpts trans. Dudley Zopp and Gerhard Probst in *Victor Hammer: An Artist's Testament*, p. 22. Originally published as *Victor Hammer: Rückschau, Gegenwart und Ausblick* (Graz: Schmidt-Dengler, 1936). I am indebted to Sophie Eisenhut, who called my attention to this passage by citing it in her lecture "Victor Hammer's Years in Europe," read at the Wells College Book Arts Center Symposium honoring the life and work of Victor Hammer (October, 1993).
[38]*A Theory of Architecture* (1952), incorporated into *Memory and Her Nine Daughters, The Muses* (1956); reprinted in *Victor Hammer: An Artist's Testament*, p. 164.

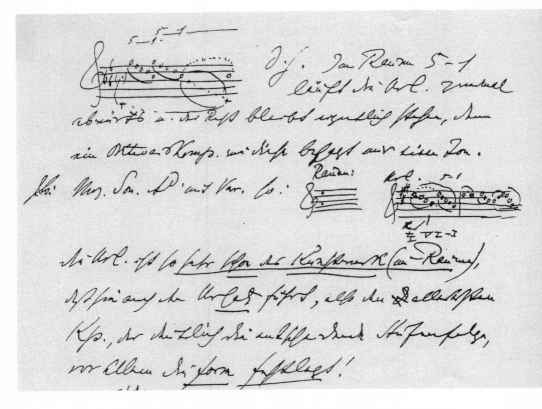

Plate 12. From Schenker's letter to Hammer, November 22, 1925, page 3.

. . . the first things which I, as a classic painter, see . . . are the square of the frame itself and all the other squares in the picture as against the triangles of the figures which I see placed on a ground plan in a definite pattern, like the pawns in a chess-board. But I can immediately switch to the aspect of a room peopled with males and females and a dog, see the expression of the faces, the light playing on the figures and the gentlemen on the steps behind the doorway looking at me. The squares and triangles constitute the skeleton of the composition, and a masterly hand has hidden it behind the human likeness of people gathered in their accustomed surroundings.[39]

Later in the same essay he explains how a "classic artist" places structural planes within the space or frame of a painting:

Within the frame, which limits the field of vision deliberately, he reduces the whole of the world symbolically, but visibly, to a comprehensible unit. The forms of the foreground, the middle plane, and the background are determined by their position on the ground plan that acts as a frame which is extended into depth. The physical eye, limited in its capacity, cannot apprehend the relation of the forms which appear simultaneously on the ground plan and the elevation—only the mind's eye can do that.

[39]*On Classic Art* (1959), reprinted in *Victor Hammer: An Artist's Testament*, p. 203.

The work of the artist who is capable of making this relation visible will turn out to be classic as compared with the work of prehistoric and modern artists.[40]

Such passages help us understand the like-mindedness that must have drawn Hammer and Schenker to each other during the time of their correspondence and discussions.[41]

Victor Hammer opened Schenker's eyes to the structural aspect of the visual arts, and may have helped shape his ideas and the imagery of his language. One of the most pervasive elements of Schenker's language is a direct borrowing from the visual arts: his use of the word *Bild* —a picture or image—for what we now call a graph or sketch. (As we have seen, Schenker characterized his sketch of the Mendelssohn song as a *Bildchen*, or little picture.) Schenker's eyesight was weak,[42] but this did not prevent him from using visual imagery and actual visual images to transmit his ideas. One of the greatest strengths of his approach is his use of "pictures"— visual representations—to convey what he saw, that is to say, heard in a piece of music. He eventually dispensed with words and relied entirely on pictures, as in the collection of five analyses he published near the end of his life.[43] It was his use of pictures that enabled him to go beyond the verbal description of surface events and depict what lay beneath.

[40]Ibid., p. 208.

[41]Their exchanges included some disagreement, especially in the area of politics, but their friendship was not diminished by Schenker's opposing views on such matters as Hammer's internationalism. See the passages from Schenker's diary transcribed in Hellmut Federhofer, *Heinrich Schenker: Nach Tagebüchern und Briefen in der Oswald Jonas Memorial Collection* (Hildesheim: Olms, 1985), pp. 317 and 327. (For further material on Hammer, see pp. 38–39, 45, 96, 102, 149–50, and 318.)

[42]In several letters, Schenker mentioned to Hammer that he felt hampered by his nearsightedness. For example, he told him (December 19, 1921): "My wife writes everything [for me] because of my eyesight." ("Meine Frau schreibt alles wegen meiner Augen.") Federhofer records that Schenker's extreme myopia measured minus 11 diopters; see *Heinrich Schenker*, pp. 45 and 270.

[43]Schenker, *Fünf Urlinie-Tafeln* (Vienna: Universal Edition, 1932; New York: David Mannes Music School, 1932); reissued, with a new introduction and glossary by Felix Salzer, as *Five Graphic Music Analyses* (New York: Dover, 1969).

IV

STYLE

Rhythmic Displacement in the Music of Bill Evans

Steve Larson

During a 1978 interview, Bill Evans told pianist and radio journalist Marian McPartland about the importance of rhythmic displacement to his artistic conception:

> As far as the jazz playing goes, I think the rhythmic construction of the thing has evolved quite a bit. Now, I don't know how obvious that would be to the listener, but the displacement of phrases and, you know, the way phrases follow one another and their placement against the meter and so forth, is something that I've worked on rather hard and it's something I believe in.[1]

Evans went on to demonstrate various techniques of rhythmic displacement in four choruses of "All of You"; the first three choruses are played solo, and in the last chorus (which follows a brief discussion) Evans is accompanied by McPartland playing the tune in octaves. These performances of "All of You" offer a particularly rich opportunity to study a catalogue of his techniques of rhythmic displacement.[2]

Rhythmic displacement (also called "cross rhythm" or "polyrhythm") arises when listeners experience an implied grouping or accent structure that conflicts with the underlying metric structure.[3] Displacement may arise

---

[1]Marian McPartland's *Piano Jazz* with guest Bill Evans, recorded November 6, 1978 (The Jazz Alliance TJA–12004).

[2]Specific instances of rhythmic displacement in Evans's recordings have been noted in Steve Larson, *Schenkerian Analysis of Modern Jazz* (Ph.D. dissertation, University of Michigan, 1987); Steve Larson, "Triple Play: Bill Evans's Three-Piano Performance of Victor Young's 'Stella by Starlight,'" in "An Analysis Symposium: Alternate Takes—Stella by Starlight," *Annual Review of Jazz Studies* 9 (1997–98), pp. 45--56; and Steven Strunk, "Melodic Structure in Bill Evans' 1959 'Autumn Leaves,'" presented at the *John Donald Robb Composers' Symposium* in Albuquerque, N.M., 1998.

[3]Rhythmic displacement has a long history in jazz, and may be found in music of various other styles. The purpose of this paper is to explore the role that displacement plays in Evans's music. On displacement in jazz, see Cynthia Folio, "An Analysis of Polyrhythm in Selected Improvised Jazz Solos," *Concert Music, Rock, and Jazz Since 1945*, edited by Elizabeth West Marvin and Richard Hermann (Rochester, NY: University of Rochester Press, 1995), pp. 103–134; Steve Larson, "Triple Play," pp. 45–56; Steven Strunk, "Melodic Structure in Bill Evans' 1959 'Autumn Leaves,'" presented at the *John Donald Robb Composers' Symposium* in Albuquerque, N.M., 1998; Keith Waters, "Blurring the Barline: Metric Displacement in the Piano Solos of Herbie Hancock, " *Annual Review of Jazz Studies* 8 (1996), pp. 19–37. For related work on non-jazz styles, see Alison Hood, *Chopin's Strategic Integration of Rhythm and Pitch: A Schenkerian Perspective* (Ph.D. Dissertation, Trinity College Dublin, 2002); Arthur J. Komar, *Theory of Suspensions: A Study of Metrical and Pitch Relations in Tonal Music* (Princeton: Princeton University Press, 1971); Harald Krebs, *Fantasy Pieces: Metrical Dissonance in the Music of (cont.)*

either through polymeter, accentual shifting, or both. *Polymeter* pits two different metric structures against one another, either as what Keith Waters calls "measure-preserving polymeter" (as in Example 1a) or "tactus-preserving polymeter" (as in Example 1b). Measure-preserving polymeter tends to create cycling gestures that call attention to the downbeats of agreement, and tactus-preserving polymeter typically creates longer gestures of suspense that anticipate a forthcoming simultaneous downbeat.

Example 1. A taxonomy of displacement (the upper line represents an improvised line, the lower represents the underlying meter).
     POLYMETER: (a) measure-preserving; (b) tactus-preserving
     ACCENTUAL SHIFT: (c) anticipation; (d) delay
     COMBINATIONS: (e) shift-shifting; (f) shift-shifting that
produces **liquidation**

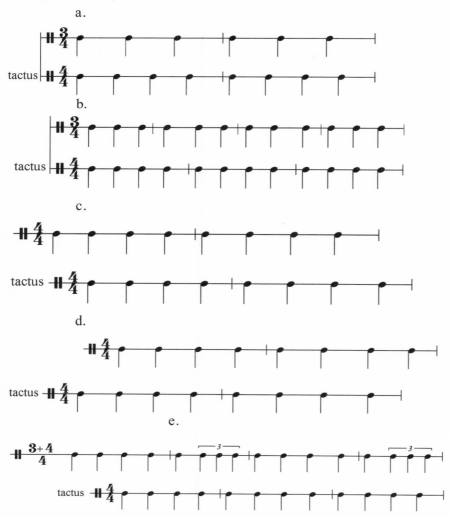

f.

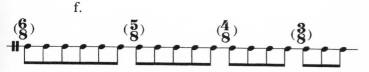

Whereas polymeter presents different meters at the same time, *accentual shift* presents the same meter at different times. Accentual shift may place a figure before (Example 1c) or after (Example 1d) its normative metric placement. Where the pitch content of an accentually shifted pattern allows us to hear it as an anticipation, it immediately heightens interest by drawing attention to its beginning and to the beat on which it "belongs." Where the pitch content of an accentually shifted pattern allows us to hear it as a delay, it may prolong intensity the way a suspension does, making us wait for the pitches it displaces. Polymeter and accentual shift may also occur simultaneously (as in Example 1e) or used with an increase in intensity so as to create an effect of liquidation (as in Example 1f).

Evans uses all of these techniques in his "All of You" improvisation. As I shall argue, the rhythmic instability created by Evans's techniques of rhythmic displacement functions not only in ways that are analogous to the ways in which tonal instability functions, but also in concert with tonal structures so as to advance dramatic, rhetorical, and gestural strategies. Much as tonal instability creates expectations for stability, so rhythmic instability creates a desire to hear agreement with the underlying meter. Detailed analysis also shows that the patterns of pitches projected by Evans's techniques of displacement create interesting and sophisticated relationships to one another, to prolongational structures, and to the theme on which he improvises.

Analysis of Evans's improvisation on the first chorus

Evans's opening statement of the melody (Example 2) subtly introduces each of the techniques of displacement that will appear (with more dramatic impact) later in the improvisation.

He reharmonizes bars 1–2 of Cole Porter's original theme, turning the opening upper-neighbor figure F–E (which in the published sheet music is supported by a neighboring six-four that immediately resolves to tonic) into an entire upper-neighbor "approach chord" that does not resolve until the following measure. The next two measures in Evans's reharmonization echo this motion by giving the dominant its own upper-neighbor approach

Robert Schumann (New York: Oxford University Press, 1999); William Rothstein, "Rhythm and the Theory of Structural Levels," (Ph.D. dissertation, Yale University, 1981); William Rothstein, *Phrase Rhythm in Tonal Music* (New York: Schirmer, 1989); William Rothstein, "Rhythmic Displacement and Rhythmic Normalization," in *Trends in Schenkerian Research*, ed. Allen Cadwallader (New York: Schirmer Books, 1990), pp. 87–113; and Carl Schachter's series of articles for *The Music Forum* on "Rhythm and Linear Analysis," which are reprinted in his *Unfoldings: Essays in Schenkerian Theory and Analysis* (New York and Oxford: Oxford University Press, 1999).

Example 2. Transcription of Bill Evans's improvisation of "All of You," bars 1-8.

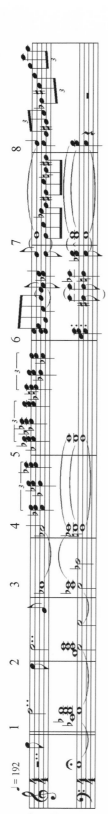

Example 3. Hypothetical version of bars 1-6.

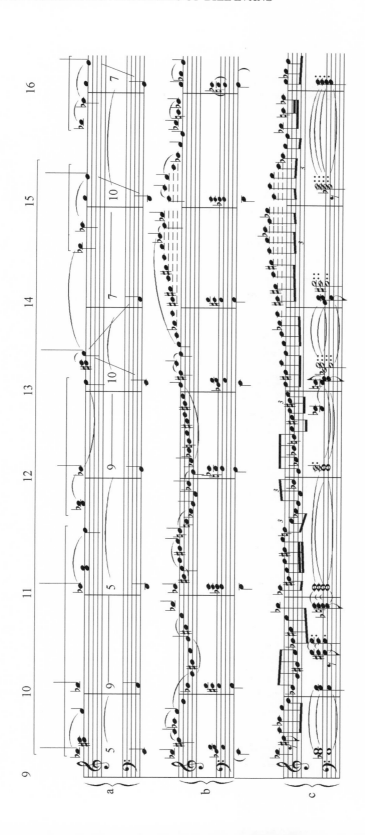

Example 4. Bars 9–16.

chord. Evans could have returned in bars 5–6 to the same harmonies of the opening two bars (and in some choruses, he does precisely this). But here (and in most analogous places), he suspends the left-hand chord of bar 4 through bar 5, turning an implicit melodic hypermetrical suspension into an entire suspension chord and thus heightening the instability.

The effect of this hypermetrical suspension is heightened by the measure-preserving polymeter of the quarter-note triplets in bars 4–5. Characteristically, Evans introduces this polymeter in the middle of a measure, and further complicates matters by having the stepwise melodic arc change direction on a rhythmically unstable note. One result is that this melodic gesture embodies the grace of smoothly joined physical gestures. Had Evans introduced the quarter-note triplets on the downbeat instead of in the middle of bar 4, and had he changed direction on a rhythmically stable instead of a rhythmically unstable note, the result (Example 3) would have been much less elegant than what he actually played.

In bar 6 Evans introduces another type of rhythmic displacement: accentual shift in the form of eighth-note anticipations.

The tactus-preserving polymeter in bar 7 is reminiscent of ragtime, in which a directional change in the melody creates groups of three notes (with accents on the G). However, the anticipation of the first eighth note sets up an alternative accentual scheme in which the third, sixth, and ninth notes of this figure are accented. That is, the accentual shift of bar 6 carries into bar 7, turning what would have been a rather ordinary ragtime figure into something more refined.

In the second section of the first chorus, beginning in bar 9, Evans settles into what becomes the basic texture for his improvisation: "shifted" left-hand chords supporting a right-hand melody in eighth notes (Example 4). The left hand rarely attacks the downbeat; most often it is shifted one eighth note late. (The other two most common shifts found in this improvisation result in a left-hand chord that comes either one eighth note early or several beats late.) The right hand moves in eighth notes and is spiced up with an occasional triplet.

Although the harmonies are complex, and the resolutions of some dissonances are delayed until the chords change, the pitches played by the right hand stand in clear relation to the chords implied by Evans's left hand. Note that the right hand typically delays changing to the pitch material implied by the left-hand chord until that chord actually enters (that is, the right hand—like the left hand—is shifted one eighth note late), and further note that the right hand often shifts accents to upbeats. The analysis in Example 4 shows the underlying counterpoint as well as the delay of chord arrival and dissonance resolution.[4] And as the brackets above Example 4a show, hidden repetitions of the figure B♭–A♭–G–F saturate the middleground of this passage.

---

[4]The Schenkerian analyses in this article follow the suggestions in my "'Strict Use' of Analytic Notation," *Journal of Music Theory Pedagogy* 10 (1996), pp. 31–71: all notes of the surface are represented (except repeated notes and the most obvious ornaments); few symbols beyond noteheads, stems, and slurs are used; all and only the noteheads that (*cont.*)

The next section (bars 17–24, Examples 5 and 6) introduces an even more sophisticated example of accentual shifting. Here shorter gestures are carried by an overall sweep that begins before bar 17, touches down briefly at the tonic of bar 22, and then moves to the cadence at the end of the next section. This long sweep may be understood either as resulting from the shifting shown in Example 6b, or as projecting the polymeter described in Example 6c. While it is unlikely that Evans perceived it both these ways as he played it, we may experience it in either way as listeners.

The rhythmic displacements here are matched by various elements of the voice-leading and motivic structure. As Example 5 shows, various shifted descending half-step resolutions (which recall and end with the F–E motion from the beginning of the original melody of "All of You") interact with hidden repetitions of a descending-fourth motive (Ab–G–F–E). As Examples 5b and 6a suggest, the first note of the arpeggiated figures in this passage are expected to appear on the first and third beats of the measure. Instead, however, Evans shifts some of these chords at different rates.

Because the pattern is shifted in different amounts, because the first chord enters 2½ beats before the bar, and because the remaining chords pair compressed and uncompressed versions of the figure, a tactus-preserving polymetric juxtaposition of seven-eight and four-four arises. The two meters come together on the downbeat of bar 19, but the figure and the process of shifting continue beyond that downbeat. What follows may easily be heard either in the underlying four-four meter or in an implied triple meter (either 3/4 or 3/8). The implied triple meter seems to continue past the tonic arrival in bar 22, all the way to the hypermetrical downbeat of bar 25. Bars 25–32 then settle back into the basic texture established in bars 9–16 as they move smoothly toward the cadence that is expected in bar 31 (Example 7). Evans's line sounds as though it will cadence on the downbeat of this measure, but at the last moment he avoids doing so.

Second chorus

The displacement techniques found in bars 33–38 (Example 8) are in many ways similar to those of bars 17–22, although now realized in a more intense manner. Like bars 17–22, bars 33–38 enter early (beginning before the downbeat with an approach chord to the approach chord) and begin with a shifted statement of the figure of the descending seventh-chord arpeggio. But whereas the anacrusis to bar 17 begins a couple of beats before its hypermetrical downbeat, the anacrusis to the passage of bars 33–38 begins more than a measure early. Another similarity between bars 33–38 and 17–22 involves the use of successive shifts. Like bars 17–22, bars 33–38 successively change the amount of shift to produce a pattern that creates rhythmic instability with the underlying meter and moves to the

---

are stemmed on a given analytic level are represented on the next more-remote level (flags are used for occasional self-evident exceptions); and slurs unambiguously indicate embellishment function only.

Example 5. Bars 16-22.

Example 6. Bars 16-25.

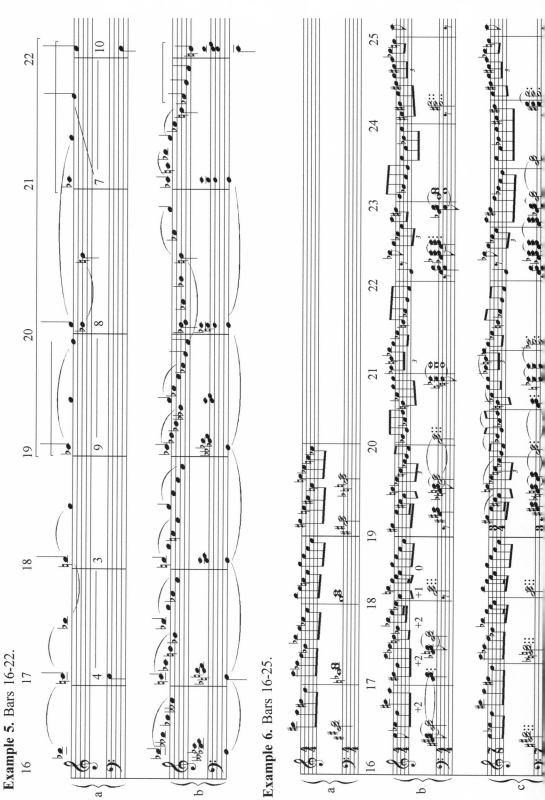

Example 7. Bars 25-32.

Example 8. Bars 31-38.

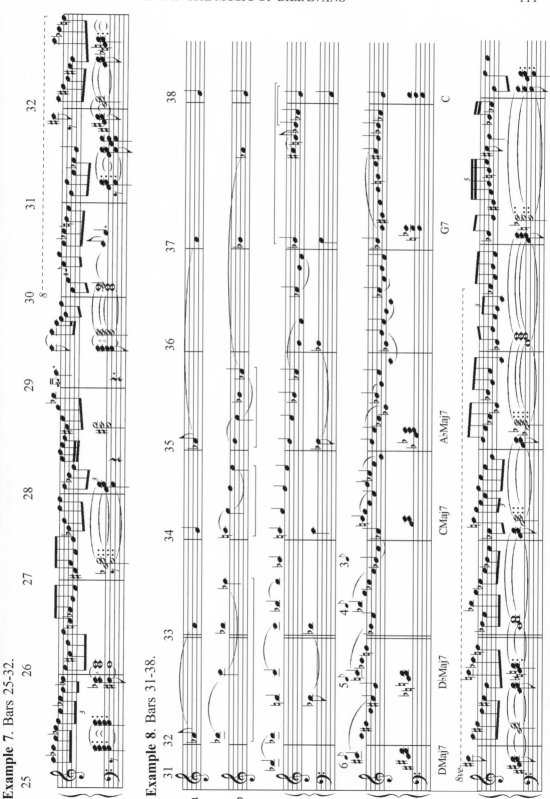

target tonic (in the sixth measure of the theme) as a point of rest. But whereas the shifting implies a seven-eight polymetric juxtaposition in bars 17–22, in bars 33–38 it creates a different effect, one of "liquidation" (see Example 8d).[5]

The motivic development found in bars 33–38 also bears certain similarities to that of 17–22. Bars 33–38 are based on a middleground structure that leads to the tonic by using a four-note motive similar to the one seen in the earlier phrase (see brackets in Example 8b). Furthermore, it enriches that middleground with hidden repetitions that confirm arrival on that tonic, much as in bars 17–22. However, whereas in bars 17–22 the four-note motive appears solely with the notes Ab–G–F–E, in bars 33–38 the motive appears at different transposition levels. Note also that the passage ends with a stepwise descent from C♯–G (bars 37–38) that may be understood as a summary of the melodic line of bars 31–38.

That Evans retains in bars 33–38 the idea of the long gesture created by shifting—yet produces liquidation instead of polymeter and a different set of hidden repetitions—suggests his flexibility in the use of these techniques of displacement. In bars 38–40, Evan sequences the idea found at the end of the previous phrase, creating a polymetric juxtaposition of three-eight against the underlying four-four. Example 9 shows how this passage creates this polymeter while expressing an exciting middleground ascent based on a deeper-level register transfer.

The "lick" in bar 41, which Evans uses in many of his solos, may be heard as an expansion of the one of bars 38–40. Like the figure of bars 38–40, the one of bar 41 has a consistently descending contour and speeds up in the middle; it is different, however, in that it contains more notes and the intervals are larger. Thus, the rising gesture of bars 38–40 sounds as though it naturally culminates in a registrally and durationally expanded statement of its own motive. The resultant motive also resembles the earlier figure in at least two ways: first, both this figure and the original melody of "All of You" are concerned with the appoggiatura figure A–G; second, both are concerned with joining motions in two different octaves.

This motive is subsequently compressed to a shape that lasts three beats and is sequenced in what follows. That sequence may be understood as the result of a "recipe" designed to create a tactus-preserving polymetric juxtaposition of three-four against the theme's underlying four-four (see Table 1):[6]

---

[5]Steven Strunk noted instances of similar "liquidations" in other Evans performances in his "Melodic Structure in Bill Evans' 1959 'Autumn Leaves,'" presented at the *John Donald Robb Composers' Symposium* in Albuquerque, N.M., 1998.

[6]This recipe could, of course, be adjusted for other combinations of meters. And more could be said about the types of motives that Evans uses in such situations, the ways in which the passages based on such recipes grow smoothly out of previous material and lead convincingly into what follows, and the strategic roles they play within the larger "story" of Evans's improvisations.

Table 1: *A recipe for smoothly introducing a tactus-preserving polymetric juxtaposition of three-four against the theme's underlying four-four.*

(1) Locate one hypermetrical downbeat that will serve as the beginning and another one, four bars (16 beats) later, that will serve as the goal.

(2) Play a figure in the first measure (4 beats). Three measures (12 beats) remain.

(3) Replace those three measures of four-four with four measures of three-four (3x4=4x3).

(4) Reharmonize, if necessary, so that each (new) three-four measure is a single chord.

(5) Play the figure of the first measure in each (new) three-four measure, adjusting it to fit the chord and duration of each measure.

* * * *

As may be seen in Example 10, bars 41–44 follow the recipe outlined above: (1) the hypermetrical downbeat at bar 41 is the beginning, and the hypermetrical downbeat at bar 45—four measures (16 beats) later—is the goal; (2) Evans plays a figure in the first bar (EØ^7, bar 41) so that three measures (12 beats) remain; (3) he replaces those three measures of four-four (bars 42–44) with four measures of three-four (3x4=4x3); (4) he reharmonizes those measures, turning A^7–DØ^7–G^7 into A^7–DØ^7–G^7–Fm^7, so that each three-four measure is a single chord (the inserted Fm^7 is an approach chord to the EØ^7 of bar 45); (5) he compresses the figure of bar 41 and adjusts it to fit the chord of each (new) three-four measure (bars 42–44). Bars 45–48 transform this figure further and return us briefly to agreement with the underlying meter. The unshifted appearance of the descending seventh-chord arpeggio in bar 47 helps to confirm this agreement.

Bars 49–56 begin by returning to the melody—that is, to Evans' version of the melody (Example 11). The D♭maj^7 approach chord (bar 49) again has its own approach chord, the Dmaj^7 (bar 48), and the ascending G–A♭ becomes an extended ascent through several octaves as Evans plays the five-note figure A♭–C–E♭–G–B♭ in quarter notes (shifted one eighth note), then compresses the pattern (with C changed to B to reflect the change of harmony to the altered dominant) with quarter-note triplets (a measure-preserving polymeter), and then in even shorter notes. The resultant acceleration supports the physical gesture of reaching over (which itself could be analyzed as a Schenkerian "reaching over") to successively higher octaves. And the use of the same figure is made possible by (and "brings out") Evans' retention of the same harmonies in bars 4 and 5 of the A section (cf. Example 2). Having arrived in the upper register, Evans settles into the agreement with the meter as he floats back down. The unshifted appearance of the descending arpeggio in bars 54–55 helps confirm this agreement.

Bars 57–64 draw the second chorus to a close (Example 12). Once again, the techniques of displacement work with and rely upon the pitch structure of Evans' improvisation. The middleground, shown in Example 12a, is the same as that of analogous measures in these performances. The simple descent expresses a relaxation toward the cadence. But, as

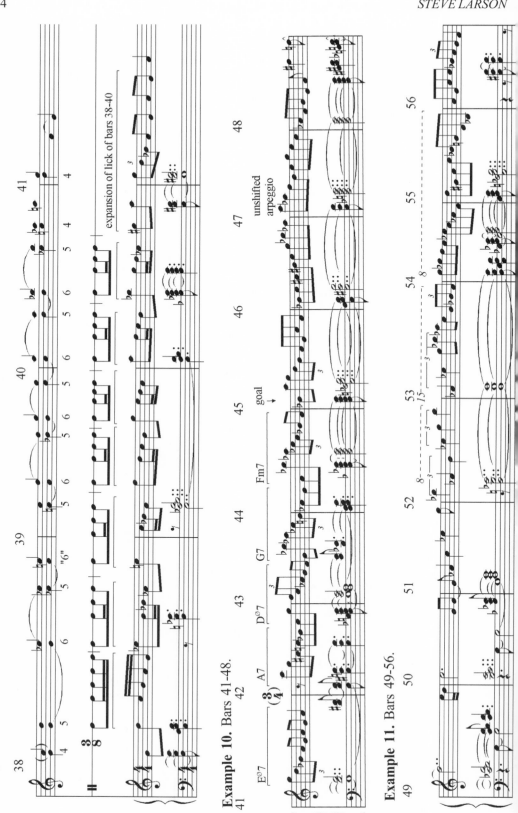

Example 9. Bars 38-41.

Example 10. Bars 41-48.

Example 11. Bars 49-56.

Example 12. Bars 57-63.

the parentheses in bar 63 of Example 12b indicate, the final note of the cadence is again withheld. For that withholding of the cadence to be effective, the music that leads to it must make us want that cadential note. The musical forces lead the tones of this linear progression securely toward that C, and Evans heightens our perception of this as a gesture of relaxation in two ways.

First, he delays the arrival on the first tone with climbing figures that make that A a goal but delay its arrival. These climbing figures are rhythmically unstable, creating a tactus-preserving polymetric juxtaposition of three-eight against the underlying four-four (see Example 12d). But the pattern suggests that A will appear on the third beat of bar 58. Instead, Evans delays the arrival on A with a new figure that embellishes B. That new figure (a hidden repetition of the B–D, see the lower bracket of Example 12c, bar 58) becomes an important motive in what follows (see the upper brackets in Example 12c).

The second way in which Evans heightens my perception of this as a gesture of relaxation is through the shifting of the final three notes of that figure. The figure eighth–eighth–quarter is usually end-accented so that the quarter note lands on the downbeat. The slanted lines in Example 11c show the delays that result from this shifting.

The "turnaround" of bars 63–64 continues the shift presented in the previous measures; nothing articulates beats one and three (Example 13). It would be possible to regard this as a standard turnaround (Cmaj⁷–E♭maj⁷– Dmaj⁷–D♭maj⁷–Cmaj⁷ is a standard way to return to Cmaj⁷), but here this progression has a motivic significance, for it echoes the chromatic descent that ends this section and it prepares the following section. Note how in this passage there is an extension of Evans's method of using approach chords: E♭maj⁷ is the (half-step upper-neighbor) approach chord of the approach chord of the approach chord.

Example 13. Bars 63-64.

Third chorus

Remarkably, the next chorus (Example 14) presents displacements that are even longer, subtler, and more powerfully disorienting than those found in the first two. In previous passages, as we have seen, Evans created tactus-preserving polymetric juxtapositions of three-four against the underlying four-four by following the recipe given above. Here, he "doubles" that recipe: (1) the hypermetrical downbeat at bar 65 is the beginning and the hypermetrical downbeat at bar 73, eight measures (32 beats) later, is the goal; (2) Evans plays a figure in the first two measures so that six measures (24 beats) remain; (3) he replaces those six measures of four-four with eight measures of three-four (6x4=8x3); (4) he reharmonizes those measures so that each three-four measure is a single chord; and (5) he compresses the figure of bars 65–66 and adjusts it to fit the chord of each (new) three-four measure (bars 67–72). Furthermore, the right hand anticipates the downbeat in each of the implied three-four bars of this passage, thus adding yet another level of rhythmic shift. I'm not suggesting that Evans consciously went through this process to create bars 65–72. But I do think that this recipe not only helps us to understand what is going on there better, but may also be useful to improvisers seeking similar effects.

The hypermetrical downbeat of bar 73 is articulated with an unshifted left-hand whole note. At this point, Evans shifts gears and accelerates with a steady stream of triplets. Given Evans's basic texture of eighth notes, and the longer notes of bars 65–72, the increased activity of uninterrupted triplets heightens the excitement. Here, too, Evans uses the "rhythmic dissonance" of displacement to heighten the effect of these more-rapid notes. The first triplet places its high note on the beat. This pattern could have continued (with triplets descending from high notes on the beat, as in Example 15a), or Evans could have gone the other direction (ascending from low notes on the beat, as in Example 15b). Either way, the grouping and accents of the right hand would have agreed with the underlying four-four to create a "rhythmic consonance." Instead, Evans creates a "rhythmic dissonance" by beginning as in Example 15a and then shifting the notes in Example 15b as shown in Example 15c. The result may be correctly described as a rotation of the triplet figure (so that x–y–z becomes y–z–x), but I would argue that it could be better understood as a disagreement between contour and beat that sounds like the right hand is shifted one triplet eighth early. The feeling that a set of accents comes in one triplet eighth early is anticipated by the pickup A that begins this lick (see Example 15d).

After the sophisticated "double portion" of the recipe in bars 65–72 and the fireworks of shifted triplets in bars 73–80, the music of bars 81–88 has the effect of a return to the basic texture, a denouement to the impressive display we've experienced (Example 16). Nevertheless, Evans once again uses shifting and compression to create a tactus-preserving polymeter of the sort seen in bars 16–19. And, once again, hidden repetitions confirm arrival at the sixth measure of this section (the pattern B♭–A♭–G appears on various levels of musical structure). In this sense, these measures are similar to those in analogous sections.

Were the analogy to continue, bars 86–88 would present an extended anacrusis to bar 89, perhaps with tactus-preserving polymeter and an ascending stepwise middleground. These measures do provide a link to the next section, but there are some differences that reflect the different strategic functions of this passage. Having passed the climactic portion of his demonstration, Evans winds down now, leading to the final cadence. Instead of a tension-building

Example 14. Bars 65-73.

Example 15. Bars 73-74.

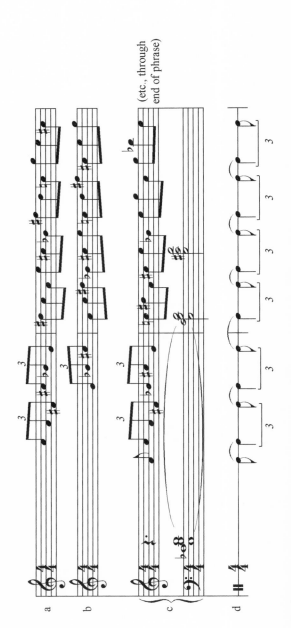

Example 16. Bars 81-86.

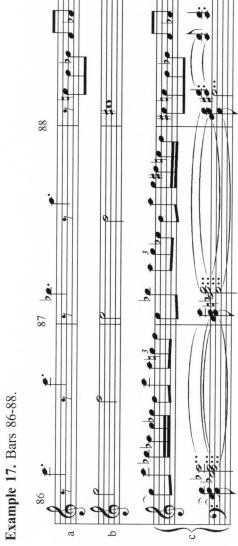

Example 17. Bars 86-88.

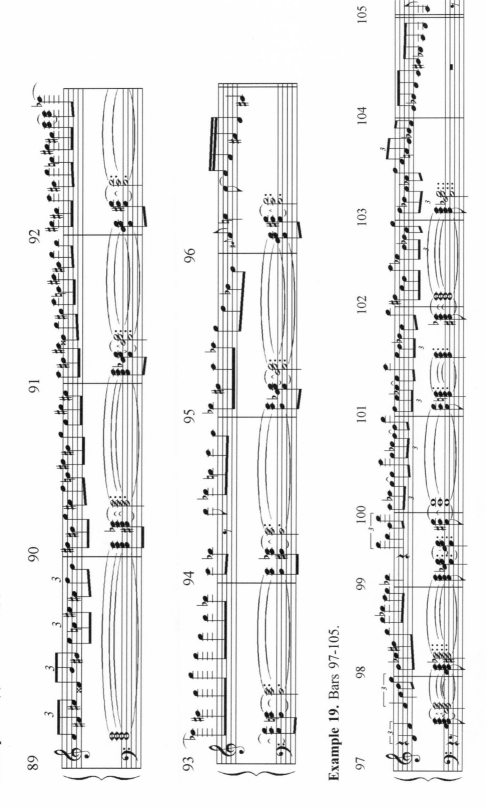

Example 18. (a) Bars 89-92; (b) bars 93-96.

Example 19. Bars 97-105.

ascent, there is a relaxing middleground descent, and instead of the strong rhythmic dissonance of polymeter, Evans plays something that is only subtly shifted. As Example 17 shows, the right hand in bars 86–88 has a compound melodic structure. The "alto" line (Example 17b) articulates the meter at the half-note level, while the soprano (Example 17a) enters an eighth note later. The effect, however, is one of anticipation by three eighth notes, as a result of the underlying pitch structure (parallel sixths) and the shape of the gesture (which leads to the following "alto" half note). Note that in bar 88 the right hand continues in the lower register with a hidden repetition of the "soprano" of bar 86–87, now an octave lower.

The harmonies of bars 89–92 are repeated three times in the following 12 bars. Jazz players also call this type of phrase expansion a "turnaround." Bars 89–92 group triplet eighth notes in pairs to suggest quarter-note triplets, yielding a measure-preserving polymeter (Example 18a). Bars 93–96 return to the basic texture (Example 18b). Once again, having arrived in the upper register, Evans settles into agreement with the meter as he floats back down, with the unshifted appearance of the descending arpeggio in bar 95 helping to confirm this agreement.

Bars 97–100 begin with quarter-note triplets, smoothly introducing the measure-preserving polymeter by omitting the quarter note that would have fallen on the downbeat (Example 19). The shifted quarter-note triplet in bar 99, however, introduces a longer gesture that spans two statements of the turn-around figure, one whose compound melodic structure recalls bars 86–88. As in bars 86–88, the "soprano" of bars 100-102 is shifted one eighth note. However, whereas the alto of bars 86–88 emphasizes beats one and three, the "alto" of bars 100-102 emphasizes two and four. This phrase leads smoothly into bar 105, which features a return to the melody as well as to metric stability.

Fourth chorus (accompanied)

After Evans concludes the third chorus, McPartland notes the dizzying effect of Evans techniques of displacement: "That was wild, you know, you displaced it so much I couldn't find the place to come in." Following a brief discussion, Evans plays one more chorus, this time with McPartland accompanying by playing the melody in octaves. The accompanied performance features many of the same techniques of rhythmic displacement, and a list of those may summarize this essay. In first phrase, Evans returns to the basic texture seen in bars 17–24 of the solo performance. Bars 9–12 of the accompanied performance, like bars 73–80 of the solo performance, explode with the fireworks of shifted triplets. The remaining four measures of this phrase create another example of tactus-preserving hypermeter by following the recipe given above. Bars 25–32 of the accompanied performance create a powerful measure-preserving polymeter. The quarter-note triplets actually begin in bar 24 (typically, they are thus more smoothly introduced than they would have been had they begun on the hypermetrical downbeat of bar 25). But again, these triplets are grouped in twos to make a deeper-level polymeter (like half-note triplets, they give us six evenly-spaced notes in the place of each measure's four beats).

Evans's demonstration of techniques of rhythmic displacement is far more than a catalogue. In addition to demonstrating examples of various types of displacement, Evans shows us how these techniques function in concert with tonal structures to advance the dramatic, rhetorical, and gestural strategies of his improvisation. Hearing Evans's masterly display here, listeners can readily empathize with McPartland, when she exclaims, at the end of Evans's performance: "Wow! . . . My goodness, that felt like swimming against the tide!"[7]

[7]Temple University supported some of my early research on displacement in the music of Bill Evans through a 1988 Faculty Summer Research Fellowship. Earlier versions of this paper were presented to the Third International Schenker Symposium at Mannes College of Music in March 1999, to the series "Lectures in the History and Theory of Music" at the University of Maryland in March 1999; to the "Temple University College of Music Lecture Series" in March 1999; and to the John Donald Robb Composers' Symposium at the University of New Mexico in March 1998. Poundie Burstein's patient and thorough editing of this article improved it in many ways. Special thanks to Winnie Kerner and Gary Versace, who proofread my transcriptions, and to Richard Herman, Henry Martin, Steve Strunk, and Keith Waters for their advice and encouragement.

Levels of Voice Leading in the Music of Louis Couperin

Drora Pershing

One of the great strengths of Louis Couperin, a neglected master of the seventeenth century, is his long-range musical thinking, his "structural hearing," in Felix Salzer's evocative phrase.[1] Musical coherence in the seventeenth century hinges on the same basic elements as does that of later periods. Meter, rhythm and phrasing, as well as contrapuntal and tonal structure—these are the foundations of all music. Of course the relationships among these elements differ in different style periods, but careful examination can discern the nature of coherence in music of any period. The Schenkerian approach used in this study promotes both a closer reading of the music and a deeper understanding of the style.

Though more scholarly attention is now being focused on this repertoire,[2] that attention still concentrates largely on matters of texture and ornament rather than on formal structure and harmonic language. Indeed, it is precisely the complex nature of its texture that tends to mask the counterpoint in the music of Louis Couperin and his contemporaries. In an article about seventeenth century lute and harpsichord traditions, David Ledbetter describes the early seventeenth-century lute style as a two-part texture of parallel thirds or tenths spiced with occasional chords.[3] In the 1630s there emerged the *style brisé,* first in lute music and then promptly absorbed into the *clavecin* language, which quickly became the new standard texture for dance music on both instruments. This "broken style," its splintered harmonies shared among the various voice parts, thoroughly disguised the contrapuntal underpinning of many of these pieces, making a scholarly focus on ornamental textures and contours all the easier.

* * * * *

Nearly a century separates the Attaingnant keyboard dance collections of the 1530s from the seventeenth-century dances that are the heart of the French "classical" *clavecin* repertoire.[4] Since very little keyboard music

[1]Felix Salzer, *Structural Hearing* (New York: Boni, 1952; Dover reprint, 1962).

[2]See especially the fine study by David Ledbetter, *Harpsichord and Lute Music in 17th-Century France* (London: Macmillan, 1987).

[3]David Ledbetter, "Aspects of 17th c. French lute style reflected in the works of the Clavecinistes," in *Lute Society Journal* (1982), pp. 55-66.

[4]Pierre Attaingnant, *Quatorze Gaillardes neuf Pavennes sept Branles et deux Basse Dances le tout reduict de musique en la tabulature. . .* (Paris, c.1530). Modern ed. by Daniel Heartz in *Corpus of Early Keyboard Music,* Willi Apel, general editor, Vol. 8: Keyboard Dances from the Earlier 16th century (Middleton, Wisconsin: American Institute of Musicology, 1965).

survives in French sources from this entire period, we depend on the contemporary lute repertoire to shed light on the evolving French dance-music tradition. Lute collections of the early seventeenth century typically contain the usual core dances—allemandes, courantes, and sarabandes, as well as some chaconnes and tombeaux (laments on the death of some favorite, similar to allemandes in both structure and texture), and occasional gigues.[5] These were regularly performed for balls at the royal court and in the great noble houses of Paris. By the time of Louis XIII in the 1620s allemandes had already begun to fade from court dance fashion, but courantes and sarabandes remained very popular. In fact, the courante was the favorite among all the dances at the court of Louis XIII, and the contemporary lute repertoire contains more courantes than any other dance. This was still the case in the harpsichord collections later in the century. The Sun King himself (Louis XIV) was lauded for his virtuoso dancing of the courante, which continued to be the favorite court dance well into his reign (1651–1715).[6]

Much insight into this era may be gathered from a fascinating seventeenth-century document, the *Lettre de Mr. Le Gallois a Mademoiselle Regnault de Solier touchant la Musique*.[7] This *Lettre* was published in Paris in 1680, and in it, the author—cleric, scholar, musical connoisseur, very free with his opinions—paints a vivid picture of the musical taste of his day. He discusses the two principal styles of keyboard composition and playing in the France of his youth more than twenty years earlier, and describes the characteristics and practitioners of each. The two are Jacques Champion de Chambonnières and Louis Couperin, and Le Gallois calls them "chefs de secte," so to speak, party heads.[8]

By 1680, the style of Chambonnières had already been current for a half century, both in his own widely circulated pieces and in the work of his pupils. As early as 1636, Marin Mersenne in *Harmonie Universelle* had praised his music and playing. And as David Fuller points out, scholars since the beginning of the twentieth century have quoted M. Le Gallois in

---

[5]In the lute manuscript collections (and later in the keyboard collections), the dances were organized by key and type. All the dances in one key were grouped together, beginning with preludes—if the manuscript had any—followed by allemandes, courantes, sarabandes and finally any others in that key. In the sixteenth and seventeenth centuries lute tunings proliferated, some of them more comfortable than others for playing in particular keys. It was far easier to group together the pieces in a single key and select suitable pieces from that key list for a performance, than to retune the lute for each piece in a different key. Thus arose the custom, continuing into the eighteenth century, of having all movements of a suite in the same key.

[6]See discussion in Wendy Hilton, "A dance for kings: The 17th-Century French *Courante*," in *Early Music*, Vol. 5/2 (April 1977), p.161.

[7]This *Lettre* appears in an extensively annotated translation by David Fuller in "French harpsichord playing in the 17th century—after Le Gallois," in *Early Music*, Vol. 4/1 (January 1976), pp. 22-26.

[8]Scholars of this repertoire refer to Louis Couperin familiarly as "Louis." This avoids the confusion that might arise from references merely to "Couperin," who might be any one of several members of that distinguished family, most likely François.

discussions of this "first phase of French harpsichord classicism."[9] A notable passage in the *Lettre* describes Chambonnières'

> . . . natural, tender and well-turned melodies which were not found in those of others [i.e., other composers as well as players] . . . Every time he played a piece, he introduced new beauties, with grace notes, . . . and various embellishments . . . [so that] he disclosed ever fresh graces in them . . . [10]

Of course we should remember that Gallois is describing Chambonnières playing his own music and his playing would therefore reflect compositional as well as performing choices. David Ledbetter points out that this contrast (i.e., "not found in others…") would have been between the shapely melodies of Chambonnieres and the "chaudronner"—clattering or rattling (Ledbetter calls it "smithying")—of purely ornamental passagework that may have been current among the virtuoso keyboard players of the day.[11] In any event, the most appealing feature of Chambonnières' music, according to Le Gallois, was the grace and delicacy of its surface, both the melodic contours themselves and the ornaments of those contours.

On the other hand, he describes Louis Couperin (in the *Lettre*) as one "who excelled in composition, that is, in his learned researches (*doctes recherches*)."[12] And this playing style was admired by savants because it was full of chords and enriched with fine dissonances, with structural niceties and with imitation."[13]

Finally, says Le Gallois, "Chambonnières spoke to the heart, and Louis Couperin to the ear . . ."[14] Since Le Gallois "preferred Chambonnières," as Fuller points out, his assessment of Louis Couperin's musical style was perhaps not as generous as it might have been. His comment that Couperin spoke "to the ear" implied that he spoke *only* to the ear, a lesser achievement, to the contemporary taste, than that of Chambonnières. Fuller himself describes Louis's music as "full of inspired contrivance," the word *contrivance* perhaps rather disparaging of these pieces with their organic power.[15] And in fact much scholarly opinion up to the present day has continued to regard Chambonnières as not only the founder of the French classical clavecin school, but perhaps its greatest practitioner.

An examination of the dances of Chambonnières reveals that his strength does indeed lie in his fluid keyboard style, a great variety and richness of decoration, and, in the best pieces, a graceful turn of melody as well. The

---

[9]H. Quittard, "Chambonnières" in *Tribune de Saint Gervais*, VII (1901), cited by Fuller, in "French harpsichord playing," p. 22.

[10]Fuller, "French harpsichord playing, p. 23, Fuller's translation.

[11]Ledbetter, "Aspects of 17th c. French lute style," p. 55.

[12]*doctes recherches*: "doctes" could be translated as skilled or clever. Davitt Moroney, editor of the new Couperin edition, translates this phrase as "intelligent esotericism."

[13]Fuller, "French harpsichord playing, p. 23.

[14]Fuller, "French harpsichord playing," p. 24.

[15]Fuller, "French harpsichord playing," p. 26, note 19.

Courante de Madame (#13 in Chambonnières's own publication of 1670) is a lovely piece, its balance and focus resulting from precise control of each phrase gesture.[16] Here are melody, harmony and rhythm united to produce the characteristic swaying, alternating duple and triple meter of courantes. But other Chambonnières dances lack one or more of these essential elements, and their effectiveness is lessened in consequence. The harmonic motion in many of his pieces often seems almost random; without directed motion to clarify the structure, and with a top voice often lacking the coordination with the bass that helps define form, we find few Chambonnières pieces with the cogency of the *Courante de Madame.*

Turning to the music of Louis Couperin, we find modern assessment of his music not very different from that of M. Le Gallois three hundred years earlier. In his 1978 survey of French Baroque music, James Anthony says that Louis, ". . . in common with most seventeenth century harpsichord composers, made little effort to unify the two sections of his dances; sometimes [the remark echoes with disapproval] the disparity is considerable."[17] Ledbetter feels that counterpoint, for Couperin, was "more a matter of the imitative development of figures at specific moments, rather than a constant underlying principle."[18] Thus Anthony's criteria for compositional unity are limited to the motivic aspect of the pieces, and Ledbetter sees counterpoint in Louis as purely textural embellishment. It is clear that neither scholar regards counterpoint as a structural resource in this music.

Example 1. Louis Couperin, Courante #18, bars 14-18.

---

[16]Original engraved edition, *Les Pieces de Clavessin de Monsieur de Chambonnieres. Se vendent a Paris…*(1670). *Livre Premier, Livre Second.* Modern edition in Chambonnières, *Oeuvres Complètes*, eds. Paul Brunold and André Tessier (Paris, 1925; reprint, New York: Broude Brothers, 1967).

[17]James Anthony, *French Baroque Music from Beaujoyeulx to Rameau*, revised edition (New York: W.W. Norton, 1978), p. 250.

[18]Ledbetter, "Aspects of 17th c. French lute style," p. 108.

Example 2. Louis Couperin, Sarabande #51, bars 13-20.

A closer examination of the Louis Couperin dances contradicts these views. Most of the pieces have in common a tight overall plan that governs the motion from start to finish. Most of them enrich this organic structure with large-scale voice-leading detail that clarifies and propels the motion. And the best of them fuse this directed contrapuntal structure with phrase and metric design in a way that makes them extremely effective, and sometimes very powerful. A few short examples of Louis's typical contrapuntal-structural technique will illustrate. At the end of this essay, a more thorough consideration of the E-minor Sarabande will give us a glimpse of the composer's larger vision at work.[19]

Example 1 shows the detail of the final dominant prolongation at the end of the B strain of Courante #18. The rising top voice is supported by a

[19]Most of the harpsichord works of Louis Couperin survive in two seventeenth-century manuscript sources:

A. The ***Beauyn Ms.***, Paris, Bibliothèque Nationale, Rés. Vm⁷ 674-675. (Facs. Geneva: Minkoff, 1977).

    1) Modern edition in: Louis Couperin, Pièces de Clavecin, ed. Paul Brunold (1935); rev. Thurston Dart (Monaco: Éditions de Oiseau-lyre, 1959). (This is usually referred to as the "Brunold-Dart" edition.)

    2) idem., ed. Davitt Moroney (Monaco: Editions de Oiseau-lyre, 1985). (*cont.*)

B. The ***Parville Ms***, *US-BE* MS 778; now in the music library at U.C. Berkeley. Selected dances from this Ms published in: Louis Couperin, *Pièces de Clavecin*, ed. Alan Curtis (Paris: Heugel, 1970).

Both manuscripts contain the works of other composers as well as Louis; the modern editions cited contain only the works of Louis.

    In the manuscript sources the dances are organized according to key and type (see note 5 above); the modern editions print them in the same order. The dances cited in this study are numbered according to the Brunold-Dart edition of 1925; the Moroney edition of 1985 uses most of the same numbering.

Example 3. Louis Couperin, Courante #92, bars 6-12.

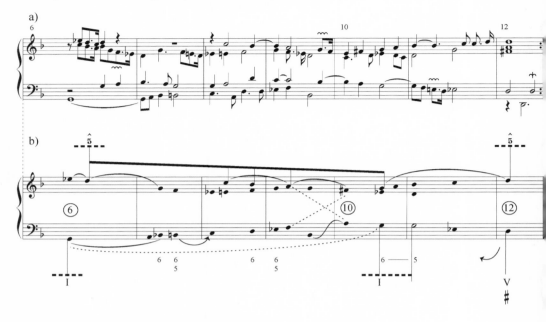

Example 4. Louis Couperin, Allemande #92, bars 17-21.

Example 5. Louis Couperin, Sarabande #65 (a) quotation; (b) voice-leading sketch.

(cont.)

Example 5: cont.

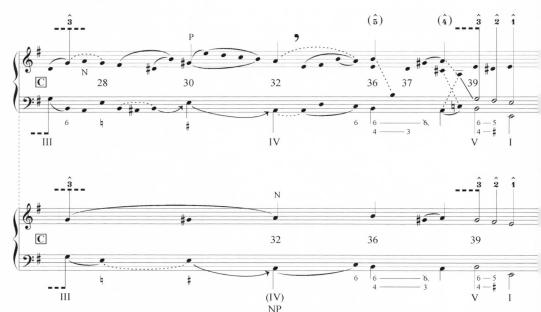

sequence of applied leading-tone and dominant chords. In Example 2 (p. 127), from the B strain of Sarabande #51, a characteristic motion in parallel tenths organizes the entire phrase. (Note the voice exchange that covers the continuing series of tenths after the top-voice C♯ in bar 18.) Example 3, (p. 128) shows an outer-voice framework in contrary motion (embellished with voice exchange, as part of an opening tonic prolongation in this imitative-texture allemande). And finally, in Example 4 (from the second strain of the same allemande), we see 7–6 suspensions between the two upper voices that intensify a chromatic motion from minor V to VII, propelling the motion toward the final dominant of the last phrase (not included in this example).

The remainder of this essay will be devoted to Louis Couperin's E-minor Sarabande (Example 5, pp. 128-30).[20] It is one of only three pieces he wrote in that key, and exemplifies his masterly fusion of design and structure in an apparently simple piece.[21] One of the longest of his dances, it is the only one in three strains; the second and third strains are each twice the eight-bar length of a typical strain. A brief overview reveals an opening tonic prolongation with outer voices moving primarily in contrary motion, with a continuation to a cadence on III. The B strain remains within the boundaries of III. Its two large phrases are balanced with respect to melody line: each consists of a preliminary four-note descent followed by a cadential rise. The final strain completes the tonal structure, moving from its opening on G (III) to a cadence in A minor (IV) before reaching the cadential phrase in bar 36.

---

[20]This piece may be found as #65 in the edition by Davitt Moroney.
[21]The comma symbols in the graph indicate phrase separations.

In most seventeenth-century sarabandes and many courantes, a regularly repeating four-bar phrase structure is standard. Cadential hemiola, that ancient trick of triple-meter pieces, often abates and softens the regularity somewhat, since its effect is to shift the recurring first-beat emphasis and to bridge the single-measure units of a phrase. Nevertheless, in these dances the four-bar phrase unit remains the norm. In this piece, Couperin takes on the challenge of expanding the normal strain length without relying exclusively on the usual recurring four-bar structure throughout.

The first strain is structurally the most conventional (and the shortest, only eight measures in length). The typical sarabande rhythm of the opening bars pauses for a moment on dominant harmony in bar 4, and then resumes its smooth motion to a cadence on III. The B strain (sixteen bars long) would normally fall into four segments—and indeed it does, both in the top line (see Example 5b) and in the bass motion. The bass note B comes at the precise dividing moment of the first phrase of the strain (bar 12). But Couperin withholds from this proto dominant its D$\sharp$ leading tone until the last beat of bar 13, well after the expected interior phrase break. To make the point even clearer, the bass note B is tied into the next measure—as are three inner voices—leaving only soprano and tenor to begin the new phrase unit. With a hemiola in bars 14–15 further disguising the expected symmetry of this phrase, the interior division is almost entirely obscured. The result is that this first phrase of the B strain moves through its full eight measures with no stops. The second half of this strain then reverts to the normal four-bar phrase units, cadencing on III. Its two four-bar melody phrases, with their hint of *petite reprise*, outline the tetrachords of the key of G (III), $\hat{4}$–$\hat{3}$–$\hat{2}$–$\hat{1}$ (ending in bar 20) and $\hat{5}$–$\hat{6}$–$\hat{7}$–$\hat{8}$ (bar 24).

The sixteen-measure third strain, also in two phrases, is even more striking. Though the melody line of the first phrase is still laid out regularly in dotted patterns like the earlier four-bar units, the internal divisions of *both* phrases are now bridged over, resulting in a final strain consisting unmistakably of two full eight-measure halves. As in the second strain, the "dominant" harmony reached at the midpoint of each phrase is denied its leading tone at the critical moment—and therefore its dividing dominant function (bars 28–29, and 36–37), and the bass note of each "dominant" is tied into the next measure. But this time there is also a hemiola athwart each midpoint, completely concealing any subdivision, and in the last phrase, there are actually three hemiola units in succession, driving the entire phrase towards the final cadence of the piece.

So far we have seen an overall harmonic plan dovetailing with phrase and rhythmic design, the internal section units spanning increasingly longer distances as the piece progresses. Now we come to the larger contrapuntal-tonal structure, which is just as clear and purposeful as the textural and phrase organization. As the graph shows, the first strain (A) moves from I to III, supporting a basic top line descent of a third from b^1 ($\hat{5}$) down to g^1 ($\hat{3}$). In the second strain (B), which is in III throughout, the two phrases are defined first by a bass motion up to D, supporting V (bars 9–16), and then by the repeated cadential progressions (bars 17–20 and 21–24). But the top voice structure, a descent of the same third b[1] to g[1], now reaches across the entire strain, spanning its two component phrases.

The last strain (C), the most complex in phrasing and metrical organization, is likewise the most complicated in linear structure, and full of rich detail. The top line of its first phrase (bars 25–32) rises essentially from G to G# to A in the one-line register, with a[1] supported by a cadence on IV in bar 32. The relatively simple motion of the earlier phrases is ornamented here: each note in the ascent now enjoys its own embellishing figures. A rising fourth, supported by the bass descent of a sixth to B, leads to the first g[1] (bar 25). A neighbor-note a[1] in bar 27 precedes the return to the same g[1] (bar 28), now supported by the E-minor harmony marking the hemiola bridge mentioned earlier. The transformation of E minor into E major, dominant of IV (bar 30), is heightened by an applied dominant, and the E-major chord itself is prolonged with a beautiful top-voice leap to e[2] (bar 31) before resolving to the cadence on IV.

But the (middleground-level) top line has not yet finished its climb. The IV is prolonged past the phrase cadence of bar 32, as the top voice reaches the structural b[1] (bar 36) for the third and last time in the piece. This climactic peak is intensified by both contrapuntal dissonance (the fourth over the bass B) and metrical dissonance (the hemiola), and Couperin sustains the tension as long as possible. The apparent cadential six-four of bar 36 arouses expectations of a cadential progression, but Couperin moves the alto E (the sixth in the six-four chord) to a D and the top-voice G to a G# (bar 37), converting the six-four chord into leading-tone harmony for the subdominant. It is not until the last beat of the last hemiola in the piece (bar 39) that the six-four chord finally returns, now supporting the true structural 3̂ of the final cadential descent. And the cadential resolution to pure dominant harmony is delayed even beyond that last beat, until the penultimate eighth note. Feel the force of that final cadential progression with its sonorous closing tonic, so powerfully enhanced by the last structural bass notes, in the lowest and richest register of the seventeenth-century French harpsichord.

I am inclined to agree with Bruce Gustafson, harpsichordist and noted scholar of seventeenth-century French keyboard music, who wrote in an early article, "no other composer of seventeenth-century France wrote such nobly conceived and harmonically arresting music. It is no wonder that harpsichordists may talk about Chambonnières, but they play Louis Couperin."[22] And David Ledbetter, admiring Louis's technical mastery in the unmeasured preludes, observed, "few preludes [lute or keyboard] can match their broad paragraphing and large-scale structure."[23]   Louis Couperin's remarkable achievement lies in his ability to apply this large-scale perspective to dance pieces with their limited and prescribed formal shapes, in such a way as to illuminate, expand and enrich those shapes.

---

[22]See Bruce Gustafson, "A performer's guide to Louis Couperin," in *Diapason*, Vol. 66 (June 1975), p. 7.
[23]David Ledbetter, *Harpsichord and Lute Music in 17th-Century France*, p. 91.

The Analysis of East Asian Music

David Loeb

Several circumstances have created greater differences within East Asian music than within Western. For instance, whereas the compact and nearly contiguous landmass of Europe facilitates travel between countries, East Asia comprises countries isolated by vast seas and high mountains over an area much larger than Europe. While for many years in the West, Latin provided a nearly universal means of communication, in East Asia there has never been a common spoken language, and Chinese has provided only limited written communication.

Moreover, the scarcity of sources presents many difficulties in the study of East Asian music. No work in a composer's hand or any other primary source predates 1900. Musicians composed mainly for instruments they played, teaching their own and other works entirely by rote.[1] The few extant historical sources rarely came directly from composers. There are no complete works sets and very few critical editions.[2] Recent anthologies of works for particular instruments are nearly all published in traditional tablature (as in Example 1), which vary with the period and school of playing.[3] Publications in Western notation begin to appear around 1880, but these vary in accuracy and comprise only a tiny fraction of the extant repertoire. Therefore we often must work from modern editions in tablature, contending with major discrepancies in some pieces.

While European countries share the same notation, scales, and instruments, East Asian countries each have their own.[4] And although some musical genres flourished more in one Western country than others, no important genre of one country is totally absent elsewhere. In Asia, on the other hand, several genres that are important in one country are not found elsewhere (such as meditative solo wind music in Japanese Buddhist temples, virtuosic solo zither pieces for Chinese literati, drum accompaniments for Korean solo string or wind works, and complex and energetic Indonesian choral music).

---

[1] An interesting semantic reflection illustrates this. Western languages have long used "write" as a synonym for "compose," but this usage only came to East Asia quite recently with the adoption of Western working methods by composers.

[2] See David Loeb, *The Music Forum*, Vol. 4 (New York: Columbia University Press, 1976), pp. 335-93, for discussion of the problems in preparing the critical edition included.

[3] One notable exception: In the 1950s the Chinese government published anthologies for solo instruments in Western notation, adding tablature symbols as necessary.

[4] Even when China and Japan use identical written characters for some instruments, their construction, tuning, and playing techniques differ greatly, as is the case with the pipa and biwa, or tseng and koto.

Example 1. A Si-Jo piece in tablature notation.

Nevertheless, certain features are found throughout much of this repertoire. Most notably, almost all East Asian music uses pentatonic scales. In many compositions, the melodic structure follows the prevalent scale of the work, a seemingly innocent principle that assumes great importance for music whose scales include intervals which Western music considers disjunct. Even in the absence of harmonic progressions, these scales allow cadences at structural points to establish a clearly audible tonic sense.[5]

The extensive use of pentatonic scales does not imply as much similarity as one might expect, however, for there is a variety of pentatonic scales found throughout this repertoire. Even countries that use identical scales may treat them so differently that the geographical origins can be readily distinguished. Furthermore, there is considerable variety in the manner and extent of the use of tones that lie outside of the scale of the composition. Often the difference in the treatment of these added tones results from the capabilities and limitations of the instruments involved. (For instance, much Indonesian music has tuned percussion which cannot produce notes outside the scale, while at the other extreme one traditional Japanese koto tuning includes two scales from a common tonic, allowing for mixture using only open strings.) Also, noticeable fluctuations of intonation and temperament can color the primary scale, though these do not seriously affect the tonal analysis.

When dealing with Eastern music—much as with Western music—recognizing the manner in which melodic motions lead to and from a tonal center can enhance our perception of that tonic. This in turn can help us identify how the tonal goals are attained and communicated, giving us deeper appreciation for the subtleties of the music. Of course, an exhaustive study of the East Asian repertoire would far exceed the bounds of this article, which offers only a basic introduction to the analytic methods that may be used in approaching this music. To this end, this essay will examine the tonal structure of three instrumental works, from China, Japan, and Korea, respectively.

The Embroidered Purse (China)

Example 2 shows the Chinese modes. As with all East Asian pentatonic scales, each of the Chinese modes divides into a perfect fifth and a perfect fourth. The fifth is divided into three intervals and the fourth into two, with no more than one semitone in each group. In addition to the fifth above the tonic, each scale includes at least one other perfect fifth, allowing occasional tonicizations. Scales with semitones also contain a tritone.[6]

Note that some of the adjacent scale degrees form the interval of a second, and other adjacent scale degrees form the interval of a third. This allows an attractive ambivalence in the treatment of thirds, which appear sometimes as leaps and sometimes as stepwise motions within passing or neighbor relationships. To make things clearer, Example 2 identifies the scale steps by analogous degrees of a Western diatonic scale. For instance, in Chinese Mode I, the fourth tone of the scale is labeled "5̂" (not "4̂"), thereby highlighting the presence of a third within the first four steps of this scale.

The Chinese Mode I merits recognition as the most basic: more works use it than all the other modes, and only Mode I allows the tones to be

[5]In this regard, an analogy may be made with analytic studies of Western music in the Phrygian mode, where contrapuntal cadences to the tonic can establish a tonal center in the absence of standard harmonic progressions. The semitone motion down to the tonic provided by the Phrygian mode is likewise a standard feature in many East Asian compositions.

[6]Chromatic intervals in East Asian scales are rare. One Indonesian scale has an augmented fifth and diminished fourth pair in addition to the main perfect fifth and perfect fourth pair. Although augmented seconds are often found in Korean music, these do not represent scale intervals.

Example 2. Chinese Scales.

arrayed in ascending fifths starting from the tonic. Within pieces in Mode I, $\hat{3}$–$\hat{2}$ –$\hat{1}$ descents occur in spans of varying scope, neighbor figures occur with these first three scale degrees or as $\hat{5}$–$\hat{6}$–$\hat{5}$ motions, and passing motions include $\hat{5}$–$\hat{6}$–$\hat{8}$ and $\hat{8}$–$\hat{6}$–$\hat{5}$.

One can derive the other Chinese modes by shifting the starting point from Mode I (much as one can derive the different modes from a major scale in Western music); this is shown by the brackets in Example 2. Mode II works very differently from Mode I. Since Mode II does not provide for a $\hat{2}$–$\hat{1}$ descent (there is no scale tone between $\hat{1}$ and $\hat{3}$), we find lower neighbors and $\hat{5}$–$\hat{7}$–$\hat{8}$ ascents creating tonic stabilization. One also finds $\hat{8}$–$\hat{7}$–$\hat{5}$ passing motions as well as passing and neighbor motions involving $\hat{4}$, although these motions have less structural importance, since they do not move to the tonic.

Modes III and IV differ from one another only in the identity of the tone between $\hat{5}$ and $\hat{8}$. The uses of $\hat{7}$ in Mode III or $\hat{6}$ in Mode IV closely resemble uses of these degrees already mentioned. Both modes have $\hat{5}$– $\hat{4}$–$\hat{2}$–$\hat{1}$ structural descents and can have $\hat{5}$– $\hat{4}$–$\hat{2}$ interruptions, and both permit sequences outlining fourths. Strong motions connecting $\hat{1}$ and $\hat{4}$ are rare, however; this preserves the independent character of these modes, rather than allowing them to become simply plagal forms of Modes I and II.

In Chinese music, most added tones continue the upward succession of fifths. In Mode I this yields $\hat{7}$, which temporarily displaces $\hat{1}$ (semitones are rare in Chinese music). This $\hat{7}$ in turn functions as $\hat{3}$ of a temporarily tonicized $\hat{5}$, and the characteristic melodic patterns will appear transposed if the tonicization lasts beyond a few notes. In Mode II, the added tone— which appears much more often than the added tone in Mode I—becomes $\hat{2}$. This scale degree can form part of $\hat{3}$–$\hat{2}$–$\hat{1}$ and $\hat{5}$– $\hat{4}$– $\hat{3}$–$\hat{2}$–$\hat{1}$ descents, occasionally of structural weight. Since this causes us to perceive $\hat{2}$ as an integral part of the scale rather than as an added tone, this tone can tend to disrupt the purely pentatonic nature of the music.

Example 3a shows *The Embroidered Purse*, a Chinese piece for the yang-qin.[7] This instrument is a diatonically tuned hammered dulcimer

---

[7]The score is from a transcription from Yen Zhia, ed. (Taipei: Pan-chio, 1977), p. 97. Another transcription by Chu-sung Jiang in *Yang-ch'in Jiang-I* (Taipei, 1971) pp. 104-5, and a recording by an unknown master *on CHINE Musique Classique* (OCO 559039) have been consulted in the following analysis. While these versions differ slightly, especially as regards that passage of bars 25-31, none of these differences critically affect the analytic comments presented here.

Example 3a.   Transcription of *The Embroidered Purse* (Chinese).

* alternate source for Interlude:

Example 3b. Analytic sketch of *The Embroidered Purse*.

somewhat resembling the Hungarian cimbalom, both instruments probably having evolved from the Persian santur. This piece uses Mode IV (one step higher than shown in Example 2) with an added tone that extends the succession of fifths downwards instead of upwards. This added tone functions as a $\hat{7}$, serving both as a whole-step lower neighbor to $\hat{1}$ and as part of stepwise descents from the ninth scale degree to the fifth (which, unlike Chinese pieces in Mode I, are not heard as tonicizations of $\hat{5}$).

Hasty perusal of the form suggests an ABA, but more careful scrutiny reveals greater subtlety. The presumed A sections each contain a twelve-bar theme with a slightly decorated restatement. Even the theme itself includes repetition, for bars 9–12 virtually duplicate bars 5–8. The purported B section (bars 25–31) should be regarded as a mere interlude; its brevity and apparent lack of a recognizable theme or motive make it seem like a digression rather than an actual contrasting section. As a result, one might more accurately regard the form as variations with an interlude.

The voice leading of this work is sketched in Example 3b. As this example shows, the theme of bars 1–12 is framed by $\hat{5}$– $\hat{4}$–$\hat{2}$–$\hat{1}$ structural descents preceded by a $\hat{5}$– $\hat{4}$–$\hat{2}$ interruption. (This structure of course governs not only the theme of bars 1–12, but also the variations in bars 13–24, 32–43, and 44–55.) We find a sequence in bars 1–2 and lower neighbor decorations of the tonic in the fourth bar of every four-bar phrase of the theme and its variations. The interlude of bars 25–31 prolongs $\hat{5}$ in a manner highly suggestive of the opening of the theme, first prolonging E by an ornate transfer of register and then pronging it by a motion through A and F$\sharp$ in an embellished reworking of the prolongations heard in bars 1–2. One should note that this piece ends on $\hat{5}$ (as does the theme and each variation). Such an ending is typical of other Chinese and many Japanese pieces, but this implies neither an inconclusive ending nor a missing $\hat{1}$.

The Cloud Well Lion Dance (Japan)

The Japanese modes are shown in Example 4a. One can see Japanese Mode I as an inflected version of Chinese Mode I (compare with Example 2a above), with $\hat{3}$ and $\hat{6}$ each lowered a semitone (although no evidence suggests that the Japanese scale evolved that way). Usages similar to those found in Chinese Mode I pieces may be found occurring in Japanese music (of course with the inflections), but they are often overshadowed by strong descents from the ninth scale degree through eight and six to five that are sometimes structural, reinforcing the idea that these are not tonicizations of $\hat{5}$. The ninths in such motions are often preceded by   upper neighbor resolutions that prepare such descents.

Mode II usually occurs as a koto tuning in obbligato parts added to pre-existent solo works rather than in solo pieces. In such pieces, $\hat{5}$– $\hat{4}$–$\hat{2}$–$\hat{1}$ descents assume a structural role. These descents are often transposed up a fifth (with a raised ninth), thereby providing much variety.[8] While most

---

[8]Transpositions in Mode I pieces down a fifth can occur as $\hat{5}$-$\hat{4}$- $\flat\hat{2}$-$\hat{1}$, although this usually is technically impractical.

Example 4a. Japanese Scales.

Example 4b. Transcription of *Cloud Well Lion Dance* (Japanese).

Example 4c.   Analytic sketch of *Cloud Well Lion Dance.*

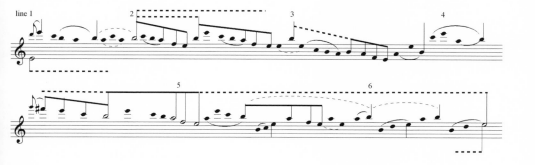

added tones arise from these transpositions, other added tones appear as whole steps below the tonic (in both Modes I and II), appearing either as lower neighbors or as passing tones between $\hat{5}$ and $\hat{8}$. Other less common added tones arise from more remote transpositions of these patterns.

The *Cloud Well Lion Dance* (Example 4b) is a Japanese piece for shakuhachi.[9] The shakuhachi, an end-blown flute derived from instruments that came via the Silk Road more than a millennium ago, has five holes tuned to the Chinese Mode II. With considerable effort, the shakuhachi can produce a chromatic range of more than two octaves, enabling it to play diverse repertoire.

This piece begins and ends with leisurely tonic prolongations (Example 4c). In the beginning of the work, the Ds appear as lower neighbors, but later they always lie within $\hat{5}$–$\hat{7}$–$\hat{8}$ passing motions.[10] After establishing the initial tonic, the melody begins to emphasize $\hat{5}$. This leads to several $\hat{5}$–$\hat{4}$–$\hat{2}$–$\hat{1}$ descents, including one in the lowest register made possible by the parenthetical low E towards the end of line 3. This note does not appear in the sources, and in fact extends the customary range of the instrument, requiring great control. Most performers do not include this note, which results in a $\hat{5}$–$\hat{4}$–$\hat{2}$ interruption lacking any eventual fulfillment. The best performances of this work, however, do include this low E.[11]

After establishing the initial tonic, the melody begins to emphasize $\hat{5}$. This in turn leads to several $\hat{5}$–$\hat{4}$–$\hat{2}$–$\hat{1}$ descents, including one in the lower register made possible by the parenthetical low E. The climax occurs in line 7 where G resolves to F$\sharp$ (a 10–9 resolution); both of these notes are added tones. The appearance of the F$\sharp$ initiates a descent from a raised ninth to $\hat{5}$. The $\hat{8}$–$\hat{6}$–$\hat{5}$ portion of this descent happens twice in groups of three eighth notes, suggesting a sesquialtera or a meter change. This vigorous rhythm evokes the lion dance most convincingly.

By catching our attention with this lion dance figure, this climax clearly prepares for the subsequent structural descent. One more descent follows, allowing a gradual release of tension. The composition concludes with a further winding down, as longer notes lead to the final tonic.

---

[9]The transcription comes from a combination of two editions: Kawase Teiji, ed., *Yuube no Kumo* and *Kumoi Jishi* (Tokyo, 1970), folds 4-6; and Harumi Sato, ed. *Koten Honkyoku Hikyoku*, Vol. 1 (Kobe, 1954), folds 2-3. The latter includes a shakuhachi duet version of uncertain origin; the best recording of this work may be found in *Shakuhachi Honkyokushu*, Vol. 2, performed by Katusya Yokoyama, Ongaku-no-tomo-sha, OCD-0912. More than a dozen Japanese lion dance pieces exist, mostly with regional names. "Cloud Well" refers to the koto obbligato tuning, showing an awareness that the piece does not use the customary Mode I.

[10]The notation does not convey the great variety in the intonation of the lower neighbor D in actual performance. In a private conversation, shakuhachi master Katsuya Yokoyama emphatically stated that playing these notes all at exactly the same pitch would make for a very insipid interpretation. This intonational variety does not weaken the sense of the neighbor function.

[11]This E does appear in the recording cited above. Many of the other performers who include the E have learned this from Yokoyama.

Pyong-Si-Jo (Korea)

Our last piece, *Pyong-Si-Jo* ("A Melody from Peaceful Times") comes from Korea (Example 5a).[12]   *Si-Jo* denotes a genre of pieces which originated as vocal melodies. In modern performances they are heard only on instruments, usually the taegum (a transverse flute) or hegum (a recent adaptation of the Chinese er-hu, brought closer to the western violin, found mainly in North Korea). This work shares with some older Korean melodies an interesting metric property of irregular alternation of bars with five and eight beats; one can see this indicated in Example 1, a tablature excerpt from a different *Si-Jo* piece.

Although eight different pitches occur in this excerpt, one can nonetheless readily discern a pentatonic character. C$\sharp$ and E$\flat$ appear infrequently, and obviously embellish D, implying that they are not members of the governing scale. The choice between A$\flat$ and A$\natural$ might seem less clear, but evidence points to the inclusion of A$\natural$ as the true scale member. A$\flat$ first appears as a neighbor to G, helping us to continue hearing it as such even when placed between B and G. On the other hand A$\natural$ functions more strongly in connecting B and G, and its significance is enhanced by the perfect fifth at the end of bar 5. Thus the piece follows Chinese Mode I with three added tones that all function as chromatic neighbors to $\hat{1}$ or $\hat{5}$.

Example 5b presents a graph of the excerpt. Its two voices reflect melodic polyphony, not melodic-harmonic structures. Note that the D in bars 3–4 lacks harmonic function, since it always occurs within the arpeggiation to or from G. Similar uses of a fifth degree below the tonic occur in China and Japan, although without any formal concept of inversion.[13] The low G in bar 3 has mere decorative status rather than significance as a tonic statement in the lower register; it occurs only once in an inconspicuous context, whereas the upper register G occupies nearly half the total duration of the excerpt (even without including the time spent on what are obviously neighbor tones).

*   *   *   *   *

The works and analyses discussed above provide a glimpse of traditional works from East Asian countries, as well as some sense of how these

---

[12]Adapted from Sa-hun Chang, "Art Song," in *Survey of Korean Arts Traditional Music* (Seoul: National Academy of the Arts, 1973), pp. 181-201.

[13]About 20% of Chinese qin pieces end on a perfect fourth. Since that interval never occurs in the lowest register (although easiest there), one can assert the existence of a large prolongation of a lower tonic into that final fourth, interpreting it as the upper fifth of an understood 8/5 sonority. In many Japanese sangen pieces the two lower strings are tuned to a fourth, with the upper one always heard as the tonic, while in pieces with these strings tuned to a fifth, the lower note functions as the tonic. See David Loeb, *op. cit.*, for instances of melodic inversions of other intervals functioning as alternative renderings of parts of thematic ideas in different statements, occurring either simultaneously (or nearly so) in polyphonic contexts or else at corresponding points in time in solo variation pieces.

Example 5a. Transcription of *Pyong-Si-Jo* (Korean, see Example 1 above).

Example 5b. Analytic sketch of *Pyong-Si-Jo.*

(bar) 1   2   3   4   5   6

pieces may be understood theoretically and analytically. In addition to considering these problems purely for their own sake, these insights might also guide our responses to Western music influenced by that of Asia. This is especially true for works that involve melodic progressions including intervals regarded as scale steps in Asian music but as leaps within Western music.

For a particularly instructive example, consider the poignant oboe melody that opens "*Der Einsame in Herbst*" from *Das Lied von der Erde* of Gustav Mahler (Example 6). An automatic reaction to the B♭ in bar 6 would consider it as an incomplete upper neighbor. But recognition of the structure of Chinese Mode II (Example 2), with its use of $\hat{8}-\hat{7}-\hat{5}$ descents, suggests that Mahler has deftly inserted these elements into a broader Western context. That is, on a local level there is a sense that the D–C–A motion in bars 3–4 is stepwise, characteristic of the scale motion of the Chinese Mode II, but in a larger sense, the C here constitutes part of a passing motion by step through the B♭ in bar 6.

In bar 15, one expects a departure from the tonic, but an extraordinary contrapuntal motion brings a tonic resolution shortly thereafter in bar 19. This I chord lacks a strong sense of resolution, even with the bass brought down to the lowest register. The real closure arrives only in bar 21, as a result of the melody literally led step-by-step from D to A. This fourth descent restates the "intercultural" treatment of bars 3–6 and overlaps with a renewed beginning of the same process. Echoes of this idea recur

Example 6. Analytic sketch of Gustav Mahler, "Der Einsame in Herbst," from *Das Lied von der Erde*, bars 1-21.

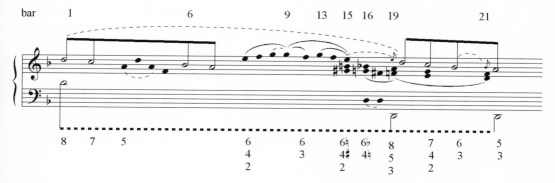

frequently throughout this piece, culminating in the B♭–A melodic sigh that concludes the movement.[14]

[14]From this same work, see also "Das Trinklied von Jammer der Erde" bars 5–14, and for characteristic Mode I practices, see "Von der Jugend" bars 3–5 and "Von der Schönheit" bars 1–2.

Baroque Styles and the Analysis of Baroque Music

Channan Willner

Following a presentation I gave in 1995 on the durational analysis of J.S. Bach's instrumental music, Carl Schachter posed a question about the prevalence of four-bar grouping in many of Bach's rhythmically irregular instrumental works. How, Carl asked, could one reconcile these contradictory features? I answered his question rather tentatively at the time, but I have since reconsidered the issue from the vantage point of stylistic diversity and stylistic mixture within a hierarchy of Baroque styles. In this essay I should like to revisit the matter by focusing on levels of style, tonal structure, and durational patterning in the music of Bach, Vivaldi, and Couperin.[1]

It is not often that Schenkerians take out the time to study the kind of Baroque music most often played on the radio—the concertos of Vivaldi, the suites of Telemann, the recorder sonatas of Loeilliet, and all the other works of the supposedly lesser Baroque composers. Openly or tacitly we believe that it shows only lopsided tonal and durational structures, that it treats basic issues incompletely, and that it just doesn't measure up to the music of Bach, Handel, or Domenico Scarlatti. I take this opportunity to dispel such misguided beliefs by rerouting our apprehensive approach to this repertoire in an altogether different direction.[2]

Let me start by suggesting that we put our value judgments aside for now, and that we rethink the music of the seemingly minor Baroque composers as a different kind of music, composed at the same time as the music of Bach and Handel but in a decidedly different style. Whether the music of Rameau and Couperin is as integral, as coherent, or as structured as that of Bach and Handel need not concern us at the moment. If we want to learn something about this repertoire—and about the stylistic environment in which Bach and Handel worked and from which they both borrowed heavily—we must be willing to suspend our preconceptions and to study this music on its own merits.

---

[1]The relation of style and structure throughout the vocal repertoire of the early eighteenth century is a more complex phenomenon, one that would require another study.
[2]I thank Bruce Gustafson for his helpful comments on an earlier version of this paper.

145

I. Bach and the mixture of styles

The Allemande from Bach's D-minor French Suite, reproduced in Example 1, offers a vivid example of Bach's way with durational patterning and stylistic diversity. Example 2 is a tonal sketch and Example 3 is a rhythmic reduction, or *pace reduction,* as I call it. The pace reduction shows quite clearly the underlying metric and periodic regularity of the reprise. The twelve measures of the reprise divide into one introductory measure and three overlapping groups, each essentially four measures long. The first two groups are both displaced from their position in the metrical grid by the introductory measure. The opening four-measure group extends from bar 2 to bar 5; the second group, overlapping, enters in the middle of bar 5 and continues up to the middle of bar 9; and the third group, overlapping as well, occupies bars 9–12.

Example 1. J.S. Bach, French Suite in D minor, Allemande, first reprise.

Example 2. Bach, D-minor Allemande, tonal reduction.

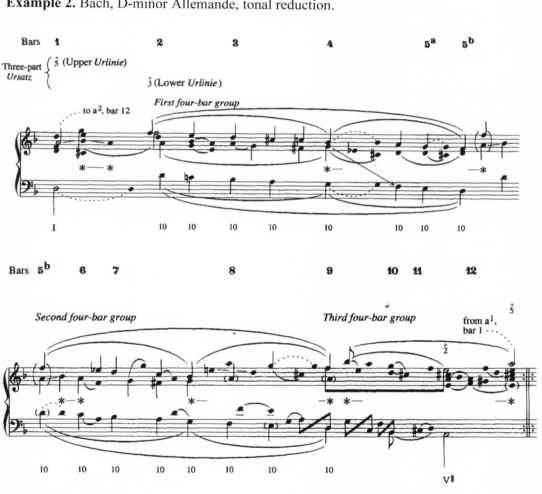

*Preparation for and superposition of b♭²-a²

(cont.)

Example 3. Bach, D-minor Allemande, pace reduction.

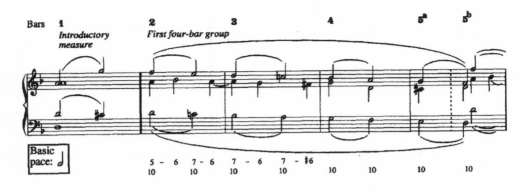

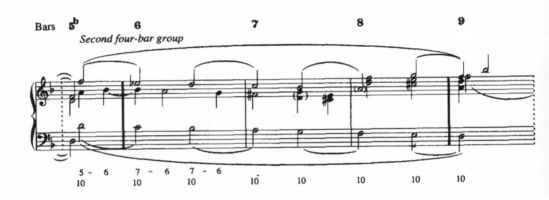

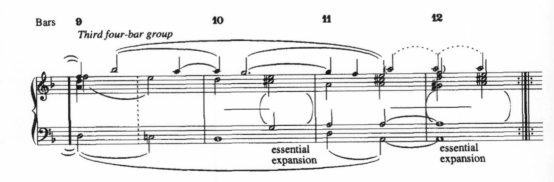

Once we clear away the many local delays occasioned by the Allemande's thick web of suspensions and by their constantly varied resolutions, it becomes apparent that the introductory measure and the first group set up a very regular outer-voice framework. In the top voice, an ascent from a^1 to g^2 gives way to a four-bar octave descent from f^2 to f^1. In the bass, a supporting neighbor-note motion, d–c$\sharp$–d , over the sustained tonic in bar 1, is followed by a four-bar octave descent from d^1 to d, which moves in parallel tenths with the descending upper voice.

As we normalize the progression of the outer voices, we realize that the two voices move evenly in half notes and that their movement is stepwise. This essentially even, stepwise movement of the outer voices embodies what I call the *basic pace* of the piece—the steady tonal and durational progression of soprano and bass that underlies the entire Allemande. Most early 18th-century instrumental compositions that sustain the densely contrapuntal fabric of the high style also display a single underlying pace which guides the piece from beginning to end. Though most often conjunct, and most readily apparent in the movement of the outer voices, it also affects the conduct of the inner voices. The basic pace allows for a moderate amount of arpeggiation and repetition, and it also lends itself to temporary expansion and contraction. In the compound 4/4, the basic pace proceeds in quarter notes; in the "small" or "simple" 4/4, as Kirnberger calls it, the basic pace proceeds in half notes, just as it does in the D-minor Allemande; and in ¾ time it fluctuates between an even one-bar movement and a moderately uneven alternation of half notes and quarter notes.[3] There are other underlying paces whose movement is conspicuous here—especially the faster figural paces of quarter notes and eighths—but they need not concern us now.

The passage illustrates the happy union of periodicity and tonal articulation one often finds in Bach.[4] Since each underlying tone occupies a half note, stepwise groups of two, four, and eight tones naturally set up a tonally based periodic design of one, two, and four bars. Thus, the eight tones of the falling octave in bars 2–5 occupy four measures since each pair of tones occupies precisely one measure.

The second group of four bars follows exactly the same pattern—an octave descent from F to F in the upper voice, and from D to D in the

---

[3]I discuss the basic pace, its fluctuations, and its relation to other paces and to Kirnberger's survey of 18th-century meter in "Stress and Counterstress: Accentual Conflict and Reconciliation in J.S. Bach's Instrumental Works," *Music Theory Spectrum* 20 (1998), pp. 286–304, and in "Sequential Expansion and Handelian Phrase Rhythm," *Schenker Studies 2*, ed. Carl Schachter and Hedi Siegel (Cambridge: Cambridge University Press, 1999), pp. 192–221. The D-minor Allemande has been the subject of at least one similar analysis in the Schenkerian literature: see William Renwick, *Analyzing Fugue: A Schenkerian Approach* (Stuyvesant, N.Y.: Pendragon Press, 1995), p. 15, Example 1-15. I first presented my reading of the Allemande, in a drastic durational reduction, in my paper, "Nascent Periodicity and Bach's 'Progressive' *Galanterien*," read at the annual meeting of the American Musicological Society in Pittsburgh, 1992.

[4]William Rothstein, *Phrase Rhythm in Tonal Music* (New York and London: Schirmer Books, 1989), pp. 136–37.

bass—even though the very beginning of the descent and its conclusion are veiled by contrapuntal and registral complexities. In all, this group represents a hidden tonal and rhythmic repetition of the first group. The third group shows a descent from d to A in the bass that is expanded twice in order to extend to four bars. These essential bass expansions are noted by small parentheses in Example 1b. During each expansion, the basic pace halts temporarily, and its activity is taken over by the more ornamental figural paces and by the diminutions that operate at the surface. Going its own way during the third group, the upper voice superimposes the $\hat{5}$—the structural a¹ which was hidden under a maze of simulated lute arpeggiations in bar 1—on top of the texture at bar 12 (Example 2).

The type of *tonal periodicity* that governs the Allemande's first reprise rarely prevails for the duration of a complete piece, nor is it the only kind of periodicity one finds in Bach. But it occurs very frequently in his music. The question arises whether a deeper reason exists for Bach's apparently deliberate decision to compose in such a foursquare way—to follow a strict periodic plan even though the plan is thrown off at the outset by one measure and is then masked by a web of suspensions and ornamental arpeggiations.

Bach's fusion of dense counterpoint and "progressive" periodicity embodies a deliberate mixture of styles. The basic pace of the outer voices and the unpatterned resolutions at the surface represent the high style of Bach's lingua franca, with heavy borrowings from the *style brisé* of the French lutenists, while the basic grouping in four-bar subphrases shows the superimposition of a lower style of composition, in this instance the emerging galant style. During the second decade of the 18th century the galant style had already begun to displace the middle style and the mixed style employed by most Baroque composers at the time. Both Bach and Handel were intimately familiar with these lower styles, and both frequently set the three—especially the galant style—in opposition to the high style, which remained their compositional mainstay. The periodic grid of the galant style offered an automatic, ready-made mechanism for writing on a scale larger than the embryonic scale of additive Baroque temporality. Its drawbacks—a very slow harmonic rhythm, a heavy emphasis on thematic repetition, and a highly simplified tonal vocabulary—could be offset by the high style.

II. The three styles

That several conflicting styles would intersect even in Bach's quintessentially Baroque Allemande tells us a good deal about the fabric of Baroque music in general. What we think of as Baroque instrumental music is actually made up of several different ways of composing. At the top, at least in terms of moment-to-moment harmonic complexity and artifice, we find the high style, the familiar contrapuntal web of Bach's and Handel's major instrumental works. At a lower level of tonal expression—incorporating simpler harmonies, and readily accessible thematic work—we have both the more casual and relatively informal middle style of Telemann's *Musique de table*, and the increasingly popular galant style. Finally, at a minimal level of complexity, we encounter the low style, whose sparing tonal vocabulary, bare textures, and roughly turned thematic outlines underline its characteristic repetition of short and blunt motives. This is the kind of explicitly programmatic and insistently repetitive writing that marks the Biblical Sonatas of Kuhnau and those pieces in which François Couperin depicts theatrical or military events or evokes the rugged contours of folk music.[5]

These are, of course, generalizations. The Baroque composer was perfectly capable of pursuing the style most appropriate to the occasion and genre at hand, and the boundaries between the three styles were not always clearly defined, especially in the vocal repertoire. Each style also had many subcategories, as well as national variants—so many, in fact, that a hierarchically tiered system of classification was needed to sort them out.[6] Among these subcategories and variants were the high style's learned counterpoint, the middle style's mixed style—a suitably tasteful union of the pleasing and the "natural" elements of the French, Italian, and German styles—and the low style's folklike simulations of pastoral drone accompaniments.[7]

To illustrate the middle style briefly, I should like to present the first reprise of the Gavotte from the Eighth *Ordre*, in B minor, of François Couperin's *Pièces de clavecin* (Example 4). The pace reduction in Example 4b shows how the thematic statement in the opening two measures follows a basic pace of quarter notes, and how the responding two-bar group, though more elaborate at the surface, follows a pace of half notes below, under the surface. The two groups and the mixture of underlying paces they embody are repeated as the Gavotte moves to the dominant. Although pace expansion and contraction is common throughout the Baroque repertoire, the extended mixture and contrast of paces—*composite pacing*—is typical largely of the middle style, and it figures prominently throughout the instrumental music of Telemann, Vivaldi, and Couperin. In composite pacing, one underlying pace seems at first to predominate, but its hegemony is soon challenged by slower and faster paces. No single pace governs the entirety of the movement, and no single pace articulates the motion of the outer voices from beginning to end.

To get an idea of what the low style is like, let us look at the first reprise of the Fanfare from Couperin's Tenth *Ordre* (Example 5). Neither its

[5]The most authoritative introduction to the study of stylistic hierarchies in Baroque music is Claude Palisca, "The Genesis of Mattheson's Style Classification," in *New Matthesoon Studies,* ed. George J. Buelow and Hans Joachim Marx (Cambridge and New York: Cambridge University Press, 1983), pp. 409-23. The foundational contemporary description of these hierarchies is Johann Mattheson, *Der Volkommene Capellmeister,* trans. by Ernest C. Harriss (Ann Arbor, Mich.: UMI Research Press, 1981). The most vivid description, however, is found in Johan Adolf Scheibe's *Critischer Musicus* (*neue, vermehrte und verbesserte Auflage*, Leipzig: Breitkopf, 1745; reprinted Hildesheim: G. Olms, 1970), pp. 126–30. For a translation with illuminating commentary and further references see Melanie Diane Lowe, "Expressive Paradigms in the Symphonies of Joseph Haydn" (Ph.D. dissertation, Princeton University, 1998), pp. 328–35.

[6]That was Mattheson's classification scheme, which is described in detail by Palisca, ibid.

[7]I retrace the origins of the threefold classification of styles in the works of the Greek and Roman rhetoricians in my closing remarks. Throughout his *Capellmeister* Mattheson offers strong advocacy on behalf of a "tasteful" and "natural" mixed style. A useful overview of the social and intellectual pressures that promoted such mixtures is Donald R. Boomgaarden, *Musical Thought in Britain and Germany During the Early Eighteenth Century* (New York: P. Lang, 1987).

Example 4. François Couperin, *Pièces de clavecin, Ordre* 8, Gavotte.

static harmonic rhythm nor its obsessive repetitions—whose striking visual outlines on paper are as remarkable as their aural effect is hypnotic when they are played—prevented Bach from using the material in the Corrente from the B-flat Partita. Bach, Handel, and especially Scarlatti often troped the lower styles and their folksy idioms onto their own distinctly personal ways of composing. They either elevated the material they troped, so that it would fit comfortably in its new environment, or they allowed stylistic friction to become a major issue in the composition.[8]

Example 5. Couperin, *Pièces de clavecin, Ordre* 10
"La Triomphante," Troisième partie: Fanfare (Bars 1-12).

*Although the note values of the upper voice appear not to be in agreement with those of the bass, it is customary to notate them in this way.

[8]On stylistic elevation and stylistic friction as compositional resources in early eighteenth-century music see my doctoral dissertation, "Durational Pacing in Handel's Instrumental Works: The Nature of Temporality in the Music of the High Baroque" (City University of New York, 2005, at *www.channanwillner.com*). An indispensable semiotic account of style relations is Robert S. Hatten, *Musical Meaning in Beethoven: Markedness, Correlation, and Interpretation* (Bloomington, Ind.: Indiana University Press, 1994).

III. The middle style: An analysis

The middle style, which concerns us here, *sounds* superficially like the high style, but it allows for more liberal changes in harmonic rhythm and for a greater number and a more varied succession of themes and textures. It also fuses the three national styles – the Italian, the French, and the German—more closely, so that tracing the provenance of each national style becomes much more difficult; hence the gradual emergence from the middle style of the "natural" and "tasteful" mixed style.[9] Received notions about Baroque music to the contrary, the middle style promotes neither affective uniformity nor motivic consistency; rather, it puts substantial emphasis on a continual play of contrasts among a variety of surface elements. Above all, the middle style frequently abandons the basic pace that a composition appears to have set up in favor of an ever-changing compendium of foreground and middleground paces which the composer highlights at will. Tonally straightforward but rhythmically unpredictable, the middle style projects an improvisatory spontaneity whose spur-of-the-moment gestures are intended to be understood and enjoyed as they occur.[10]

For an example of the middle style, let us turn to the opening ritornello from Vivaldi's well-known Concerto in G minor for Viola d'amore and Lute, RV. 540 (Example 6). Like so many Vivaldi ritornellos, our excerpt does not employ the "textbook" three-part ritornello format: There is little sense of an orderly progression from an expository *Vordersatz* to a developmental *Fortspinnung* or to a closing *Epilog*.[11] Instead, two large and fairly equal periods, sixteen and fourteen bars in length, balance each other out. The first period, in its larger outlines, ascends, and the second period descends. The first period turns from the tonic to the mediant, and the second period extends the subdominant—through an apparent return to the mediant and, at a deeper level, through a large voice exchange within the subdominant; the second period then continues on to the dominant and to the tonic.[12] The first period divides into seven- and nine-bar phrases

---

[9]An outgrowth of the middle style, the mixed style put greater emphasis on pleasing the listener by subjecting the listener to fewer musical demands. Its principal advocate, who also wrote about it eloquently, was Johann Joachim Quantz; see his *Versuch einer Anweisung, die Flöte traversiere zu spielen*, trans. Edward R. Reilly (2nd ed., London and Boston: Faber and Faber, 1985).

[10]Contemporary writers emphasize the pleasure and enjoyment that the accessibility of the middle style provides; see Scheibe, *Critischer Musicus*, p. 128, and Lowe, "Expressive Paradigms," p. 331.

[11]This quintessential three-way division, a perennial of historical musicology, is finding ever greater use among music theorists. It was introduced by Wilhelm Fischer in "Zur Enwicklungsgeschichte des Wiener klassische Stils," *Studien zur Musikwissenschaft*, Vol. 3 (1915), pp. 32–33. Among its most sustained analytical applications is Laurence Dreyfus, *Bach and the Patterns of Invention* (Cambridge, Mass.: Harvard University Press, 1996). Dreyfus argues persuasively that the plastic modification of the ritornello's three parts is one of the Baroque composer's fundamental ploys of invention. One might say that the absence of the three parts in a Vivaldi ritornello embodies an important inventive and stylistic statement.

[12]Extended subdominants and large-scale voice exchanges of comparable complexity are very frequent in the music of Bach and Couperin.

and, further, into four more-or-less equal subphrases—three, four, and five bars long; the second period divides, similarly, into six- and eight-bar phrases and, further, into four subphrases three and five bars long. The division into brief, dovetailing subphrases is a matter of great importance for there is a striking disjunction in the articulation of these short groups. Notwithstanding a general affinity between the phrases and the subphrases, and a fluent melodic continuity from one subphrase to another, almost every subphrase introduces semiautonomous thematic and rhythmic material. This relatively independent material contrasts, sometimes quite dramatically, with the material in the adjacent subphrases.

Surprisingly, perhaps, it is the tonal structure of the ritornello (Example 7) that contributes most substantially to the ritornello's cohesion. The climactic emphasis on the high tones c^3 and a^2 near the end of the first period in bars 12 and 13, and, during the second period, the prominence of the high tones bb^2 and g^2 (bars 17–19), then a^2 and f^2 (bars 20–22), and finally g^2, f^2, and $c\#^2$ (substituting for e^2, bars 26–29) indicate that an octave descent from an implicit d^3 to d^2 governs the entire ritornello, and that much of the descent is accompanied, in typically Baroque fashion, by a quasi-structural line a third below.[13]

The most improvisatory features of the ritornello are its ever changing durational design and, conversely, its kaleidoscopic succession of thematic fragments. This kaleidoscopic quality extends to Vivaldi's articulation of the basic pace. Were one to trace the progress of the basic pace, as I have done in Example 8—and, directly under the music, in Example 6—one would find that it moves at a steady one-bar rate up to the climactic appearance of c^3 and a^2 in bars 12 and 13, where, without warning, it expands to two-bar movement. In fact, one could say that in these measures the basic pace suddenly stops dead in its tracks. As the ritornello picks up speed and approaches the central cadence on the mediant in bars 14 and 15, the pace accelerates wildly to movement in quarter notes and eighth notes. During the two sequential subphrases that open the second period, the basic pace slows to three-bar movement through *sequential expansion*, a phenomenon I discussed in several recent publications.[14] For the first three sequential measures the basic pace extends the bass G, and for the second three sequential measures it extends the bass F. The basic pace resumes its essential one-bar movement for only one measure, during the dramatic leaps in bar 23; it then accelerates to quarter-note movement in

---

[13]Octave descents, like the descent which underlies Vivaldi's ritornello, are common over short spans of time in Baroque style but not, in my experience, across entire movements. Longer octave descents usually represent thematic enlargements at the middleground that are superimposed, with little help from the bass, over descents from $\hat{5}$; I discuss this issue at length in "Durational Pacing." David Smythe offers a very different view in "Schenker's Octave Lines Reconsidered," *Journal of Music Theory,* Vol. 43, No. 1 (Spring, 1999), pp. 101–34. The basic introduction to fundamental structures which, like those in Example 2 and in Example 7, show more than one descending line, is David Neumeyer, "The Three-Part *Ursatz,*" *In Theory Only,* Vol. 10, No. 1–2 (August, 1987), pp. 3–29.

[14]See my "Sequential Expansion" and "Stress and Counterstress."

Example 6. Vivaldi, Concerto in D minor for Viola d'amore and Lute, RV 540
I: Allegro, opening ritornello (bars 1-30).

Example 7. Vivaldi, D-minor Concerto, tonal reduction.

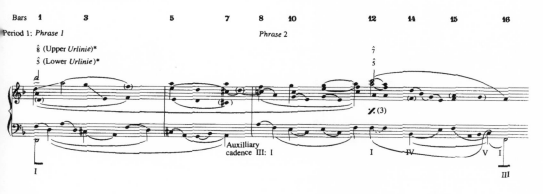

(*cont.*)

(Example 7, cont.)

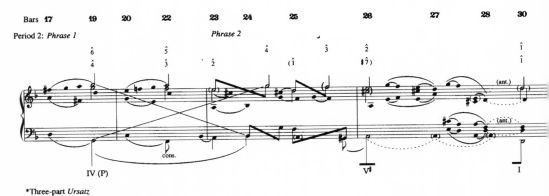

*Three-part *Ursatz*

Example 8. Vivaldi, D-minor concerto, pace reduction.

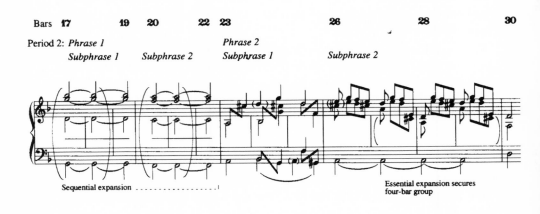

Example 9. Vivaldi, D-minor Concerto
Beginning of first solo episode (bars 30-40).

(etc.)

bars 24 and 25, and, further, to movement in eighths during the extension of the dominant in bars 26–29. Evidently, the sense of an essential one-bar movement established in bars 1 through 11 is lost shortly after the climactic repetitions in bars 12 and 13.

What has happened here is quite typical of the middle style: The one-bar basic pace has essentially dissipated in the course of the ritornello and has given way to *composite pacing*. Composite pacing, a notion I introduced briefly when I discussed the larger rhythms of Couperin's B-minor Gavotte (Example 4), signifies the frequent alteration of the underlying pace described by the outer voices; when composite pacing prevails during a substantial stretch of music, it prevents any one pace from predominating over its companion paces. As Vivaldi's ritornello proceeds, the underlying pace established by the outer voices changes so often that the variable figural paces of the foreground become far more consequential than any sustained or underlying durational movement. Even in these opening measures the rhythms of the foreground—the eighth-note leaps and the dotted sixteenths in bars 1 through 4, as well as the figural quarter notes that underlie the eighths—cover up and obliterate the articulation of a steady one-bar movement relayed by the underlying harmonies. The rhythmic outlines that emerge most readily from under the surface of the music—the composites of quarter notes and eighths marked as "the most prominent pace" in Example 6—thus take precedence over the slower half-note basic pace, to which the movement of the outer voices ultimately reduces (Example 8).[15] The same could not be said about the web of foreground suspensions and the lute-style arpeggiations in Bach's D minor Allemande, where the half-note basic pace of the outer voices remains the composition's most conspicuous tonal and durational attribute (see Example 3 above). If Bach's Allemande resembles a kind of composed-out first and fourth species counterpoint, Vivaldi's ritornello resembles fifth species counterpoint, writ large.[16]

IV. The middle style and the high style: Larger issues

Awareness of the difference in pacing between the high style and the middle style impinges on our interpretation of each style's larger compositional environment. Despite much expansion and contraction, the steady progress of the basic pace in the high style promotes an orderly temporality, a consistent thematic design, and a textural uniformity that characterize each movement from beginning to end. The more precarious and adventurous progress of composite pacing in the middle style exerts no such influence—it promotes a deliberately uncontrolled temporality and in so doing it fosters frequent changes in texture and in thematic design. Consequently it also allows for a less patterned tonal and formal structure.

It may have been this kind of spontaneous and improvisatory temporality, rather than just the powerfully affective concerto setting as such, that attracted Bach to Vivaldi's music. After all, the three-part ritornello and its Italianate working out were compositional resources which Bach and other German composers had encountered years before making the acquaintance of Vivaldi's *L'Estro armonico* in 1713. It would be tempting to think that in the same way Bach later on took over and elevated the galant style, Bach also somehow tried to incorporate Vivaldi's rhythmic freedom (along with Couperin's) in his own much stricter durational practice. But certainly any attempt to retrace a thread of influence along such lines would be a daunting task. For one thing, Bach's temporality shows a long-range consistency throughout his oeuvre that one does not easily associate with the notion of unfettered rhythmic freedom.[17]

[15]Because a new subphrase begins at the upbeat to bar 5, I parse bars 4 and 5 differently, despite the similar looks of their first halves.

[16]To be sure, Bach and Handel employ composite pacing also, especially in thematic and cadential areas of the composition and when they call upon the middle style, above all in vocal music. But they do so in a more controlled, less extravagantly spontaneous manner, and within the framework of brief and idiomatic departures from the basic pace. An altogether different issue, which must await further study, is the mixture of paces that obtains when a slow-moving cantus firmus underlies a choral movement, or when a moderately-paced vocal line combines with animate obbligato instrumental lines.

[17]Not that Bach didn't try. He was under severe pressure from Scheibe and his circle to accommodate his artifice to the more easygoing practice of the times, and he in fact did what he could—even in his most severe contrapuntal works from the 1740s—to attune (*cont.*)

Looking briefly again at the thematic design of Vivaldi's ritornello, we may wonder how one might reconcile the wide leaps in bars 1–8 with the much more sustained small intervals in bars 9–16 during the first period, and how one might also reconcile the corresponding but far more drastic contrasts throughout the second period. Up to a point, these contrasts represent an instrumental simulation of vocal gestures, fluctuations in affect and intensity that realize the ritornello's emotional *Gestalt* and define its formal outlines. Furthermore, any ritornello will contain features that are in some way unclear, incomplete, or undeveloped; these might be worked out and explained later on. But the first solo section of the D minor concerto shows that Vivaldi does not explicate or expand on his ambitious ritornello. Instead—and this is by no means unusual—he simply branches off in a different direction to satisfy the virtuosic demands of the two solo parts; see Example 9.[18]

The essence of Vivaldi's ritornello, then, resides in its lively foreground—in the colorful and theatrical contrasts between and among its eight subphrases, each of which Vivaldi highlights in turn. Such explicit thematic disjunction does not confine itself to Vivaldi's ritornellos or to his concertos: The improvisatory mélange it embodies is the order of the day in most music of the middle style, and it straddles the boundaries of many instrumental genres, forms, and media. In the long run, one might think of this music as a collection of promissory notes, in Edward T. Cone's sense of the term.[19] But whereas Cone's nineteenth-century notes are usually paid up, our early eighteenth-century notes remain largely unpaid. Given a free rein, the kind of short-breathed, casual, and sometimes even chaotic durational setting that results from extended composite pacing almost inevitably leads the composer to make promises that cannot be kept.[20]

Among several composers who turned this potentially precarious situation to their advantage was François Couperin. Couperin's keyboard miniatures encapsulate many extraordinary riches in very short spans of time. They are paradigmatic of the middle style's hidden treasures. That is probably why they served as a gold mine of thematic sources not only for the two major composers of the high style—Bach and Handel—but also for many later composers, most of whose borrowings from Couperin remain largely

---

himself to the needs of contemporary practice. For a fascinating and detailed account, with many further references, see David Yearsley, "Ideologies of Learned Counterpoint in the North German Baroque" (Ph.D. dissertation, Stanford Universiy, 1994).

[18] William Rothstein (personal communication) is certainly correct in pointing out that in his solo episode Vivaldi does maintain and even cultivate the one-bar basic pace of bars 1–11.

[19] Edward T. Cone, "Schubert's Promissory Note: An Exercise in Musical Hermeneutics," *Nineteenth-Century Music*, Vol. 5, No. 3 (Spring, 1982), pp. 233–41.

[20] Ever searching for material or just for stylistic issues he could appropriate, Handel sometimes turned precisely to this kind of durational chaos and reorganized the fracas along proper elevated lines. For an example of what I call "elevated chaos" see the closing movement of the A minor Concerto Grosso, Op. 6, No. 4.

Example 10. Couperin, *Pièces de clavecin, Ordre* 5, "La Flore."

*Thematic enlargements and diminutions of e¹-a¹-d¹, bars 3ª-6ᵇ.

Examples 11. Haydn, Piano Sonata in E minor, Hob. XVI: 34.

a) Bars 1-8 (the first theme)

b) Bars 30-42 (the second theme)

unknown.[21] In Example 10 I reproduce a short piece entitled, appropriately enough, "La Flore"—Flora, the Roman Goddess of flowers, fruits, and springtime—from Couperin's Fifth *Ordre*. Despite a frequently contrapuntal texture, several hemiolic stretches, and recurring chromatic conflicts, the

[21]The influence of Couperin on later eighteenth- and nineteenth-century composers is hard to document because the *Nachlass* of most of these composers—for instance, Schumann's library of scores at the Robert-Schumann-Haus in Zwickau—contains no trace of Couperin's music. But Couperin's music was widely available in published editions dating back to Couperin's own day, and it is quite possible that many of the composers whom Schenker revered studied Couperin in their youth, when they were learning to play the fortepiano or the pianoforte. The principal exception was Johannes Brahms, who together with Friedrich Chrysander edited Couperin's complete *Pièces de clavecin*.

In a future study I hope to show that the internal evidence of Couperin's influence on the music of later composers is strong enough to stand on its own.

Example 12. Beethoven, Piano Sonata in D, Op. 10, No. 3
      III: Menuetto, bars 1-16.

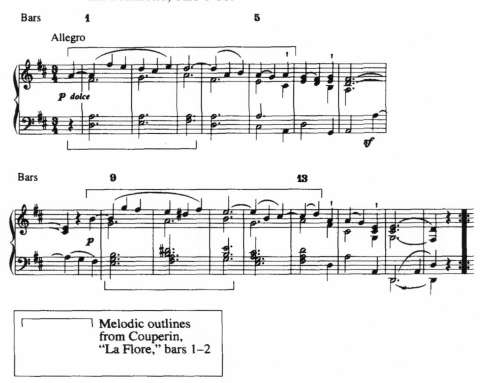

Example 13. Brahms, Piano Concerto No. 2 in B♭, Op. 83
      I: Allegro non troppo, bars 81-85.

Bars   **84**

piece is firmly grounded in the middle style. It begins with a short, tonally closed theme, and during its second reprise it emphasizes the disjunction between a string of relatively abrupt subphrases; it closes with several subphrases that chart a relatively similar territory, and with a harmonically angular and insistent coda. Below several of the score's systems I list a few of the borrowings from—and the allusions to—this miniature that I found in the keyboard music and in the orchestral works of Haydn, Beethoven, and Brahms. In Examples 11, 12, and 13, I quote from these borrowings. The three composers must have sensed that Couperin's music contained more basic material, suitable for further elaboration, than Couperin (or, for that matter, any other composer) could work out singlehandedly.

For all its brevity, "La Flore" contains enough material for each composer to focus his attention on a different part of its design. During the opening Presto from the E-minor Piano Sonata (Hoboken XVI:34) Haydn gradually expounds on the suggestion of a hemiolic overlay made by the upper voices in Couperin's bars 5–7 and 10–12 as he transforms his own first theme into the second theme, on the mediant (Example 11b). Haydn also allows the second theme to assume the outlines of Couperin's opening theme. Beethoven, by contrast, elevates Couperin's gesturally twirly opening three-bar theme into a lyrically serene vision, which emerges out of the preceding "Largo, e mesto" at the opening of the Menuetto from the D-major Piano Sonata, Op. 10, No. 3 (Example 12). And Brahms alludes to Couperin's pastoral extension of G (during the tonicization of the mediant) in the course of the stormy and turbulent developmental pages of the first-movement exposition from the B♭ Piano Concerto, Op. 83 (Example 13). Like many composers, Brahms sublimates both the gestural and the orchestral qualities of Couperin's intimate keyboard setting. The angular rhythms of Couperin's eighth-note motives combine with the density of ornaments (especially the suspensions, in the evocative low register) and with the rich harmonic implications over the sustained bass pedals to present an irresistible invitation for orchestral transformation.

These examples are only the tip of the iceberg. The music of our canonical composers is replete with substantial borrowings from Couperin's 220 keyboard vignettes and portraits, and from his Franco-Italianate ensemble music. Further study will, I believe, bring many additional borrowings to light—from Couperin, from the other composers of the middle style, and especially from Rameau. So at least until the beauty, the significance, and the influence of the middle style have been more completely gauged and understood, I suggest that we leave the radio on when that recorder sonata by Loeilliet or concerto grosso by Manfredini is playing, and I recommend that we listen attentively.

V. Value judgment and historical perspective

When at the beginning of this paper I issued a call to revisit and rediscover the treasures of the middle style, I suggested that we put aside our value judgments in order to focus on what the middle style had to offer. Let us pick up these value judgments now and return to the music of the high style—to the Allemande from Bach's D-minor French Suite and, more generally, to the works traditionally associated with the canon of great composers that Schenker revered. How does the high style, with its even contrapuntal pacing and densely linear fabric, reflect Schenker's notion of the masterwork composed all at once, as if in a fit of daemonic inspiration?[22] Is there a common denomenator between the high style and the middle style? A look at the emergence of stylistic classicification during the golden age of Greek and Roman rhetoric might lead us to a few answers.

The division into three styles of rhetoric had its origins in the two polar opposites of ancient oratory, the plain style and the grand style. These two styles embraced a wide range of styles described as appropriate to the occasion.[23] For greater precision in classification, the two styles eventually split into four—the grand into grand and forceful, the plain into plain and elegant. The four-way division is the centerpiece of the major treatise, *On Style*, attributed to Demetrius.[24] The reformulation of the four-way division

---

[22]Ian Bent offers an exceptionally pithy but lively overview of Schenker's vision in his introduction to Heinrich Schenker, "Essays from *Das Meisterwerk in der Musik,*" *Music Analysis*, Vol. 5 Nos. 2–3 (July–October, 1986), pp. 151–91.

[23]Though often associated with Aristotle, the twofold division into plain and grand styles came into being earlier. The literature on this subject is vast; a standard introduction is George A. Kennedy, *The Art of Persuasion in Greece* (Princeton: Princeton University Press, 1963). A compelling and widely available account can be found in the introduction by Doreen C. Innes to Demetrius, *On Style* (Cambridge, Mass.: Harvard University Press, 1995), pp. 311–42.

[24]*Ibid.*, p. 325. The attribution to Demetrius is probably mistaken, and the author remains unknown.

as a set of three occurred when the Romans adopted the art of rhetoric; it took final shape in the works of Cicero, above all in *Orator*.[25]

Preoccupied on the face of it with fine-tuning the eloquence of speech, the division into three styles, just like the earlier divisions into two and four styles, was of necessity inextricably bound to the depth of thought that underpinned the eloquence of orations and the presentation of cases at courts of law.[26] Simple though it appears, Cicero's description of "the plain style, for proof, the middle style, for pleasure, the vigorous style for persuasion," embodies a commitment and a pledge on the part of the orator, the lawyer, the writer, and the composer—any artist for that matter who invokes the rigor of the high style—to present a coherent, unified, and consistently sustained piece of work.[27]

By its very nature, the contrapuntal environment of Bach's and Handel's high style, and especially its hierarchically tiered and evenly articulated realization of imitative textures, promotes just this manner of sustained, deliberately coherent composition. The ubiquitous, indeed overwhelming presence of imitation in their music fosters a kind of contrapuntally regimented thematic economy—a "fugal ethic"—which in turn leads to the constant transformation and enlargement, across various levels of structure, of a small font of motives and themes. The tonally grounded support of the basic pace guarantees an orderly temporal arrangement of this multi-level thematic play. And the evenly paced tonal support of large-scale progressions like the parallel tenths in bars 2–5^a and bars 5^b–9^a of Bach's D-minor Allemande (see again Example 3) helps the evenly laid-out thematicism reach the deeper levels of tonal structure.

I mentioned at the outset that in bars 9–12 of the D minor Allemande Bach brings the structural $\hat{5}$, a^2, on to the top of the Allemande's maze of arpeggiated sixteenths, and that Bach carries out the superposition with the help of the long-range neighbor-note motion b♭^{2}–a^2, which begins on the second beat of bar 9 (see the asterisks in Example 2). The superposition is a major event in the Allemande's first reprise, and it paves the way for an extensive composing out of a structural descent from a^2, which takes place in the course of the second reprise. Because it is a major event, Bach

---

[25]Cicero, *Orator,* trans. by H. M. Hubbell (Cambridge, Mass.: Harvard University Press, 1939); see especially paragraphs 20ff (pp. 357ff).

[26]For a particularly good account of the many tensions between content and expression, especially during the early days of rhetoric, see Graeme Nicholson, *Plato's Phaedrus: The Philosophy of Love* (West Lafayette, Ind.: Purdue University Press, 1999), pp. 35–55.

[27]Cicero, *Ibid.* The first consequential application of the three-style division to musical composition, and by extension to analysis, seems to have emerged during the late Renaissance, within the extraordinarily wide stylistic framework of madrigal composition; see Martha Feldman, *City Culture and the Madrigal at Venice* (Berkeley: University of California Press, 1995). Style analysis of instrumental music along similar lines plays an essential role in Robert S. Hatten's *Musical Meaning in Beethoven* and in the recent work of Elaine R. Sisman; see especially Sisman's *Mozart, the "Jupiter" Symphony, no. 41 in C major, K. 551* (Cambridge and New York: Cambridge University Press, 1993). A recent comprehensive historical survey is Marina Lobanova, *Musical Style and Genre: History and Modernity,* trans. by Kate Cook (Amsterdam: Harwood, 2000).

prepares the superposition, elaborately, during the first eight measures of the first reprise.

The principal steps in the preparation for the superposition of bb^2–a^2 include the prominent movement of the inner voice, a^1–bb^1–a^1, under the preliminary superposition of g^2–f^2 in bars 1–2^a; the "peek preview" of a^2, thrown atop a supporting inner-voice bb^1–a^1 immediately following the superposition of g^2–f^2 on the last beat of bar 2; the underlying outer-voice descent in tenths in bars 2–5, which is conspicuously subdivided at bb^1–G in bar 4 and has its subdivision colored by an inner-voice eb^1; the replacement of f^2 by bb^1–a^1 at the beginning of the second set of descending tenths in the second half of bar 5, which recalls and intensifies the introductory gesture of bar 1; and the prominent subdivision at bar 7 of the second set of descending tenths, where bb^1 again positions itself over a contrapuntal G.

As the second descent of outer-voice tenths ends at the turn of bar 9, g^2–f^2 appears on top once more, substituting for the expected g^1–f^1 and reestablishing the registral, thematic, and structural circumstances that prevailed at the turn of bar 2. As if to intensify the connection, the entrance of bb^2 on the second beat of bar 9 is promptly imitated by the bass in bar 10. All in all, the arrival of bb^2 has the effect of a climactic gesture: In the long run, it supersedes the hidden repetition of the descending tenths as the guiding idea of the first reprise.

It is the evenly paced contrapuntal environment of the Allemande—its high style—that facilitates and promotes such careful motivic preparation across several levels of structure all at once. And it is the high style's *noblesse oblige* that compels Bach to saturate the Allemande's texture and its structure with contrapuntal parallelisms which eventually burst their bubble and come into their own at bar 9. If the leading composers of the middle style—Couperin, Rameau, Telemann, and Vivaldi—rarely felt compelled to saturate their music to quite the same extent, they nonetheless often did enrich the colorful fabric of their tapestries with underlying thematic associations and structural inventions.

A brief example will illustrate what I mean. I observed earlier that Couperin's "La Flore" (Example 10) is firmly grounded in the middle style. Couperin begins the developmental spinning of "La Flore" at bar 3^b with an ascent from e^1 to a^1 and a descent from a^1 to d^1: The resulting contour e^1–a^1–d^1 spans the *Fortspinnung* group in bars 3^b–6^a (see the asterisks in Example 10).[28] Much of the figural spinning that follows the double bar expands on this contour, using the same chromatic incipit, the eighth notes e^1–$f\sharp^1$–g^1, as its point of departure.

The movement from the temporary mediant in bar 8^b (2.*volta*) to the subtonic in bars 15^a shows an ascent to a^1 (bar 10) that is followed by slower, more extempore descents to g^1 (bar 13^a) and to d^1 (bar 15^b), with a

---

[28]Like many solo and concerted Baroque compositions, "La Flore" shows the influence of ritornello structure even though no orchestra is in sight. During the first reprise, the opening theme in bars 1–3^a represents a *Vordersatz*, the developmental spinning in bars 3^b–6^a a *Fortspinnung*, and the cadential progression in bars 6^b–8^a an *Epilog*.

nested descent to e^1 (bar 11^b) thrown in for good measure. The preliminary cadential progression, which spans the departure from the mediant at bar 19^b and the arrival at the tonic at bar 27^a, then presents a second but incomplete improvisation on the same shape. The upper voice rises in its now-familiar way from e^1 to a^1 (bar 21^a), but it glides over g^1–f^1–e^1–d^1 as is rushes down to the dominant's g♯ (bar 23^a; see the ellipsis sign in Example 10). A repetition (bars 23^b–27^a) brings in the tonic, yet it fails to secure a more substantial statement of these tones.

To make up for the omission, Couperin adds an urgent, dramatically charged coda (bars 27^b–35^a) whose principal mission it is to reach up to d^1, twice, and to mark the arrival at d^1 each time by means of a caesura that halts all activity (bars 29^a and 33^a). The emphasis on d^1, coupled with its echo—a similar emphasis on e^1 at the downbeat of the measures that follow (bars 30^a and 34^a)—compensates for the earlier lacuna.[29]

The short span, light three-voice texture, and quick tempo of Couperin's elfin piece hardly foster the type of thematic density that pervades Bach's Allemande. But the same kind of intimate conversation between surface motives and larger outlines—a dialogue, however informal, between structural levels—shapes its outlines too. The difference between Bach's fabric and Couperin's, then, is a difference in weight, in degree of intimacy. It is essentially the difference between deliberate saturation and opportune improvisation.

[29]Couperin's repetitions and transformations of tonal contours have not gone unnoticed; see David Tunley's fine monographs, *Couperin* (London: British Broadcasting Corporation, 1982), and *François Couperin and the Perfection of Music* (Aldershot, UK, and Burlington, VT: Ashgate, 2003).

V

WORDS AND MUSIC

Schumann's "Das ist ein Flöten und Geigen"
Conflicts between Local and Global Perspectives

Lauri Suurpää

A conflict between appearances and reality seems to play an important role in Heinrich Heine's "Das ist ein Flöten und Geigen" and also in Robert Schumann's setting of this poem as part of his *Dichterliebe* song cycle. In his setting, Schumann expresses tonality in a way that creates ambiguities that in turn mirror aspects of the text. At times the music of this song establishes the tonality with a tonic that is absent; at other times, a tonic that might initially suggest a structural function will ultimately be recognized as subordinate; or else a seemingly subordinate chord will ultimately be recognized as a structural tonic. As a result, the local tonal impressions here often differ from structural functions at later levels.

These strategies for creating tonal conflicts have been discussed at length by Carl Schachter in several of his writings. For example, in his article "Analysis by Key" Schachter uses the notion of "apparent center" to describe situations where the governing of a certain key is suggested even though there is no tonic chord present. In such a situation

> [t]he 'tonic' is an expected center that is never confirmed; in no sense is its harmony a matrix for the pitch content of the passage. When we use the word 'tonic' in analysis, we should do well to remember that it can represent quite different kinds of musical structure. We can quickly infer a tonic as center from signals given by other pitches; neither the tonic chord nor even the tonic note need be present. We can infer a tonic as matrix, however, only through the presence of at least two (and typically all three) of the tonic triad's constituent notes, and these notes must be spread out through time as the beginnings or goals of significant linear and harmonic structures.[1]

This quotation suggests that in order to be able to speak about a tonic as a real center, rather than as an apparent one, we must have a structural tonic, a chord functioning as a matrix for a given musical span. There is a subtle yet important distinction between structural and apparent tonics. According to Schachter's formulation given in "Either/Or," an apparent tonic is

> a chord constructed like a tonic but without a tonic's function. It does not form the beginning or goal of a significant prolongational span, and

---

[1]Carl Schachter, "Analysis by Key: Another Look at Modulation," *Unfoldings: Essays in Schenkerian Theory and Analysis*, ed. Joseph N. Straus (New York: Oxford University Press, 1999), p. 140.

it does not connect convincingly with another similar chord that does function as beginning or goal. Therefore it represents a relatively low-level event.[2]

Since an apparent tonic does not represent a true structural center—a matrix for a given span—we must speak about apparent centers in situations where there are only apparent tonics, rather than structural ones.

But even the status of a structural tonic may initially be uncertain. In "The Triad as Place and Action" Schachter describes the arrival of the tonic in bar 111 of the "Storm" movement from Beethoven's Sixth Symphony as follows:

> This F [the bass note of bar 111], which goes on as a bass pedal for nine measures, constitutes, in fact, a return to the movement's structural tonic. When it first appears, however, it supports a dissonant formation. . . . As the pedal persists, we become increasingly convinced of the importance of the F, but at first we cannot be sure that it represents a true tonic arrival rather than, say, a V of IV. Only with the F major of bar 119 is its status evident beyond a doubt. . . .[3]

This analysis shows that there may also be structural tonics that initially have the air of a relatively low-level element.

All of these aspects of tonal organization suggest possible divergences between moment-by-moment and global perspectives. An apparent center implies the governing of a structural tonic that does not actually appear. An apparent tonic, in turn, may suggest a deep-level role for a chord that is ultimately understood to function as a relatively local contrapuntal element. The kind of situation Schachter explains in Beethoven's "Storm" movement, on the other hand, includes a conflict of an opposite kind: an element that first suggests only a local function is ultimately understood to have a deep-level role.

Such tonal conflicts all may be found in Schumann's "Das ist ein Flöten und Geigen," helping to constitute its sonic quality and dramatic character. The song consists of an A section (bars 1–34) which is repeated with minimal variation (in bars 35–68), and of a coda (bars 69–84) that begins like yet another A section. The harmonic content of the A section is highly original. It both begins and ends with a dominant chord, and it includes only one brief statement of the tonic chord (in bar 9). There is a large-scale sequential repetition within the A section (bars 1–16 and 17–32) where more or less the same music is heard twice, first underlining the dominant of D minor and then the dominant of G minor. This repetition further obscures the tonal focus, for the relation between the dominant of D minor that opens and closes the section and the underlined dominant of G minor that begins the sequential repetition is not immediately apparent.

[2]Carl Schachter, "Either/Or," *Unfoldings: Essays in Schenkerian Theory and Analysis*, ed. Joseph N. Straus (New York: Oxford University Press, 1999), p. 126.
[3]Carl Schachter, "The Triad as Place and Action," *Unfoldings: Essays in Schenkerian Theory and Analysis*, ed. Joseph N. Straus (New York: Oxford University Press, 1999), pp. 179–80.

Example 1 presents my reading of the voice leading of bars 1–34. In Example 1b, I indicate at the beginning an A-major triad in parentheses. This reading suggests that the seventh and ninth of the opening chord are local decorative elements coming from an elided octave and that the underlying triad is heard for the first time in bar 4. Incidentally, the elision of the opening triad creates a beautiful connection to the previous song: the seventh and ninth can be understood—in an associative rather than strictly structural sense—as coming from the A-minor triad that ends the previous song. Bars 5–8 repeat the material of the first four measures, with the singer joining in. At this point, the seventh and ninth of the chord of bar 5 do actually come from an A-major triad, a feature that supports the interpretation of an elided triad at the outset of the work.

In bar 9 the music arrives at a D-minor chord. The function of this chord is far from straightforward. Though it momentarily forms a point of resolution of the previous A chord, this D-minor chord is a very brief element and it begins a sequential passage that leads the music away from the opening D-minor key area. Owing to this brevity and instability, I would suggest that the D minor is an apparent tonic, rather than a structural tonic functioning as the resolution of the preceding dominant.

In sum, the opening of the song creates a multi-faceted dramatic situation. Though the governing key area of the opening clearly is D minor, the D minor is only an apparent center, since there is no structural D-minor chord that provides a matrix for the pitch content here. As a result, the beginning creates a sense of ambiguity, as it is initially not clear whether the work is going to establish D minor as a true tonal center or whether the primary tonic is going to be some other chord.[4]

The continuation of the music indirectly underlines this impression of ambiguity. The sequential passage beginning with the D-minor chord of bar 9 leads to a cadence in F major (bar 15–16). The F-major chord results from a 5–6 motion above the opening A (Example 1a), so the music—up to this point— may be regarded as being in the gravitational field of the opening harmony. This F-major chord does not stand out as a significant center, however, for the music is abruptly torn away from it in bar 17, where the arrival of a D-major ninth chord suggests G minor as a new tonal center. The D-major ninth chord begins the large-scale repetition of bars 1–16, transposed a fifth lower. As such, G minor, too, turns out to be an apparent center: even by the end of the A section, an explicitly stated tonic has still not yet appeared.

The large-scale repetition of the opening measures (in bars 17–32) prolongs the D-major chord with a 5–6 motion, ending in bar 32 on a B♭-major chord (Example 1a). From this B♭-major harmony the music moves via an E-major triad (bar 33) to an A-major chord. This chord concludes

---

[4]The foreground graph of the large-scale repetition of bars 1-16 in bars 17–32 (Example 1b) requires one comment. In bars 26 and 28 I show in the top voice suspended sevenths rather than the octaves that appear in the music. I would suggest that the sevenths form a more consistent voice-leading continuity. Moreover, these sevenths do actually appear in the repetition of the opening A section, see bars 60 and 62.

Example 1. Analytic sketches of Robert Schumann, "Das ist ein Flöten und Geigen," from *Dichterliebe*, Op. 48, bars 1-34.

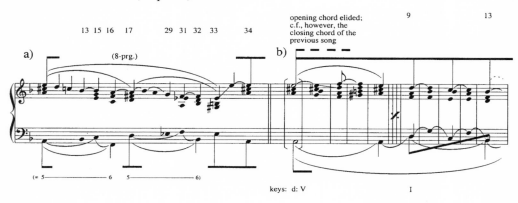

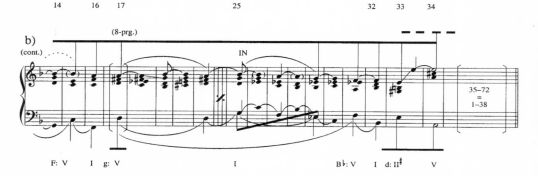

the first A section and then also begins the second (Example 1a). At the deepest levels, the entire A section prolongs an A-major chord. The D-major chord that begins the large-scale repetition (in bars 17–32) is a contrapuntal element that leads to the following E-major chord. As such, even though it is vastly prolonged, this D-major chord is structurally subordinate to the brief E-major triad of bar 33, a triad which serves as the upper fifth of the middleground A chord. The top voice consists of an octave-progression, so that E both begins and ends the top voice of the first A section, allowing for a smooth transition to the second A section.

After the repeat of the A section, the music arrives (in bar 73) at a D-major ninth chord—the same chord that began the large-scale repetition of the opening material in bars 17 and 51 of the A sections. This D chord could again lead later to an E-major chord, as did the analogous D chords of bars 17 and 51 at deep middleground, and hence continue the prolongation of the A-major harmony. No such motion to A ensues, however, and it eventually becomes clear that the D-major chord represents a tonic, the first structural tonic of the work (Example 2). The dissonant ninth and seventh here come from an elided octave in a manner similar to the opening of the song discussed above (see the D-major chord in parentheses in Example 2), and the first tonic triad is heard in bar 76. The situation here is rather similar to that discussed by Schachter in bars 111ff. of the "Storm" movement from

Example 2. Bars 72-84.

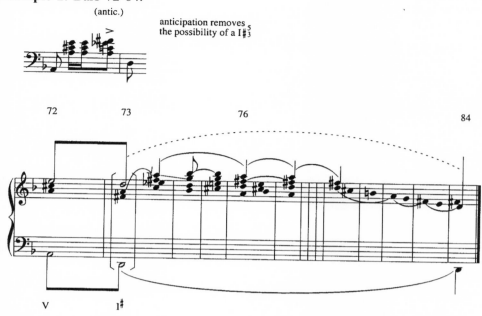

Beethoven's Sixth Symphony: in both cases, a dissonant sonority actually represents the structural tonic, even though it initially suggests some other function.

We are now in a position to form an overview of the entire song. Example 3a shows that at the remotest level the song consists of an auxiliary cadence V–I supporting a top-voice descent E–D. Example 3b indicates that the top voice consists of an implied neighboring motion prolonging the top-voice E, which is elaborated by a motion to an inner voice by means of octave-progressions during the A sections.

The apparent center and apparent tonic of the beginning, the overarching auxiliary cadence, and the initially equivocal closing tonic can all be argued to create programmatic implications that mirror the poetic text. The song cycle of *Dichterliebe* begins with love awakening, only to be lost presently.[5] In the following songs the lost love is recalled with changing emotions, ranging from anger and rage to nostalgia. "Das ist ein Flöten und Geigen" presents the protagonist as an outsider, one who is observing at a wedding party where his beloved is dancing.[6]

Das ist ein Flöten und Geigen,	There is playing of flutes and fiddles
Trompetten schmettern darein	Trumpets blaring forth;
Da tanzt wohl im Hochzeitreigen	there in the wedding party
Die Herzallerliebste mein.	my dearest love is dancing.

[5]I have examined the manner in which the love first awakes and is then lost in my "Schumann, Heine, and Romantic Irony: Music and Poems in the First Five Songs of *Dichterbliebe*," *Intégral* 10 (1996), pp. 93–121.

[6]The translation is by Philip L. Miller and has been taken from *Dichterliebe*: Norton Critical Scores, ed. Arthur Komar (New York: W. W. Norton, 1971), p. 33.

Example 3. Entire song.

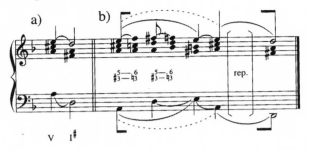

Das ist ein Klingen und Dröhnen,	There is sounding and roaring
Ein Pauken und ein Schalmein;	of drums and pipes
Dazwischen schluchzen und stöhnen	and in the midst of it
Die lieblichen Engelein.	the dear angels sob and groan.

The bitter tone of the poem is anticipated, and further underlined, by the end of the previous poem: "Sie hat ja selbst zerissen, Zerissen mir das Herz" ("she herself, indeed, has broken, broken my heart"). The way in which this poem grows out of the previous one parallels the way in which the opening dissonant harmony of "Das ist ein Flöten und Geigen" grows out of the A-minor triad that ends the previous song.

The emotional turmoil of the protagonist is conveyed by the reference to the "sounding and roaring of drums and pipes," sounds which are inappropriately noisy for wedding music. Juxtaposed with these are the quiet sobs and groans of angels. This juxtaposition suggests that the narrator feels the situation that he is describing is unjust: he should not be an outsider but rather united with the beloved, and he seems reluctant to accept the reality of the circumstances.

The protagonist's reaction against reality seems to be reflected in the tonal structure of the song. Much as the protagonist resists reality, so the large-scale auxiliary cadence postpones the arrival of the structural tonic—the matrix or reality of the tonal system—until the very end of the song. This is vain, however, since the reality is suggested already at the very outset of the song by the hints of D minor, even if only in the form of an apparent center and apparent tonic. The impression of postponement that the auxiliary cadence creates is underlined by the form of the song: the repetition of the A section, which prolongs the avoidance of a concluding tonic, seems to suggest that the protagonist likewise is eager to avoid confronting his situation.

That the final tonic of the song is first heard as a dissonant chord—as a harmony that could still continue the prolongation of the dominant—might be seen as the final attempt to resist reality. But the D-major chord does unavoidably represent the tonic, its initial disguise notwithstanding, and similarly the protagonist must accept that he has lost his beloved.

Reinterpreting the Past:
Brahms's link to Bach in the setting of
"Mit Fried und Freud ich fahr dahin"
from the Motet Op. 74 No.1

Robert Cuckson

"—But you sit at your window when evening falls and dream it to your-self."

Franz Kafka, "An Imperial Message"[1]

The message of the past comes down to us encrusted with its ever-growing patina, further compounded by each generation as it brings to bear its own concerns and experience. In the arts our sense of the past has particular weight, for to be fully grasped an artwork needs to be understood in relation to its period as well as to its place within an evolving tradition.

Occasions where a composer reinterprets material from earlier periods hold special significance. Even if undertaken with scholarship and expertise, such reinterpretations are not primarily antiquarian in nature, but rather the product of a creative act; the living context of the composer's own experience inevitably plays a part. Composition relies as much upon associative as upon logical thought processes, and without them its fruits are likely to be academic and sterile. It is in this light that a movement such as the chorale setting in Brahms's *Warum ist das Licht gegeben dem Mühseligen*, Op. 74 No. 1 (1877) should be viewed, for in this work Brahms brings his modern consciousness to bear on a tradition reaching back through J. S. Bach to Martin Luther, and beyond.

In writing this motet, Brahms added to the great series of elegiac works that already included the German Requiem, the *Schicksalslied* and the Alto Rhapsody. He assembled the text for this composition from both Testaments (Job 3:20–23; Lamentations 3:41; James 5:11), and concluded with the first stanza of Martin Luther's hymn "Mit Fried und Freud ich fahr dahin":[2]

---

[1] From Franz Kafka, *Parables and Paradoxes*, trans. Willa and Edwin Muir (New York: Schocken Books, 1958), p. 15.
[2] From Luke 2: 29 –32, *Nunc dimittis*, adapted by Martin Luther; translation by J. Letterton, from liner notes to *Brahms Motets*, Harmonia Mundi France 901122.

Mit Fried und Freud ich fahr dahin	In peace and joy I depart
in Gottes Willen,	in God's will;
getrost ist mir mein Herz und Sinn,	my heart and mind are comforted,
sanft und stille.	sweet and mild.
Wie Gott mir verheissen hat,	As God has promised me:
Der Tod ist mir Schlaf worden.	Death has become a slumber unto me.

Brahms's choice of a four-part chorale setting (albeit *a cappella*) evokes the music of Bach, who is indelibly linked to this genre. Brahms underlined his debt to Bach here by dedicating the motet to his friend Phillip Spitta, the celebrated Bach scholar. Indeed, Bach himself set this same chorale on at least five separate occasions: in his Cantatas BWV 83, 95, 106 and 125, and also in Chorale No. 49, presumably taken from a lost cantata. Of these, Cantatas 95 (1723) and 106 (1707) are known to predate Cantata 83 (1724), the chorale setting of which I shall compare to Brahms's. By the time he wrote Op. 74, Brahms certainly knew some of these settings from Chorale collections, and it is likely that he would have closely studied Bach's settings of this Chorale before embarking on his own version.

Furthermore, as a subscriber to the Bach *Gesellschaft,* Brahms was in all likelihood acquainted at the time with Cantata 83 (Vol. XX, 1872) and Cantata 95 (Vol. XXII, 1875). Like all Bach's settings of the chorale, the Cantata 95 version is similar in overall harmonic plan to that of Cantata 83, but in Cantata 95 the chorale is rendered in concertato style with an elaborate instrumental accompaniment in imitative counterpoint. The Cantata 83 version is in typical four-part style and is certainly among Bach's finest settings.

Indeed, it is possible to suggest that there is a specific connection between Brahms's Op. 74, No. 1 and Cantata 83, supposing that Brahms had studied Vol. XX of the Bach *Gesellschaft* with his customary thoroughness. A review of the text of Bach's Cantata (Hebrews 9:15; Luke 2:29–32; Hebrews 4:14–16; Hebrews 2:14–15) allows interesting comparisons to be made with the motet text. Brahms's motet chorale text (the first verse of Luther's Hymn) is a paraphrase of Luke 2:29–32. (Bach, as usual, takes Luther's final verse for his closing chorale text.) The texts of the two middle sections of the motet taken together present many of the same ideas as the text of the tenor aria from Cantata 83. Brahms's use of James 5:11, with its reference to Job, is tied to his choice of the opening text (Job 3:20–23). With Job, Brahms portrays a suffering man in the prime of life, in contrast to the old man Simeon of Luke 2:29–32. (Perhaps this lends some credence to Walter Niemann's claim that Brahms intended the motet as a memorial to the composer Hermann Goetz, who died at an early age in December 1876.[3]) Brahms's choice of the more open-minded James text, as compared to the more narrowly focused Hebrews text used by Bach for much of

[3] Walter Niemann, *Brahms* (New York: Knopf, 1929), p. 339.

Example 1. "Mit Fried und Freud ich fahr dahin," various settings.

(a)   Martin Luther, original chorale

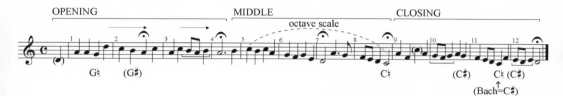

(b)   J.S. Bach, chorale setting from *Erfreute Zeit im neuen Bunde*, Cantata BWV 83

(c)   Johannes Brahms, from *Warum ist das Licht gegeben dem Mühseligen*, Op. 74, No. 1

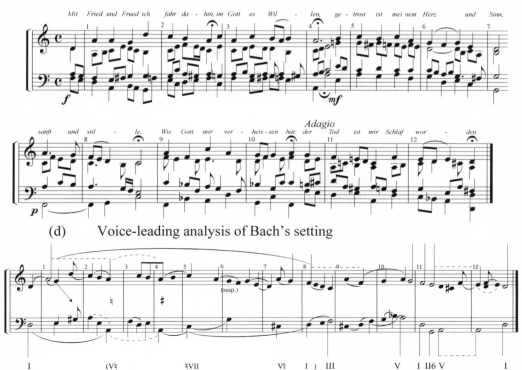

(d)   Voice-leading analysis of Bach's setting

(*cont.*)

(e)   Voice-leading analysis of Brahms's setting

Cantata 83, lends added point to his pronouncements and those of his friends as to the ecumenical character of the work.

Example 1 shows the chorale and the settings from both Bach's BWV 83 and Brahms's Op. 74, No.1, along with voice leading sketches of each work. Comparison of Bach's setting with Brahms's provides a perspective that bears upon aspects of musical and even philosophical approach. Moreover, in appreciating their different solutions to technical issues, we may hope to learn something of how each experiences and treats the tonal space as an entirety, and how each uses types of harmonic articulation characteristic of his time.

Like Brahms's setting, Bach's setting of this chorale also represents a type of engagement with the past. Luther's chorale melody, which was almost two hundred years old in Bach's day, is itself probably a conflation of phrases from mediaeval German song, and thus derives from some of the oldest material in western music. Stemming as it did from Luther, this chorale melody was not subject to the rationalizing efforts of Johannes Crueger, who in the 1640s remodeled a number of other sixteenth-century chorales to make them more amenable to setting in the newly emerging major and minor keys. As a result, in Bach's time it already stood out as a vestige of a bygone era.

The chorale melody has several features that deserve study (Example 1a). It is in the Dorian mode, the mode Luther generally employed for meditative texts. Its cadences are on $\hat{5}$, $\hat{7}$, and $\hat{1}$, with the major $\hat{6}$ of the mode contributing to the melodic cadencing on $\hat{5}$. The third A–C, which tends to promote the use of III in harmonizations, plays a prominent role in Bach's setting.[4] The chorale melody falls into three principal sections: bars 1–4, 5–8, and 9–12. With the exception of one note in each case, the first and third sections expose exclusively the upper fourth and lower fifth segments of the mode respectively, while the second section outlines the tones of an octave scale, and forms a registral bridge between the outer sections. The third section is a variation of the first, with rhyming neighbor-note figures at the cadences.

[4]See discussion in Lori Burns, *Bach's Modal Chorales* (Stuyvesant, N.Y.: Pendragon Press, 1995), p. 128.

The chorale, therefore, explores the whole ambitus of the Dorian mode, but in comparison to other modal chorales carrying Luther's imprimatur, such as "Verleih uns Frieden gnädlich," it is open to tonal treatment in a much fuller sense. This is not to say that it does not present difficulties for tonal harmonization. For instance, the prominent C♮ of bar 8, which follows the octave registral descent from the C♮ in bar 5, threatens to obscure the important events of bars 10 and 11, which would seem to require a structural dominant harmonization and thus demand a C♯. The C♮ right before the end, in bar 11, creates similar tonal conflicts,[5] and the neighbor-note cadence decorations in bars 3, 10, and 12 prevent convenient II$^{6/5}$–V harmonizations (which would result in parallel fifths). Most salient of all, the emphasis on the upper tetrachord in the opening section of the chorale melody suggests a tonicization of A minor, but this tonal motion is countered by the emphatic G♮ of bar 1.

In Cantata 83, the A-minor tonicization near the opening of the chorale relates to strong emphases on A minor in previous sections of the composition. Not only does a cadence in A minor conclude the preceding recitative, but there are also several prominent occurrences of A minor in both of the F-major arias.[6] Brahms's chorale setting, on the other hand, places less stress on A minor. Perhaps significantly, the preceding movements of his motet likewise largely avoid A minor. The opening section of the motet is in D minor, the middle section is in F major, and the final chorale is in D minor. The key of A minor occurs only in the opening section of the motet and briefly within the final chorale. The overwhelming weight of the motet's F major middle section, with its final tonic pedal point, prepares the bass tone of the I^6 with which Brahms begins the opening phrase of the chorale (in place of the customary root-position I).

The settings of the opening phrase in the Bach and Brahms settings differ greatly from one another. In the first phrase of the Bach setting, as noted above, there is a direct tonicization of A minor. Bach establishes this tonicization by means of a G♯ in the bass of bar 1, part of transferred chromatic passing motion from the G♮ on the preceding beat (see Example 2a). Brahms's motion to A minor in the opening of his setting is more ambiguous. In his version, the G♯ is relegated to a secondary status on the second beat of bar 2, leading to a deceptive cadence. The cadence to A minor is delayed until the end of the second phrase, prepared by a G♮–G♯ passing motion that is begun in the bass and completed by the tenor.

In the middle section of the chorale melody (bars 5–8) there is a motion from high to low C. The manner in which this is accomplished prepares the ground for the final cadential progressions. In his setting of this passage, Bach proceeds with a contrary-motion octave in the bass prolonging ♮VII. This prolongation embraces a dividing dominant in bars 6–7, which is

---

[5]Perhaps partly for this reason, Bach substitutes this C♮ for a C♯ in Cantata 83, though he does not do so in his other settings of this chorale.

[6]No doubt these were keys in the episodes from lost violin concerto upon which this cantata was based; see discussion in W. Murray Young, *The Cantatas of J. S. Bach: An Analytic Guide* (Jefferson, North Carolina and London: McFarland and Company, Inc., 1989), p. 52.

Example 2. Voice leading analyses of bars 1-4.

(a) Bach's setting

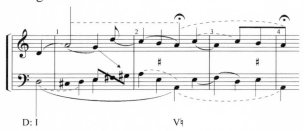

(b) Brahms's setting

decorated with an implied suspension of IV (Example 3a). This highly
unusual suspension is created by the combination of the voice exchange
between the outer parts from the fourth beat of bar 5 to the second beat of
bar 6 and the tonicizing IV-VII⁶/IV-IV⁶ motion which together contrive to
delay the appearance of the V harmony implied by the bass G on the first
beat of bar 6 to the third beat. At the end of bar 7, the bass motion resumes
from the retained C♮ by chromatic passing motion through the C♯ to D at
the beginning of bar 8 as the upper voice moves down to F. At the end of
bar 8, the motion to C♮ in the melody is supported by an imperfect authentic
cadence in III.

Brahms achieves an entirely different effect in this section by casting
all four measures of this middle section as a tonicization of C. In contrast
to Bach's use of V of C as a dividing dominant in bars 6–7, Brahms prolongs
the V as part of a progression originating with the F of bar 5 (Example 3b).
He repeats this IV–V progression with a full close in C in the following
phrase. Bars 5–6 are based on a sequential pattern that is illustrated in
Example 3c. The setting of this descending sequence initially produces a
set of outer-voice tenths, but departs from this sequence in the beginning of
bar 6, where a V substitutes for a VII⁶/II (Example 3c). The inner-voice
figuration in bar 5 falls into a pattern of four eighths, in some sense a
diminution of the four quarters of the chorale melody. It may also be intended
as a commentary on the text, for there is a momentary evocation at this
point of the beginning of *Ein Deutsches Requiem* VI, "Denn wir haben hie
keine bleibende Statt," with its meandering, near-sequential harmony and
its text which refers to the search for comfort and rest.

Example 3. Voice leading analyses of bars 5-8.
   (a)   Bach's setting;

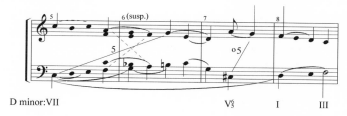

   (b)   Brahms's setting;

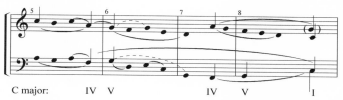

   (c)   comparison of potential sequence with actual pattern found in bars 5-6 of Brahms's setting.

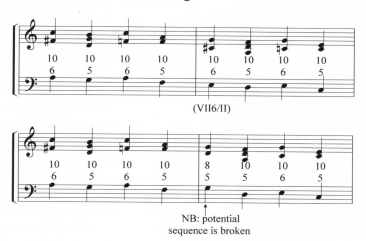

    In the final section of the chorale melody (bars 9–12), diverse features play a part. An overall relationship can be felt with the opening section (bars 1–4): each section consists of a pair of phrases of comparable lengths, and makes use of some similar motivic elements. The middle section (bars 5–8) presents a combination of a longer three-bar phrase (bars 5–7) and a short cadencing phrase (bars 7–8), creating a need for the longer and more regular concluding span (bars 9–12). In conjunction with this, the turning point in the second half of bar 10, with its powerful harmonic implications, lends emphasis to the downbeat of bar 11, which in turn makes credible the intricate contrapuntal prolongation of the cadence found in both settings.

After the cadence on III in bar 8 of the Bach setting, the bass revisits the motion from I to III and continues on to V as the upper voice returns to A (Example 4a). This V prepares the tonic on the downbeat of bar 11, with the *Urlinie* moving down through $\hat{4}$. The final cadence has a contrapuntally prolonged V, a main feature of which is the polyphonic imitation of five notes of the chorale in the bass (see the brackets in Example 4a). The unusual voice crossing of the alto to an F above the chorale neighbor note in bar 12 (see Example 1b) forms part of an implicit motion $\hat{4}$–$\hat{3}$–$\hat{2}$ motion (stemming from the G of bar 10), thereby echoing the larger $\hat{4}$–$\hat{3}$–$\hat{2}$ motion of bars 10-11. (This voice leading, incidentally, is explicit in the instrumental parts in the Cantata 95 setting.)

In Brahms's setting, III is resumed in bar 9 (Example 4b). The tenths between the outer voices in bars 10–11 provide the first part of the final cadence, and a contrapuntally prolonged V completes it. Brahms also has a four-note polyphonic imitation of the chorale in bar 11, and in bar 12 he uses again the composite chromatic passing-tone voice leading seen earlier in bar 3.

Viewed as a totality, Bach's setting has strongly contrasted cadences, and more direct opposition between C♮ and C♯. Brahms's cadences are not all as strongly tonicized or as complete, but he follows Bach's practices, even his voice-leading patterns, very closely in most respects. It is clear, however, that he has different stylistic goals. In creatively reshaping the principles of chorale setting, Brahms, like Bach before him, has boldly made use of innovative features of his mature style, in particular his own individual approach to harmonic prolongation and a number of voice-leading devices found in his later works.

The principal novel element in Brahms's setting is the extended prolongation of III, derived from the initial I⁶ by a 6–5 motion (Examples 1c and e). The symmetrical position of the I⁶–III axis permits a more uniform and evenly balanced harmonization, and the many subsequent employments of 5–6 as an engine of progression lend great fluidity to the voice leading. Viewed more generally, the 6–5 motion whereby I⁶ moves to III constitutes a reconciliation of the two regions of the chorale melody, the fifth D–A and the third A–C. By founding his harmonization on the bass note F, which is retained until just before the close, Brahms has rendered consonant the entire ambit of the Chorale melody. This is clear from the succession of outer-voice tenths (see Example 1e). While the upper voice of the succession outlines the III triad, the bass, moving in parallel with it, outlines I. That this succession of 10ths reaches as its final element the low register C–A on the third beat of bar 11 is an important justification for reading a contrapuntally prolonged V from the third beat of m.11 to the second beat of bar 12.

Additionally, variants of a particular harmonic progression—F (or D); G; C (or C♯ diminished) triads—characterize the setting throughout. The progression of bars 1–2, I⁶–IV⁴/² – VII⁶ (D minor), reappears in bars 7–8 in the form IV–V–I (C major), and in bars 9–10 as I–II–V–(I) (F major). In bars 5–6 another repetition is implied by the substitution of V for the VII⁶/II (C major) on the 1ˢᵗ beat of bar 6 (see Ex. 3 [c])—the implication is IV (V)

Example 4. Voice leading analyses of bars 9-12.

(a)   Bach's setting;

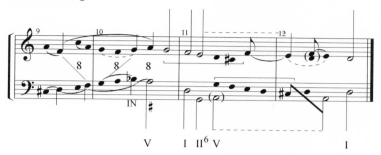

(b)   Brahms's setting.

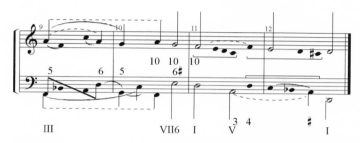

(VII⁶/II) (C major). A final allusion to the harmonic progression of bars 1–2 underpins the structural events of bars 10–11 in the form III–IV$^{4/2}$–♯VII⁶. The progression of bars 10–11 coincides with the large-scale conclusion of the F–E motion that constitutes the background bass from bar 1 to the close of bar 10. This large-scale motion to the bass E in bar 10 represents the first uprooting of the I⁶–III axis that has thus far governed the bass, preparing for the first deep-level appearance of the root-position I chord, which comes in bar 11. Significantly, the articulation at this point in the bass, where it finally moves down to the tonic, initiating the concluding cadence and the elements of the structural descent, serves to underline the final clause of the text: "Wie Gott mir verheissen hat, *der Tod ist mir Schlaf Worden.*"

*   *   *   *   *

It is fascinating to consider how both Bach and Brahms have remade the tonal space of Luther's Chorale in a more modern spirit, albeit in different ways. Bach's setting, with its strongly tonicized cadences, each moving a stage further along the road to the final cadence, not only establishes tonality in the modern sense, successfully encompassing the modal features of the melody, but also exemplifies Baroque vigor and contrast.[7] Brahms's setting is more transparent, with less determinant cadences than Bach's and a flowing and yet more polyphonic style of voice leading. At the same time,

---

[7]See discussion in Arnold Schoenberg: *Theory of Harmony*, trans. Roy E. Carter (Berkeley: University of California Press, 1978), p. 290.

Brahms utilizes the surging, wave-like, harmonic phrasing so beloved by composers of the second half of the nineteenth century, from Schumann and Wagner onwards. Evolving tonal meaning afforded by variations of progressions that intensify in wave-like succession, and which culminate in a move of clear structural significance, is indeed a vital feature of a number of Brahms's later compositions.[8]

Brahms's own interest in treating modal material was life long and formed a distinct element in his musical thought. Besides working with modal chorales and writing movements in the style of Renaissance motet as in Op. 74, No. 1,[9] he also made many folk-song settings in which he treated melodies with modal elements. These settings range from the essentially tonal to the entirely modal. Schenker indicates his awareness of this: "I view Brahms's arrangements as essays in which our system is applied also to melodies stemming from earlier periods and originating with people for whom the 'system' was basically something unknown, or at least unconscious."[10]

As disparate as these various techniques and interests may appear, it is nevertheless the case that in summer 1877 as Brahms was writing the motet at Pörstschach, he was also putting the finishing touches to the Second Symphony as well as working on settings of folk texts (Op. 69). One may suppose that his beautifully flexible and resonant chorale setting owes much to an amalgam of these conceptions that come from several different musical worlds.

Both Bach and Brahms seem to have addressed the task of setting Luther's chorale not only with great reverence, but also in the hope that they might reveal by their efforts underlying musical, and perhaps theological, truths. In this light Bach's setting can be seen as reflecting at least in part that rationalizing Pietist spirit by which, it is generally agreed, he was often influenced despite his declared opposition to it.[11] The chain of cadential tonicizations can be felt as elements of logical argument and discourse; while the strong contrasts wrought by this procedure are in a larger sense manifestations of the juxtapositions of opposites typical of the Baroque style.

In full consciousness of its lineage, Brahms chose the same chorale to conclude a work that he and his friends all regarded as a kind of "summa," a nondenominational comment on the traditions of both Protestant and Catholic liturgical composition.[12] Brahms based much of the motet upon his early Mass movements, the so-called *Missa Canonica* (1856-57). The

[8]For instance, see discussion in Carl Schachter, "The First Movement of Brahms's Second Symphony: The Opening Theme and its Consequences," in *Music Analysis* 2/1 (March 1983), p. 55. See also Brahms's Intermezzo in B♭ minor, Op. 117, No. 2, and Ballade, Op. 118, No. 3.

[9]See Virginia Hancock, *Brahms's Choral Compositions and His Library of Early Music* (Ann Arbor: UMI Press, 1983), page 157.

[10]Heinrich Schenker: *Counterpoint* (1910); trans. John Rothgeb, (New York: Schirmer, 1987), p. 29.

[11]See Albert Schweitzer, *J.S. Bach*, Vol. I, trans. Ernest Newman (London: Adam and Charles Black, 1911), p. 168.

[12]Malcolm McDonald, *Brahms* (New York: Schirmer, 1990), p. 256.

four sections of the motet have roots as diverse as Baroque cantata (as in the opening choral fugue and the closing chorale) and multi-part Renaissance motet recalling Lassus (as in the third section of the composition). Brahms's chorale setting itself shows this same blending in its combination of chorale-style figuration and voice leading with free-flowing counterpoint and more open-ended cadence progressions.

In both the Bach and Brahms settings, however, it is the modern touch of their own time that is determinant. Bach's unified succession of cadences gives full tonal structure to his setting of the modal melody, and the recurring wavelike successions that Brahms derives from the music of his own day provide him with the technical means to form his stylistic synthesis. Brahms's attitude in this regard is perhaps expressed in a letter he wrote to Elisabeth von Herzogenberg: "But shall I never shake off the theologian?" he asks, anxious as always to avoid the mantle of a composer of orthodox sacred music. "Here are all these new things going—and what comes my way? This Psalm, of course! I have just finished one which is actually 'heathenish' enough to please me and to have made my music better than usual, I hope."[13]

---

[13]Johannes Brahms, *The Herzogenberg Correspondence*, trans. Hannah Bogart (New York: Vienna House, 1971), p. 174.

Hinauf strebt's
Song Study with Carl Schachter

Timothy L. Jackson

Among my most prized possessions are a considerable number of graphs with Carl's hand-written corrections dating from the early 1980s. Over the years, in the course of my teaching career, I have continued to return to my sketches and notes stemming from my work with Carl. It seems appropriate to celebrate my experience of Carl's teaching by reproducing a few of these graphs with a brief commentary.

Like all great teacher-researchers, Carl drew extensively on his own developing research for the material used in his classes. In the early eighties, he tested his ideas on rhythmic reduction in his seminars on rhythm. Another important interest at this time was the relationship between text and music in opera (especially Mozart) and *Lieder*. In the seminar on "Words and Music" in 1983, Carl presented analyses of about fifteen Schubert songs and some parts of *Don Giovanni*, taking the same approach as in his then recently published article "Motive and Text in Four Schubert Songs."[1]

My own route to study with Carl was rather circuitous. I began my student career in composition rather than theory. After completing a Bachelor's Degree in Composition in 1979, I decided to pursue a further study at the Masters level at the University of Toronto. As an elective, one could take an introductory course in Schenkerian Analysis taught by Edward Laufer. I had been introduced to some of Schenker's basic ideas at my undergraduate school, but from a hostile perspective. Influenced by some of my teachers there, I had written an essay highly critical of Schenker for a course in the History of Music Theory. But although I was skeptical of Schenker's theories, I was nevertheless intrigued by Laufer's offering; so I enrolled.

For the first two weeks in Laufer's class, I sat in something like a daze. I felt that, as a composer, I already heard intuitively in these terms; here, at last, was a way of conceptualizing and notating that hearing in strictly musical terms. I found myself in awe of Laufer's ability not only to explicate voice leading, but through it to penetrate to the motivic heart of the compositional idea. It was time to make a move, and Laufer recommended that I continue my Master's Degree at Queens College in New York, where I would be able to pursue my studies in Schenkerian analysis with Carl Schachter and composition with George Perle.

---

[1]Carl Schachter, "Motive and Text in Four Schubert Songs." *Aspects of Schenkerian Theory*, ed. David Beach (New Haven: Yale University Press, 1981), pp. 61–76. Reprinted in *Unfoldings*, ed. Joseph Straus (New York: Oxford University Press, 1999), pp. 209–220.

At Queens College, things were very different than at my previous schools, where Schenkerian analysis was still largely regarded with suspicion. At the University of Toronto during the late seventies, Schenkerian analysis had been regarded as a necessary, but preferably avoidable, evil; but at Queens, which was closely allied with Mannes, the first bastion of Schenkerian theory in America, Schenkerian analysis was treated as a *sine qua non* of advanced study in theory.

One of my early and lasting supporters at Queens College was Saul Novack, whose generosity hardly knew any bounds. For example, shortly after my arrival in New York, Saul lent me $700 to buy an electric piano so that I would have an instrument on which to work. Saul, like Edward, recommended that I study with Carl. After my first year at Queens, although I had enjoyed my work in composition, I found my studies with Carl more rewarding. I decided that obtaining a terminal degree in music theory (rather than composition) henceforth would be my professional goal. From that point, I followed Carl from class to class, watching how he thought, attempting to assimilate his every move. In about 1983, largely as a result of Carl's teaching, my hearing and conceptual abilities began to unite in a logical synthesis so that I could make coherent graphs. As my ability to make worked-out graphs suddenly improved, I began to submit them to Carl prior to class discussion; he would mark them up in various colors of pencil.

A turning point for me came in 1983 with an analysis of Schubert's song *Ganymed*, which I prepared for Schachter's above-mentioned "Words and Music" class.[2] At this point I had only about three years of serious study of Schenkerian analysis under my belt. Schachter's annotations clarify details of the voice leading. Significant in my reading is the suggestion that the song is structured as a single "upward sweep" from ♭III to V in F major. As I show in a middleground graph of the song (Plate 1, page 194), a unified tonal process of ascending 5–6 sequences links the ♭III (A♭) with V (C). The ascending 5–6 sequence is disguised as the root position E major (bars 46ff.) and F major (bars 75ff.) chords substitute for six-three chords in the 5–6 sequence.

Here we encounter the kind of deep-structural response in the music to the textual idea, which Schachter has done so much to elucidate: the "ascending" sequence expresses Ganymed's "ascent." As is clear from my graph, I read the whole song as an extended auxiliary cadence, ♭III–IV–V–I in F major. In his comments on this graph, Schachter cautioned that "... the 'unification' of the whole into 1 key is problematic here – *only* in *retrospect* can we think of A♭ as F: ♭III."

---

[2]It is important to recall that Ernst Oster had specialized in text-music relationships in Schubert; indeed, Oster had been remarkably perceptive of the way in which structural nuances can reflect textual ideas. While Oster never published his work in this area (and Carl did not formally study with him), nevertheless, through private discussions with Oster and by attending his lectures, Carl learned much from Oster in this regard. Furthermore, Carl was able to further develop this special aspect of Oster's thinking. In his own teaching, Carl demonstrated remarkable text-music connections to his students, including myself. Indeed, my own doctoral dissertation on songs of Richard Strauss also fits into this tradition.

Another crucial feature of my interpretation is that the F chord of bars 75ff. does not yet function as the tonic, but rather as a passing chord (V7 of IV) inserted between A♭ (bar 1ff.) and B♭ (bar 79). Notice that, in terms of the texture, the F in bar 75 is "passed through"; a change in design does not arise until bar 79, thereby marking the arrival of B♭. The definitive tonic arrival is saved for the end of the song (bar 116). In his annotation Carl called attention to the rising third F–A (bars 78–79) filled in chromatically, F–G♯–A, clarifying the prolongation of the F chord.

Of course, I am proud that Carl emphatically approved of my graph. This is not to say that my readings were invariably on the mark. Sometimes I would miss the essential compositional idea. However, in such cases, it is interesting to see how Carl indicated the stronger reading while taking account of good points in my graph. For example, Plate 2 presents my graph of Schubert's great song *Der Atlas* from *Schwanengesang* with Carl's comments in orange pencil (prepared for the same class in 1983). As is evident from my graph, I read the piece from $\hat{5}$ (D), while Carl's annotations suggest that it is preferable to read the *Kopfton* as $\hat{3}$, in the form of a B♭ (♭$\hat{3}$) in bar 9 which is displaced to B (♮$\hat{3}$) in bar 20. Reading $\hat{3}$ as the *Kopfton* also changes the reading of the bass. I had taken the B♭ in bar 36 as the divider of the fifth G–D, with B♮ (bars 26ff.) functioning as C♭, that is, as an upper neighbor to B♭. One significant problem with my graph is that by reading the upper voice as leading to $\hat{5}$ at bar 36, I failed to bring the *Urlinie* convincingly down to $\hat{1}$. Carl's annotation shows how the $\hat{3}$–line can move down B–B♭–A–(G) beneath the motion up to the high d^2, which (as Carl notes) functions as a cover tone. As he observes, the B♭ chromatic passing tone in the bass represents a registral displacement.

Carl's reading clarifies a number of important points. In his analysis, the "painful" contradiction between the G minor mode of the song as whole and B (♮$\hat{3}$), which functions as the *Kopfton*, depicts Atlas's "suffering" at a background level. In the top voice, then, the initial $\hat{3}$ (B♭, bar 9) functions as an A♯ leading tone to the "real" $\hat{3}$ (B♮, bar 20); this large-scale chromatic motion then prepares the transposition of the opening three-note motive B♭–F♯–G to D♯–A♯–B, whereby B♭ is transformed into A♯ as a leading tone to B♮. Even more remarkable, then, is bar 36, where the B♭/A♯ in the bass takes a "wrong turn" to C (rather than to B♮). Again, this "painful" chromatic "deformation" of the motive is a tonal consequence of the textual idea of "suffering" ("elend"). Where I had gone astray was in placing too much emphasis on the D–E♭–D motive, with E♭ enharmonically related to D♯. However, Carl did like my large slur from the d♯^{2} (bar 28) to the d^2 (bar 36), commenting "Yes, it equals e♭."

When I recall my studies with Carl at this point in the early eighties, especially my semester of private instruction, I am struck by the brevity of some of our meetings. Each week, I would struggle mightily with the piece I was assigned to analyze. If I were stuck, Carl would make a few quick comments and send me on my way; often, he would give me just enough to open up a new, or better line of reasoning. Or, if I were completely wide of the mark, he would quickly sketch an alternative reading—sometimes on the back of an envelope and leave me to fill in the details.

Plate 1. My voice-leading sketch of Schubert, "Gaynemede," with written comments by Carl Schachter.

My last example, Brahms's great song *Immer leiser wird meine Schlummer*, Op. 105, No. 2, is a piece that I worked on during my private study in September 1983. I continue to ponder issues that Carl and I discussed twenty years ago. This song, composed in 1886–88, seems programmatically connected with the slow movement of the Second Piano Concerto (1878–81), which is also related to the song *Todessehnen*, Op. 86, No. 6 (1877?–79). The opening of *Immer leiser* quotes the first measures of the Concerto's slow movement; the middle section (bars 59–70) of the Concerto's slow movement in turn cites *Todessehnen* (bars 36–43), more precisely where the protagonist cries: "Hör es Vater in der Höhe aus der Fremde fleht dein Kind:/ Gib, dass er mich bald umwehe, deines Todes Lebenswind ("Hear it, Father in Heaven, in the wilderness your child cries;/Let your life-giving wind of death quickly waft through me"). These interrelated pieces all seem concerned with the paradoxical possibility of love outliving death.

In my view, the complexity of *Immer leiser* is related to its deliberate projection of musical paradoxes that are motivated by the poem. The very first measure presents a dilemma. Certainly, by the end of the first complete measure, it is possible to hear the initial sonority as a six-four chord. But what kind of six-four? Is it a consonant (tonic) six-four? In this case, the bass would simply arpeggiate the tonic chord, and the dominant seventh on the downbeat of bar 3 would be a passing chord caught within the opening tonic prolongation (Example 1a). Or, is the six-four chord to be understood as a cadential six-four, in which case the opening would have to be construed as an introductory dominant prolongation (Example 1b). In this connection, I refer the reader to my discussion of "structural plurality" in my study of Brahms's Haydn Variations in *Schenker Studies 2*, which Carl coedited. These comments are appropriate to the dualism at the opening of *Immer leiser*:

....the contradiction highlights an essential aspect of the theme whereby both of Schenker's readings are simultaneously valid. This unusual situation results from structural duality....Although the view of Brahms as a Classical composer (or at least as a Classicist) has persisted, in the past decade the term ambiguity—hardly a Classical characteristic—has enjoyed a certain vogue in reference to Brahms's music. This study, however, is not concerned with ambiguity but with structural plurality in which internally self-consistent but mutually exclusive interpretations are simultaneously suggested by the same music....Schenker had no conceptual way of dealing with such contradictions; therefore, when he came to publish a reading, he was compelled to eliminate them.[3]

Since a single graph cannot show paradoxically simultaneous "tonic" and "dominant" prolongations at the beginning of *Immer leiser*, I have vertically aligned two different readings.

When I first approached the song in 1983, I was already aware of the song's paradoxes. For my lesson, I produced different readings, which are reproduced in Plates 3–4. In my first reading, the III chord (E major) is prolonged with a 5–6 exchange (Plate 3). This is close to Carl's own interpretation of the middleground, shown in his graph (Plate 5, top system).

The paradox of the initial six-four is developed in the "strange" six-four chords in bars 17 and 19 (and their parallel six-fours in bars 44 and 46), the *dualism* of the fourth in these chords being an outgrowth of the opening. The G natural in the six-four chord in bar 17 (derived from its enharmonic alter-ego F double-sharp in bar 14) seems to prepare the G natural of m. 21, which may be understood as a chromatic passing tone leading down from G♯ to F♯ ($\hat{5}$–♭$\hat{5}$–$\hat{4}$, Example 1a). But, in the local context of bar 17, the G♮ may be heard in two ways: either as a stable tone (that is, as a *consonant* fourth above the bass D) in a consonant six-four with the subsequent F♯ as a chromatic passing tone, or as a dissonant 4–3 suspension resolving to F♯ as the main note (Example 1b).

The reader will notice that in 1983 (Plate 3) I interpreted the "strange" six-four chords as consonant, in other words, as standing for root-position chords (moving down by whole step). I also understood the six-four chord with which the song opens as a consonant six-four (thus, I considered the six-four chords in bars 16 and 18 to be analogous to the six-four in the pickup to bar 1 and bar 1). In my second reading (Plate 4), I followed this idea in another direction, proposing that the first of these "strange" six-fours, the G-major chord in bar 16 represents a move to the lowered dominant G major—albeit in six-four position—that would be "corrected" by the diatonic dominant G♯ major at the end of the first stanza (bar 23).

Carl, on the other hand, argued that the sonorities in bars 16, 18, 43, and 45 are to be interpreted solely as accented six-fours resolving to five-three chords. Today, however, I would contend that these six-four chords are

[3]Timothy Jackson,"Diachronic Transformation in a Schenkerian Context: Brahms's Haydn Variations," *Schenker Studies 2*, ed. Carl Schachter and Hedi Siegel (Cambridge: Cambridge University Press, 1999), pp. 247–9.

Example 1. Voice-leading sketches of Brahms, "Immer leiser wird meine Schlummer," Op. 105, No. 2.

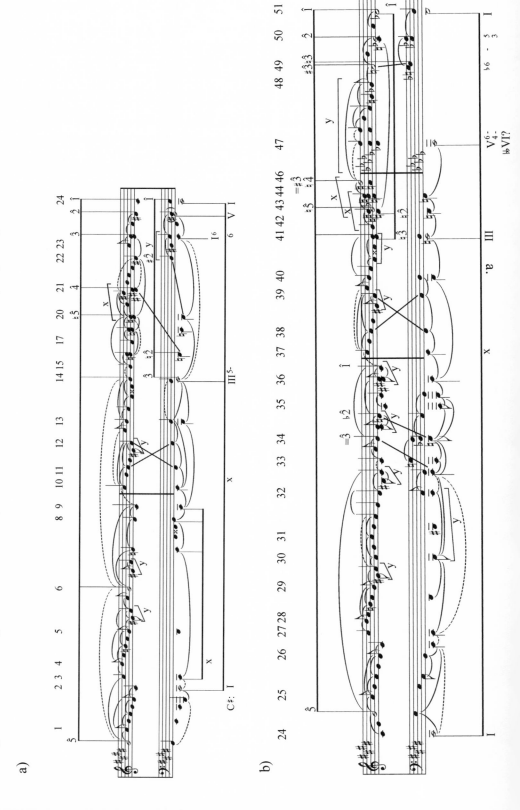

Plate 2: My voice-leading sketch of Schubert, "Der Atlas," with comments by Schachter.

Plate 3: My voice-leading sketch of Brahms, "Immer leiser" (September 30, 1983, rejected).

Plate 4. My subsequent voice-leading sketch of Brahms, "Immer leiser."

Plates 5. Voice-leading sketches of Brahms, "Immer leiser," by Carl Schachter.

"strangely" dualistic— paradoxical "both/and" sonorities. Furthermore, the role of the Neapolitan ($b\hat{2}$) in this song requires careful consideration; the "painful" Neapolitan, of course, represents the anguish of parting at death. Indeed, there is, I believe, considerable emphasis on *two* Neapolitans in this song: F natural, the Neapolitan of E major, and D natural, the Neapolitan of C♯ minor. Let us first consider the role of the F.

In the analysis shown in Plate 3, I proposed that, if we understand the F major six-four chord in bar 18 as a consonant six-four, the projected harmony is the Neapolitan of E major. I heard an inner voice line g♯¹ (bar 14)–g♮¹ (bar 15)–f♯¹ (bar 17)–f♮¹ (bar 18) resolving to e¹ (bar 23). Thus, beneath the 5̂–line in C♯ minor, I heard an inner voice 3̂–line in E major: 3̂–♮3̂–2̂–♮2̂–1̂. In a typical Phrygian progression to 1̂, $b\hat{2}$ descends through a diminished third to ♯7̂, to approach 1̂ successively by semitone from above and below. This is the case here: the F♮ (♮2̂, bar 18) moves through a diminished third to D sharp (♯7̂, bar 21), before resolving to E (1̂, bar 23). At the point where 1̂ arrives, the harmony is shifted deceptively to VI⁶ of E, or I⁶ of C♯ minor.

In this analysis, I further suggested that in the second part of the song (bars 25–end), Brahms's compositional intention is to transform this "painful" F♮ (the Neapolitan of the first stanza) into a "peaceful" E♯, the ♯3̂ of C♯ minor (see the lower system of Plate 3). More specifically, I suggested that, in the second stanza, by understanding the B♭ major six-four of bars 45–46 as a consonant six-four, the F♮ (the $b\hat{2}$ of E♭) is now given strikingly new harmonic support. In E major, F first functions as the fifth of ♭V (B♭ major) instead of the root of ♭II (F major, as in the first stanza), and then becomes the sixth above the bass in the D♭ major cadential six-four. Thus, at the conclusion of the second stanza, the inner voice 3-line of the first stanza is compelled to "collapse" (into the realm of death) as the d♯¹/ e♭¹ (bar 48), and—instead of resolving as a leading tone to e¹ (as in the first stanza, bar 23)—descends to c♯¹/d♭¹ (bar 51). Remarkably, the transformation of F into E♯ is prepared early in the song by the "rising" semitone e♯1–f♯1 (bars 5 and 11). In the end, the idea of "collapse" is realized through the recomposition of this previously rising semitone motive in the final cadence: through a dramatic downward registral shift, the "rising" second is inverted to a "falling" major seventh f² (bar 47) – g♭¹ (bar 43, Example 1).

Let us now consider the role of D♮, the Neapolitan of the overall tonality C♯ minor. This was the problem that I had tried to address in my second reading (Plate 4). In a complicated way, an inner voice 3̂–♮2̂–1̂ in C♯ minor is woven in beneath the upper voice 5̂–line. This second reading was an outgrowth of the first, since I considered this 3̂-line in C♯ minor, with its emphasis on D, to be a transference of the 3̂-line in E major, with its accentuation of F. As I propose in my recent reading (Example 1), the D♮ in the bass (bar 16), does seem to be "corrected" by D♯ in the upper voice (bars 21–22)—an extended cross-relation which I had already indicated in my second reading in 1983 (Plate 4). Example 1 also indicates that 3̂–2̂–1̂ is worked into the first stanza (bars 15–24). This descent is then recomposed in compressed form in bars 34–36 (here, the Neapolitan D♮ represents the

description "pale and cold" as the protagonist imagines her dead body: "bleich und kalt"). Finally, in the last stanza, the $\hat{3}-\flat\hat{2}-\hat{1}$ descent is extended through the final cadence (bars 41–52). Specifically, the D♮ of the B♭ major six-four (♮$\hat{2}$, bar 46) resolves to the C♯/D♭ ($\hat{1}$, bar 51).

Another "strange" aspect of *Immer leiser* is the notation of its conclusion in D♭ major. One might say that Brahms's shift to D♭ major is simply a notational convenience, and the song ends in the parallel major, C♯ major. However, I hear the harmony from bars 41 ff. as leading to a true D♭ major, which is then paradoxically revealed—in a moment of peripety—to be identical with C♯ major. For me, then, the turn to flats is more than simply notational convenience: Brahms's notation is to be taken literally. The *path* is all-important: the road into the realm of death "sinks down" from the "bright" domain of the living (four sharps) to the "dark" region of the dead (five flats): from C♯ minor/E major with four sharps (bars 41–42), through G major with one sharp (bars 43–44) and B♭ major with two flats (bars 45–46), to D♭ major with five flats (bars 47–end). As Bruckner's student, Friedrich Eckstein observed:

> Therefore, much more important than the sensual, real embodiment of a mathematically purely tuned scale is that its inner sense not be lost and that this sense be realized through strictly correct voice-leading and its principles, the true spirit of which can be maintained by precisely observing the hidden musical demands implied by a pure tuning. If one treats these holy things of art lightly, then one misses its true and deepest being and has willfully barred oneself entry to the holiest of holies. Astonishing innovations and freedoms in handling tonal structure only find their inner justification when their author is equal to all these subtleties....[4]

Following through Eckstein's observation, one might say that given a choice, the ear tends to hear rational—rather than irrational—intervals (for instance, a rational minor third rather than an irrational augmented second). Thus, as the harmony descends progressively from the sharp to the flat region, the vocal line ascends sequentially through minor thirds from G♯ to F♮: a minor third g♯^{1}–b^1 (bars 41–44), another minor third b^1–d^2 (bars 44–45), and *another* minor third d^2–f^2 (bars 46–47) – *not* an augmented second d^2– e♯^{2}. And yet, it *is* an augmented second – but only *retrospectively*: the journey from C♯ minor to D♭ major is like that through a Moebus strip; because D♭ major, paradoxically, *is* C♯ major, the apparently two–dimensional space of flats and sharps is suddenly—*peripetically*—reduced to a single dimension.

Of course, all of these musical paradoxes relate to Brahms's interpretation of the poem. The protagonist is a woman suffering from a terminal illness. As she lies on her deathbed, she becomes anguished as she considers the possibility that her beloved might be happy with another woman after her death. The only thing that can bring her solace is to be united with her beloved once again. The final line—"Willst du mich noch einmal sehn,/ Komm, o komme bald!" ("If you wish to see me once more/Come, O come

[4]Quoted from my article "Schubert as 'John the Baptist to Wagner-Jesus:' Large-scale Enharmonicism in Bruckner and His Models," *Bruckner Jahrbuch 1991–/92–/93* (Linz: Österreichischer Akademie der Wissenschaften, 1995), p. 73.

soon!")—can be interpreted in at least two ways. According to a more literal interpretation, the woman exclaims that, if her beloved wishes to see her alive, he must come to her quickly. A more figurative reading suggests that her beloved can find eternal comfort with her only by immediately following her into the realm of death. Although both interpretations are possible, I would argue that Brahms's setting strongly advocates the second by converting the "painful" Phrygian F♮ of E major (♭$\hat{2}$, the pain of parting) in the first stanza into the "peaceful" major third, E♯/F of C♯/D♭ major (♯$\hat{3}$, the *solace* of the lovers' eternal companionship in death) in the concluding stanza. Furthermore, the striking paradoxes in the music—the dualistic meaning of the six-four chords and enharmonic dualism—eloquently depict the inscrutable paradox of love alive in death.

At my lesson on this song, which lasted only a few minutes, Carl made the pair of quick pen sketches shown in Plate 5 on the verso of my first graph. Carl was uncertain as to the *Stufen* in the first part – at least in September 1983. In its larger outlines, the top sketch is close to my initial reading, except that Carl shows the *Urlinie* descending to $\hat{3}$ earlier than I did. The second sketch wonders whether the dominant six-five chord (bar 22) just before the tonic six-three (bar 23) might not function as a dominant *Stufe* in a I–III–V–I progression. This was one of those rare occasions where Carl seemed to entertain two different readings simultaneously.

Carl just dashed off these two sketches, gave me my new piece for the coming week's lesson, and sent me on my way. Like all great teachers, Carl never spoon-fed; rather, he considered where I was in my development and always threw the ball out in front, sometimes quite far out in front. He did not tell me everything he knew, or even a fraction of it; rather, I was supposed to earn my insights on my own. Therefore, he gave broad indications, suggesting some possibilities and critiquing others. His quick sketches gave me the confidence to better work out my own readings, and also think through his interpretations fully, filling in the details by myself.

In his teaching, Carl would often leap deep into a piece, seizing upon some telling motivic feature, and then leveraging that insight to fill in the structure and elucidate the details. Thus, what Carl offered was not simply the gift of knowledge; rather, he provided models for how to obtain it.

I should note again that the final analysis of *Immer leiser* presented above is my own, and one that Carl might not necessarily agree with. I nevertheless offer it as an example of his influence, for it is a measure of Carl's greatness as a teacher and a human being that he has been able to encourage and support independent-minded thinkers. In my experience of Carl's teaching, of less importance to his entire pedagogical enterprise was the "what" than the "how." As in any rigorous discipline, the crux of the issue is not only knowing which questions to ask, but—if not as importantly— the best sequence in which to ask them. By watching Carl teach for an extended period, the sensitive student could become ignited by his intuitive spark and learn to ask the "right" questions in the "right" order. No statement of gratitude can ever suffice to thank a teacher like Carl for providing the means to attain knowledge; the true acknowledgement of his teaching always will be the new discovery itself.

Intimate Immensity in Schubert's
The Shepherd on the Rock

Frank Samarotto

Music theorists have long been concerned with measuring distance. Of course, distance in music is really a kind of metaphor, but it is a deeply ingrained one: for centuries, much of the language of music theory has been imbued with this metaphor. The transparent acceptance of this metaphor has served as a foundation for the discipline in that the precise reckoning of distance gives music theorists a scientific power. However, the experience of music is more than just an objective register of facts. Ideally, music analysis should take into account ways in which music's measurable parameters might be imbued with a deep subjectivism that does not lend itself to exact calculation. In this approach the lack of numerical precision might be compensated for by exactness of the poetic image and its ability to elicit very specifically defined emotional resonances. It is with this aim that I shall consider some of the meanings that "distance" might convey in Schubert's great song, *The Shepherd on the Rock (Der Hirt auf dem Felsen)*, D. 965.[1]

To be sure, the word "distance" can mean simply a neutral measurement, but in human experience it can have other connotations, among them estrangement, detachment, the pain of separation, as well as exhilaration at the experience of monumental space. And the poetic imagination suggests still more possibilities, some of which receive eloquent exploration in the writings of the eccentric philosopher Gaston Bachelard (1884–1962). Bachelard's earlier writings were a fairly traditional examination of the philosophy and history of science, but one in which a dialogue between reason and experience allowed a fluid picture of scientific investigation as a creative act. Perhaps this was the seed of the apparently radical departure that followed: a series of books that explored the role of the poetic imagination as an essential complement to rationalist explanation in our understanding of the world. In such startlingly titled works as *The Psychoanalysis of Fire, Water and Dreams, Poetics of Reverie,*

---

[1] To be sure, distance has often been identified as the defining essence of Romanticism. For recent discussions, see Richard Kramer, "A Poetics of the Remote: Goethe's Entfernte," in *Distant Cycles: Schubert and the Conceiving of Song* (Chicago: University of Chicago Press, 1994), pp. 85-101; Charles Rosen, "Mountains and Song Cycles," in *The Romantic Generation* (Cambridge: Harvard University Press, 1995), pp. 116-236; and Berthold Hoeckner, "Schumann's Distance," in *Programming the Absolute: Nineteenth-Century German Music and the Hermeneutics of the Moment* (Princeton: Princeton University Press, 2002), pp. 51-114. In Hoeckner, see especially the discussion of Novalis's "distant philosophy" (pp. 51-4) for an anticipation of Bachelard's subjectivist turn, discussed below.

Bachelard took an innovative stance that embraced the role of the reverie and emotion as equal partners in the construction of rational truth.[2] In his introduction to *The Poetics of Space*, Bachelard clearly noted both his relation to traditional philosophy and his departure from it by declaring that,

> A philosopher who has evolved his entire thinking from the. . . nationalism of contemporary science. . .must forget his learning and break with all his habits. . . , if he wants to study the problems posed by the poetic imagination. . . . The idea of principle or "basis" in this case would be disastrous, for it would interfere with the essential psychic actuality, the essential novelty of the poem.[3]

In his foreword to this volume, Etienne Gilson noted that it "establish[ed] the *specificity* of the philosophy of art in the general family of the philosophical disciplines."[4] (Italics original.) It is the idea of specificity that interests me and that suggests fruitful analogies to music and its ways of recreating imaginative realms of distance. In *The Poetics of Space*, Bachelard investigates a world of spatial imagery available to our internal conceptual experience as it is made vividly specific through poetic language. Among chapters on the poetic spaces of houses, nests, shells, and corners, one is devoted to what Bachelard calls "intimate immensity." His description is typically elusive and at the same time very exact in its attempt to pinpoint a very particular emotional state. A quotation at length is will illustrate:

> One might say that immensity is a philosophical category of daydream. Daydream undoubtedly feeds on all kinds of sights, but through a sort of natural inclination, it contemplates grandeur. And this contemplation produces an attitude that is so special, an inner state that is so unlike any other, that the daydream transports the dreamer outside the immediate world to a world that bears the mark of infinity... it flees the object nearby and right away it is far off, elsewhere, in the space of *elsewhere*. [...]
>   Immensity is within ourselves. It is attached to a sort of expansion of being that life curbs and caution arrests, but which starts again when we are alone. [It] is the movement of the motionless man. It is one of the dynamic characteristics of quiet daydreaming.[5]

The poetic image of natural surroundings can be a particularly acute evocation of this type of space. As an example, Bachelard characterizes the immensity of the forest as "a body of impressions which, in reality, have little connection with geographical information" but rather with "the always rather anxious impression of 'going deeper and deeper' into a limitless world."[6] The connection he draws between this sort of imaginative space

---

[2]*La Psychanalyse du feu* (Paris: Gallimard, 1938); *L'Eau et les rêves* (Paris: J. Corti, 1942); *La Poétique de la rêverie* (Paris: Presses Universitaires de France, 1960).

[3]Gaston Bachelard, *La poétique de l'espace* (Paris: Presses Universitaires de France, 1957); trans. by Maria Jolas as *The Poetics of Space* (Boston: Beacon Press, 1964), p. 1.

[4]Bachelard, *Poetics of Space*, p. x.

[5]Bachelard, *Poetics of Space*, pp. 183–4.

[6]Bachelard, *Poetics of Space*, p. 185.

and images of nature certainly remind one of German Romantic sensibility, and thus it takes us easily into Schubert's aesthetic world. Still, its artistic expression is arguably quite ancient. As an example, Illustration 1 provides an evocative example of intimate immensity from Chinese landscape painting. The monumentality of mountains in contrast to tiny human figures was long a common theme in this tradition; the aim, however, was not to depict natural scenes but rather imaginative mental states.[7] The inscription on the painting is by the artist and reads:

White clouds encircle the mountain waist like a sash,

Stone steps mount high into the void where the narrow path leads far.

Alone, leaning on my rustic staff, I gaze idly into the distance.

My longing for the notes of a flute is answered in the murmurings of the gorge.[8]

The inscription's final line seems as if it could be a direct precursor of the poetic imagery that inspired Schubert. The text of the work known as *The Shepherd on the Rock* is shown in Figure 1. The first and last sections are from Wilhelm Müller; here one finds the image of the shepherd high on a mountaintop looking down into vast space. This distance is not really geological but emotional: our protagonist is far away from a beloved. The key line that Schubert dwells on is telling: "The further my voice carries, the more clearly it echoes back to me." This of course is not an assertion about acoustics, but rather a belief that separation can be bridged from within. It is the shepherd's voice, his song that collapses space, as music has power to invoke at once both distance and immediacy. Quite a different spatial imagery is suggested by the strophes marked with thick lines. These were interpolated by Schubert into the Müller poem, undoubtedly to create an opportunity for musical contrast.[9] And they do: the sense of estrangement, of distance unbridgeable, is nowhere stronger than in the setting of these interpolated strophes, which describe a place from which hope has gone.

The text provides Schubert with two opposing experiences of space, one that opens gladly into a world of intimate immensity, the other that feels a keen and painful isolation. As general mood painting, it is not hard to superficially connect the former with the opening Andantino in B♭ major, and the closing Allegretto in the same key, and to connect the latter with the G-minor middle section. But my concern here is to recover the specificity of Schubert's musical imagery, to find what Bachelard called, "the sudden salience on the surface of the psyche."[10] The concreteness of Schubert's

[7]Even in the earliest treatises on landscape painting, it was recognized that "the picture came not from an observation of external phenomena…, but from within the heart/mind of the artist." Craig Clunas, *Art in China* (Oxford: Oxford University Press, 1997), p. 55.

[8]Translation from Mary Tregear, *Chinese Art* (London: Thames and Hudson, 1980; rev. ed. 1997). She comments that, "Shen Zhou's evocation surely aims to transport the viewer into the open space high up." (p. 158)

[9]Their authorship is usually attributed to poet and librettist Helmina von Chezy (1783–1856).

[10]Bachelard, *Poetics of Space*, p. 1.

Illustration 1. *Shen Zhou (1427–1509),* Poet on a Clifftop. *[By permission of the Nelson Gallery-Atkins Museum, Kansas City, Missouri]*

particular senses of distance is focused on the pitch F♯/G♭ in various ramifications: its potential resolutions to either F or G, its role in a conflict between B♭ major and G minor, its enharmonic reinterpretation within a major third cycle, its constriction within a ninth chord. From the center point of F♯/G♭ one can derive a host of musical embodiments of distance: the neighboring figure F–G–F, the ninth chord bounded by these tones, the third from D leading up to that F, the tenth that is an expansion of that third, the major third cycle already alluded to, and more. These musical devices are imbued with richly textured meanings not accessible by scientific calculation but rather through the poetic imagination, which we must now traverse and experience in detail.

The sense of distance-as-estrangement is immediately evoked by the work's brief piano introduction (Example 1).[11] The despairing emptiness of the opening octaves is subsequently fleshed out by harmonies that strongly imply the key of G minor. But that key remains unfulfilled; we are left with an acute sense of pointing towards a distant place that seems beyond reach. As noted, the key of G minor will in fact arrive later, as the key of the bleak interpolated lines. Schubert locates distance-as-estrangement in a specific

[11]The clarinet has been renotated at concert pitch throughout.

Figure 1. "Der Hirt auf dem Felsen," text, translation, and key scheme of the musical setting.

Der Hirt auf dem Felsen	The Shepherd on the Rock	The setting
		Andantino, 3/4
Wenn auf dem höchsten Fels ich steh',	When I stand on the highest rock,	B-flat major
In's tiefe Tal hernieder seh',	Look down into the deep valley,	
Und singe,	And sing,	
Fern aus dem tiefen dunkeln Tal	Distantly from the deep, dark valley	
Schwingt sich empor der Wiederhall,	The echo rises up,	
Der Klüfte.	[The echo] of the ravines.	
Je weiter meine Stimme dringt,	The further my voice carries,	G-flat major
Je heller sie mir wiederklingt	The more clearly it echoes back to me	
Von unten.	From below.	
Mein Liebchen wohnt so weit von mir,	My love lives so far from me,	
Drum sehn' ich mich so heiß nach ihr	So I ardently yearn for her	
Hinüber.	[Who is] over there.	
Je weiter meine Stimme dringt,	*The further my voice carries,*	D major
Je heller sie mir wiederklingt	*The more clearly it echoes back to me*	
Von unten.	*From below.*	
Wenn auf dem höchsten Fels ich steh',	*When I stand on the highest rock,*	B-flat major
In's tiefe Tal hernieder seh',	*Look down into the deep valley,*	
Und singe,	*And sing,*	
Fern aus dem tiefen dunkeln Tal	*Distantly from the deep, dark valley*	
Schwingt sich empor der Wiederhall,	*The echo rises up,*	
Der Klüfte.	*[The echo] of the ravines.*	
		[Andantino, 3/4]
In tiefem Gram verzehr ich mich,	I am consumed by deep sorrow;	
Mir ist die Freude hin,	My joy is elsewhere.	G minor
Auf Erden mir die Hoffnung wich,	My hope on earth has gone;	
Ich hier so einsam bin.	I am so alone here.	
So sehnend klang im Wald das Lied,	So longingly the song rings through the forest,	
So sehnend klang es durch die Nacht,	So longingly it rings through the night;	
Die Herzen es zum Himmel zieht	It draws hearts toward heaven	
Mit wunderbarer Macht.	With wonderful power.	
		(G major)
Der Frühling will kommen,	Spring will come,	Allegretto, 2/4
Der Frühling, meine Freud',	Spring, my joy;	B-flat major
Nun mach' ich mich fertig	Now I shall prepare	
Zum Wandern bereit.	To go on a journey.	
		D major
Je weiter meine Stimme dringt,	*The further my voice carries,*	
Je heller sie mir wiederklingt.	*The more clearly it echoes back to me.*	
Der Frühling will kommen,	Spring will come,	B-flat major
Der Frühling, meine Freud',	Spring, my joy;	
Nun mach' ich mich fertig	Now I shall prepare	
Zum Wandern bereit.	To go on a journey.	
Je weiter meine Stimme dringt,	*The further my voice carries,*	più mosso
Je heller sie mir wiederklingt	*The more clearly it echoes back* to me.	

Adapted by Schubert from Der Berghirt by Wilhelm Müller.
Strophes with dark lines are interpolations attributed to Helmina von Chézy.
Italic type indicates text repeated by Schubert.

Example 1. The piano introduction as emblem of distance.

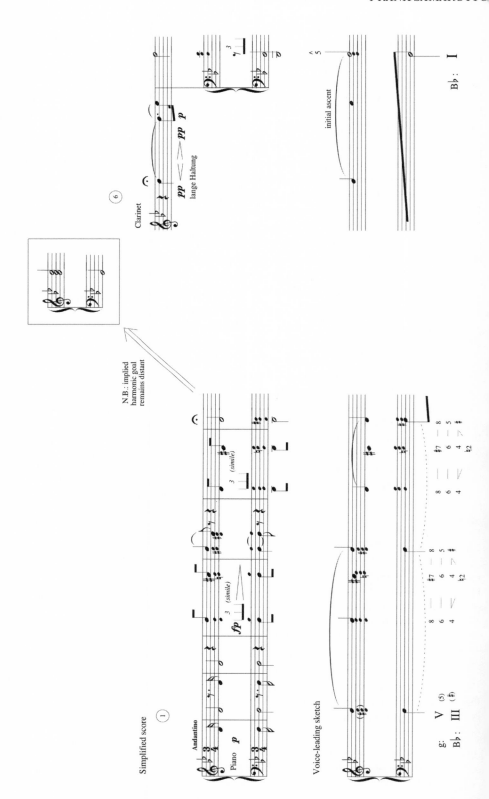

tonal context. Even the fifth of the G-minor tonic, the upper voice D, with its attendant neighbor-note C♯, takes on the character of a place from which one desires release. It is the clarinet that takes this on, with its long-held D, marked *crescendo-decrescendo*, that seems to approach and recede, evoking distance through dynamics. The clarinet's D emerges from G minor into the world of B♭ major, the work's true key. From this perspective the prior harmony is revalued as an unfolded upper third of the tonic B♭ triad.[12]

However, the escape into the world of B♭ major is not so easily accomplished. The clarinet's long introduction makes two attempts at stating the song's opening melody, but twice it falters, seemingly disturbed by vagrant thoughts. Example 2 shows the first phrase. As it begins, things go smoothly, the clarinet bridging registral distance with an easy fluency well suited to the instrument. But after four bars, it seems to encounter difficulty in the form of a brief harmonic digression. The insistent C♭–B♭ neighbor figure, with its half-step borrowed from minor, faintly recalls the estrangement and immobility associated with opening G minor; its restatement as B♮–C leads to a renewed sense of motion and facilitates a return to B♭ major.

On its second attempt, more serious difficulties arise (Example 3). Again the fifth bar (bar 23) brings a digression, a more jarring one that freezes on D major, the same triad that evoked estranged distance in the song's opening. The clarinet falls through octave leaps that stretch like yawning chasms, then struggles through half steps to ascend a chromaticized 6–5 sequence. Though it moves through foreign harmonic realms with agonizing slowness, this sequence eventually covers the same D–F third as the first digression (see the long brackets in Examples 2 and 3); thus, we are in fact retracing the same steps, the clarinet's D to F, that took us out of the opening G-minor area (See Example 1, bars 6–7). The turning point of this phrase comes with the dynamic climax on the high F♯–G. This also refers back to the implication of G minor in the desolate opening, but it also suggests a way out, in that here the tonal landscape clearly places us in B♭ major.

This is the landscape in which the singer first appears. (Examples 4 and 5). Unlike the previous passages, the first two vocal phrases seem to negotiate distance with a relaxed transcendence. The character of this ease is also evident in the free flow of motivic thirds that permeate the passages. Digressions still occur, but they are momentary responses to verbal cues. *In's tiefe Tal hernieder seh'*: we look down into the valley and the music points the way toward C minor but without leading us there. Note, however, that the brief digressions are much more registrally contained than the tenths and ninths that frame each phrase. The sense of melodic distance has subtly changed; the clarinet's huge gaps were recovered only with agonizingly difficulty, but the singer's leaps are treated as effortless (or at least must seem so). Indeed, the whole nexus of musical meanings shifted when the singer began, a change that I will now try to describe.

---

[12] The unique addition of a clarinet to the *Lied* is not, I think, merely an opportunity for virtuosic display, nor is the clarinet to be taken as necessarily representing a distinct persona. Nonetheless, its sharing of some (but not all) melodic material with the vocal part allows the idea of separation versus closeness to be expressed at another level.

Example 2. The clarinet introduction: the first digression.

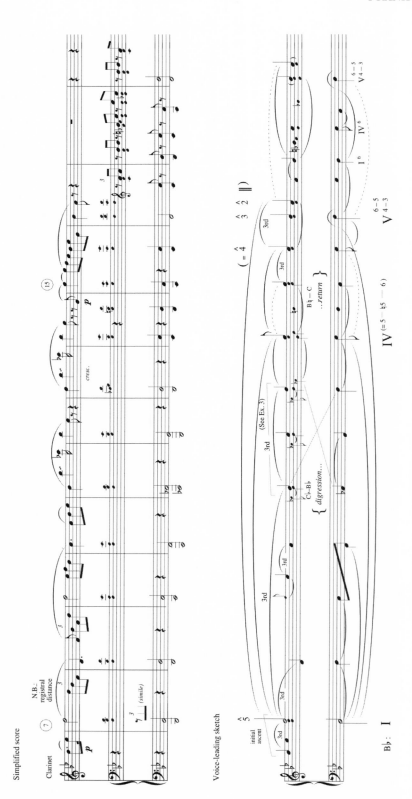

Example 3. The clarinet introduction: the second digression.

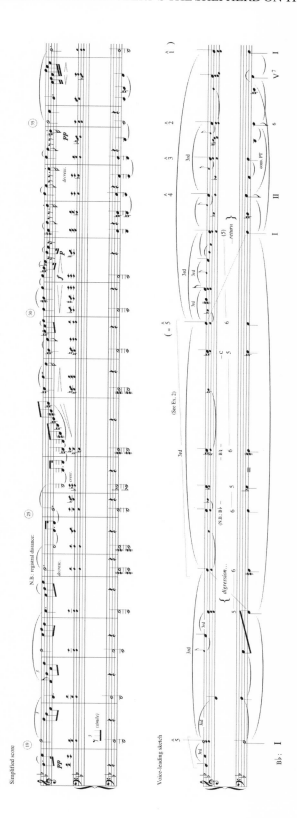

These first two vocal phrases are placidly periodic versions of the roving clarinet introduction. For the first time, we begin to approach that poetic space of expansiveness, that imaginative state that Bachelard called intimate immensity. Here great distances are not felt as insurmountable; one's spirit expands from within to easily encompass vast spaces. How is this embodied musically? Example 6 shows some details of tonal space in these vocal phrases. The main melody opens with a precipitous drop through the tonic arpeggio that spans the tenth from f^2 to d^1, which can be heard as representing an octave expansion of a third (Example 6a). The fact that the *low* D sets the word "highest" ("höchsten") indicates that Schubert means this as no simple text-painting. The meaning is deeper: it conveys the ability of the imagination to expand as if to fill a vast landscape. More specifically, the tone D was tied to the previous sense of estranged distance. In the present world of intimate immensity, D becomes an offshoot of F; recall that we escaped from the dominant of G minor by relegating the upper-voice tone D to the status of an inner voice of the B♭ triad, thus making it subordinate to F. The contrast of meanings is clear: the clarinet introduction imposed a sense of distance as a kind of estrangement, whereas the vocal section invokes a sense of distance as a kind of intimate immensity.

The F arrived at through initial ascent plays a crucial role in the vocal section, and so, by association, does its upper neighbor. As noted earlier, the clarinet struggled out of its second digression through a climax on F–F♯–G (see Example 3). This neighboring motion continues its significant role through the beautiful yodel-like leaps of a major ninth that bring the vocal phrase out of its small digression. This ninth leap can be understood as an expression of a true dominant ninth, stabilized by filling in the intervening space with thirds (Example 6b). However, it can also be understood as a neighbor tone to the root; both senses together suggest a small distance expanded into a much larger space. It is particularly the *major* ninth that makes this harmony seem open and expansive. (The sharper dissonance of the minor ninth would certainly negate this effect.)

The easy expansion of small distances into vast, even infinite spaces captures exactly Bachelard's intimate immensity. The following music (bars 64–94, shown in Example 7) goes deeper into the resources of the tonal system to find possible expressions of this expansiveness, as it sets the poem's most vivid image: "The further my voice carries, the more clearly it echoes back to me." This passage employs one of Schubert's favorite harmonic procedures, a descent through major thirds. There are two important elements: the bass descends by major thirds, B♭–G♭–D–B♭, and the top voice rises to highlight G♭ as a significant neighbor tone (Example 8; note in the score the dynamic emphasis given both to G♭ and to the F♯ that occurs later). There is no struggle in these harmonic transformations: we move easily and with conviction through the cycle of thirds. A necessary part of the feeling of magical relocation is our ability to hear an enharmonic reinterpretation of function (Example 8b). The upper voice G♭ is reheard as an F♯ that will later be reinflected to F♮ within the embracing tonal context. If the major third cycle were continued

Example 4. The first vocal phrase.

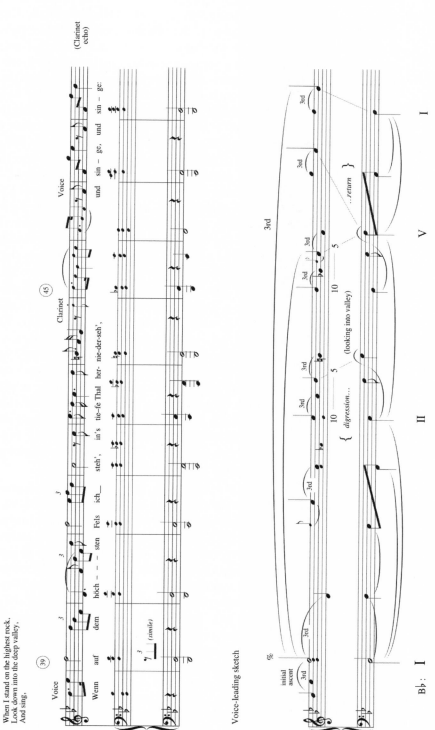

Example 5. The second vocal phrase.

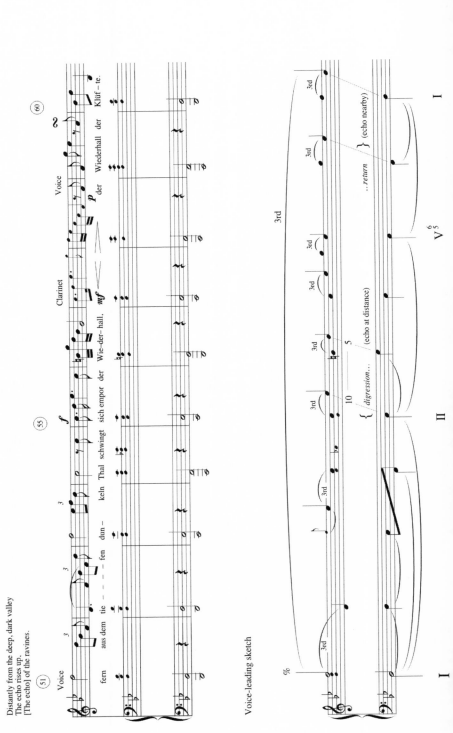

Example 6. Melodic and harmonic spaces.

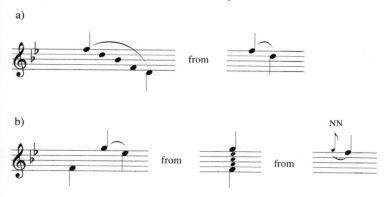

mechanically, there would be thirds *ad infinitum*, and no return to the tonic (Example 8c and d); tonal closure requires an enharmonic reinterpretation of one of these steps.

Of course, in the usual musical universe, there is no space smaller than that between G♭ and F♯, which are in principle identical in equal temperament. Nonetheless, and tuning notwithstanding, harmonic context can actually cause G♭ and F♯ to sound as functionally different tones; in a way, it creates a space, albeit a conceptual one. The perfect aptness of this metaphor is realized when this space-that-is-not-a-space, between G♭ and F♯, is spun out into much larger harmonic space, the cycle of major thirds, which by its nature suggests an infinite expanse of unending tonal motions (see again Example 8c). This thereby creates a sense of infinity-within-unity, a compelling expression of intimate immensity. The text speaks of the distance between the protagonist and the beloved. But the music does not bemoan it; rather, it celebrates that distance as one that can be instantly collapsed, suggesting that literal distance is not psychic distance.

How different this is from the piano opening, whose implied G-minor tonic seems somewhere else, off in the distance, an unbridgeable distance. Schubert fully actualizes that sense of estrangement in the bleak middle section of this work, set in G minor. There is more to this than the minor-key mood. The contextual power of this characterization is all the greater in that G minor should normally seem a close and familiar relative to B♭ major. But in the opening of this section, the singer, who had negotiated space so easily before, seems constricted by the dominating motive of a minor second (Example 9). The most significant of these is a half-step neighbor to this section's primary upper-voice tone d². One cannot help but recall the bleak vision of distance, from which B♭ major provided such welcome relief, presented by the piano's brief introduction (which also featured a half-step neighbor to D in a G-minor context). A brief digression even recalls the disturbances of the clarinet's introductory phrases. (Compare Example 9 with 2 and 3.)

Later in this section, a dominant ninth chord makes an insistent appearance, a chordal rendering of the previously prominent D–E♭–D neighbor (Example 10). This sound makes a marked contrast to the major

Example 7. The evocation of immensity.

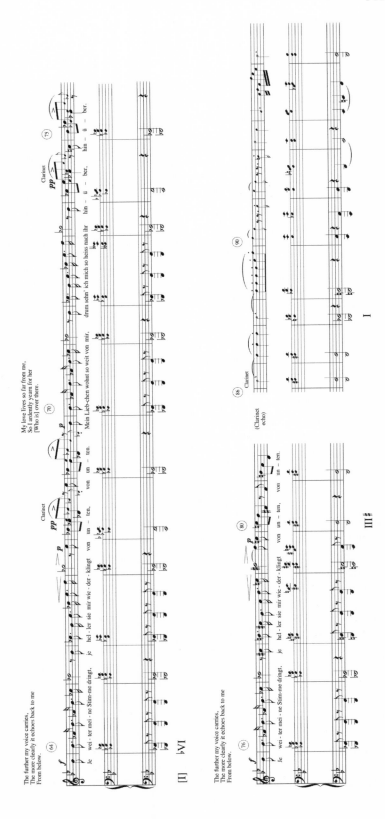

Example 8. The descending third cycle.

ninth sonorities that had occurred in B♭, in that there the vocal part freely articulated the full space of this chord (see again Examples 4–6). The pathetic minor ninth here, on the other hand, is nothing but a painful reminder of the prevailing minor seconds, and suggests a critical need for escape from the constricting depression of the G-minor space. A way out is found out shortly after, prompted by the text: the song that rings through the forest has the power to "draw hearts toward heaven," that is, to take us to a place that transcends the limitations of literal space. This is realized by a turn to major, but more potently by the f♯²s profiled in the upper voice, by both register and dynamic emphasis. (Note that the second F♯ in bar 200 is still the dynamic peak even though preceded by a higher b².) As though cued by these F♯s and the resonances they carried earlier in the piece, the clarinet is inspired to effect a transition out of the G minor. Example 11 shows it rising to G–G♭–F, and dwelling in that significant tonal space through a languid cadenza, as if savoring the reinterpretation of F♯ as G♭; the role of F♯/G♭ as neighbor tones in B♭ major was especially instrumental in creating that open space to which return is now desired.

Example 9. The beginning of the G-minor section.

I am consumed by deep sorrow;
My joy is elsewhere.

[My hope on earth has gone;
I am so alone here.]

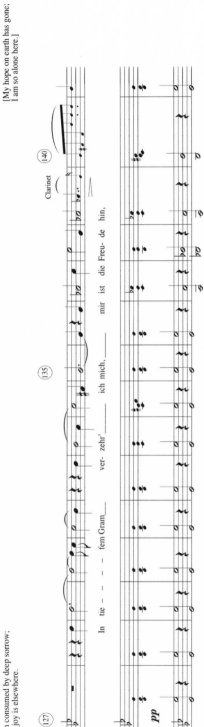

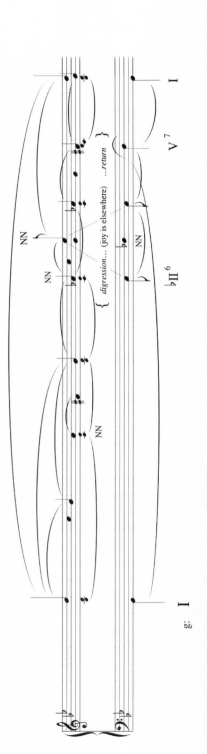

The return to B♭ major brings not the opening material, but rather something quite new. Still it reveals its sympathy with the opening by recomposing the previous third ascents from D to F (see the end of Example 11; prefigured by the earlier bracket in the same example). In this new section, the text promises that Spring will come, but the music tells us that it is already here, showing us that our experience of time can be collapsed just as our sense of distance can. The new faster tempo and the *più mosso* later on also serve to embody this. Spatial immensity is likewise evoked in this new section, where the effortless movement in and out of D major (along with the prominent featuring of F♯) underlines the repetition of the poetry's key idea (Example 12).

This final section takes on the character of a triumphant affirmation, as if Schubert is asserting that for the soul to expand, doubt and fear must be expunged. Example 13 shows how the very minor ninth chord heard in the constricted middle section is transformed by a sequence into the major ninth chord heard in the expansive first section. This final affirmation ties up one more loose end: the same diminished seventh sonority heard in the piano introduction reappears in bar 335 (see Example 13 and compare Example 1). With the reinterpretation of C♯ as D♭, the diminished seventh chord no longer points to G minor (where absence is keenly felt). Instead, it resolves emphatically to B♭ major, allowing the bass to form the motive G–F that has been so significantly referential.

My reading of this piece has attempted to show how its structure can be characterized by two nearly opposite types of space, or rather of the imaginative experiences of space: the coincidence of expansiveness and immediacy that Bachelard called intimate immensity and the sensation of constraint and loss that characterizes separation from a beloved. The first is concretized by Schubert within the tonal world of B♭. It employs the smallest of tonal spaces, a neighboring figure involving the tones F, F♯/G♭, and G, to suggest vast expanses, most simply through registral expansion but most remarkably through a harmonic cycle of major thirds. The confluence of all of these techniques brings about an exquisite sense of a familiar and immediate musical entity that is at once a fluent negotiator of immense space. Ironically, the sense of distance-as-separator is associated with the closely related key of G minor, which is characterized by a kind of paralysis of the spirit brought on by minor seconds and minor ninths and where the locus is D and its associated half-step neighbors. Otherwise ordinary and common musical relationships are given a particularity of poetic meaning that cannot be gauged by structural description alone, but one that nonetheless can be very specifically delineated.

Clearly, these characterizations are strongly contextual and the elucidation of their specific meaning is greatly assisted by the actualities of the verbal text; in an instrumental work, that degree of specificity would certainly be harder to argue. To be sure, the standard reckoning of musical structure is not irrelevant to this analysis; it has provided the reference points that allow meaning to be located in the "facts" of the musical score. However,

220

FRANK SAMAROTTO

Example 10. The minor ninth and the turn to major.

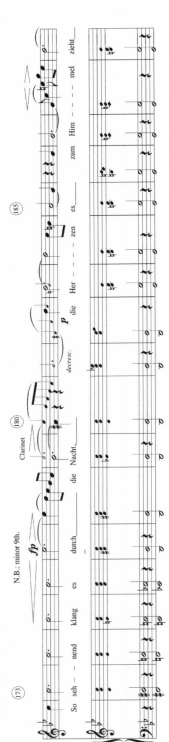

[So longingly the song rings through the forest,]
So longingly it rings through the night;

It draws hearts toward heaven
With wonderful power.

Example 11. The clarinet transition.

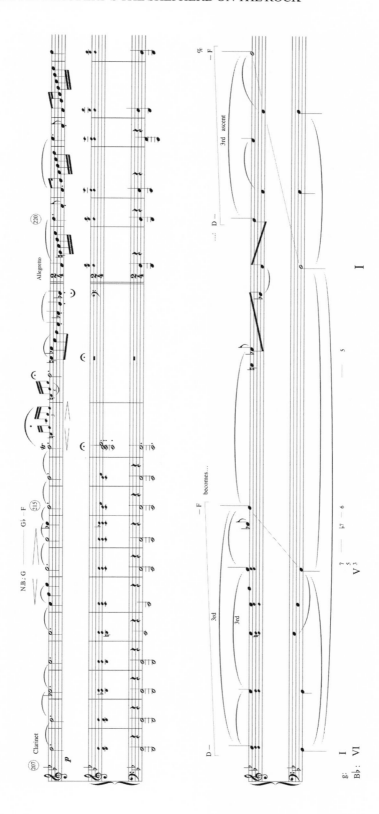

somewhere between the infinite world of possible expressive inferences and the fixed calculation of music's pre-compositional properties lies a meeting place where an individual work can come into its own. This sort of individuality is (I believe) what Bachelard was referring to when he spoke of "the essential psychic actuality, the essential novelty of the poem."[13] I would suggest that Schubert's beautiful setting is in its essence about revaluing and reinterpreting musical distances to create a unique imaginative space that is more than the measure of its parts.

Example 12. The re-evocation of immensity.

The further my voice carries,
The more clearly it echoes back to me.

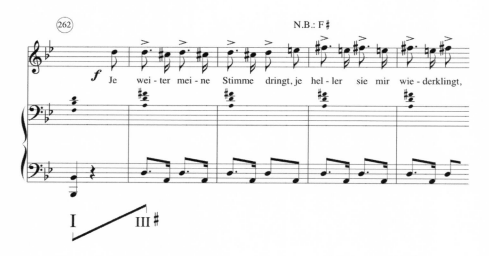

[13]See p. 204.

Example 13. The final affirmation.

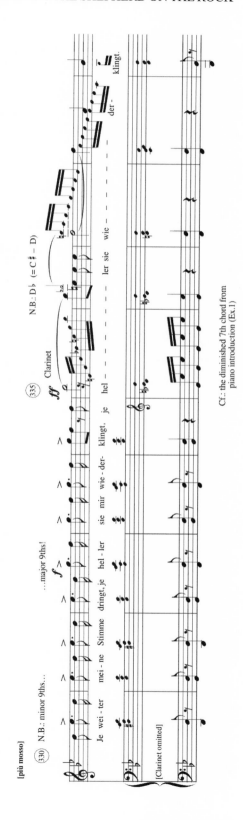

VI

FORM

Tonal Conflicts in Haydn's Development Sections: The Role of C Major in Symphonies Nos. 93 and 102

Mark Anson-Cartwright

A number of Haydn's developments are characterized by an apparently incommensurable tonal element—a chord or key whose relation to the movement's global tonic is difficult to define. A well-known example occurs in the first movement of Symphony No. 103 in E♭ ("Drum Roll"). Toward the conclusion of the development section the closing theme returns (for the first time since the exposition) in the remote key of D♭. Even so perceptive a musician as Donald Tovey apparently could make no sense of this key's function: he bluntly refers to it as "quite irrelevant."[1] And yet the key of D♭ has a definite, if not immediately obvious, function: it acts as VI of F minor which in turn serves as II of E♭.

Like the opening movement of the "Drum Roll," the first movements of Symphonies No. 93 in D and No. 102 in B♭ contain tonal conflicts in the development that dramatize and enliven, but do not negate, the movement's underlying structural unity. Near the end of each development there is a modulation to C major which marks a turning point not only because of the remoteness of C major from the respective tonics of D and B♭, but also for thematic reasons. Moreover, the disruptive effect of C major in these developments seems to contradict the "pure" or "neutral" quality that is often attributed to that key. Although these C-major passages have different structural and thematic functions, they both epitomize Haydn's art of counterbalancing centripetal (or unifying) and centrifugal (or disruptive) forces of tonality. Haydn cultivated this art perhaps more conspicuously— and ingeniously—in his development sections than anywhere else in his instrumental forms.[2]

Symphony No. 93: Parenthesis and Rational Deception

Example 1 illustrates the opening melodic phrase of the second theme of Symphony No. 93. This theme, like the closing theme of the "Drum Roll," returns near the end of the development (bar 161). Most of the development preceding this return is saturated by a motivic fragment of this theme, labeled *x* in Example 1. Motive *x* appears in the development embedded within a larger motive, *y* (see Example 2).

---

[1]Donald Francis Tovey, *Essays in Musical Analysis*, Vol. 1 (London: Oxford University Press, 1935), p. 172.

[2]This essay draws material from Chapter 4 of my dissertation "The Development Section in Haydn's Late Instrumental Works" (Ph.D. diss., City University of New York, 1998).

227

Example 1. Haydn, Symphony No. 93 in D, first movement, bars 76-79.

Example 2. Haydn, Symphony No. 93 in D, first movement, bars 111-12.

The texture of the development up to bar 153 is intensely contrapuntal—except for a brief passage in bars 122–27. The counterpoint reaches its peak of sophistication in bars 145–50, where motive *y* enters in stretto by ascending fifths. All this developmental activity provides a foil for the return of the second theme in bar 161. Although this theme is truncated after three measures, it lasts long enough to restore motive *x* to its original homophonic context.

The return of the second theme stands out not only because of the contrast of texture, but also because the key in which it is set, C major, sounds remote in the context of B minor, and is even more remotely related to the global key of D major. To make sense of this C major, one must consider the development's tonal structure, shown on two levels in Example 3. As one can see from Example 3b, the initial phase of the development, bars 110–36, contains a rising bass motion from E minor (II) to its upper fifth, B minor. Although the key of B minor predominates for several measures after bar 136, it is not prolonged by a complete cadential progression. Instead, there is a climactic deceptive cadence on G in bar 152. Following two *fortissimo* G major chords played tutti, there is a fermata, and then a quiet echo of motive *x* in the violins and flutes. The implicit tonal context is still B minor, confirmed by the C♯s in the second violin and second flute. Then, in bar 160, after three more measures of G-major harmony, the first violin adds F♮ to the chord, implying V⁷ of C, at least on paper.

The notational implication is, indeed, confirmed by the resolution to C major in bar 161. To the ear, however, the F♮ added to the G-major chord could just as easily imply E♯, part of a German augmented-sixth chord in B minor. And that implication is eventually fulfilled by the diminished-seventh chord on E♯ in bar 168, which is underscored both dynamically and by the change of rhythmic figuration (from eighths to a dotted half note).

On a deep structural level, shown in Example 3a, the diminished seventh on E♯ represents a chromatic intensification of the E-minor chord from the beginning of the development (compare bars 111 and 168). The F♯-major chord to which it resolves in bar 169 sounds at first like a dominant of the B minor that was established in bar 136, and then disrupted by the turn to C major. But this putative dominant never goes to B minor. Instead, the bass continues to ascend by step

Example 3a. Graph of Haydn, Symphony No. 93, first movement, exposition and development.

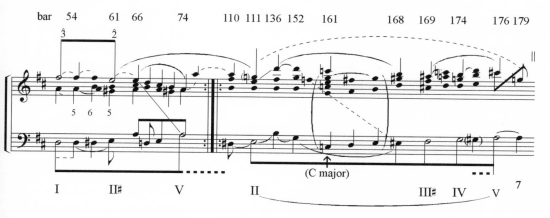

Example 3b. Detailed view of development (to bar 169).

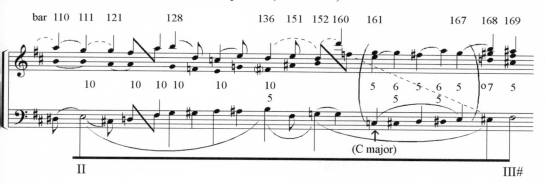

from F♯ in bar 169, first to G in bar 174, recalling the deceptive cadence in bar 152, and then on to A, the structural dominant.

The tonicized C major and the sequential progression that follows until the arrival of the E♯ diminished seventh may be viewed (at least in retrospect) as parenthetical. The abrupt shift away from C major towards the diminished seventh on E♯ reveals the parenthetical function of that key. Yet the parenthetical C-major passage is clearly a dramatically important phase of this development, a playful detour or fissure within its otherwise straightforward structure. C. P. E. Bach, in his well-known description of the free fantasy, called similar phenomena "rational deceptions" (*vernünftige Betrügereyen*), of which one kind is enharmonic reinterpretation.[3] In Symphony No. 93, the enharmonic E♯/F♮ is the agent of deception, and the C-major parenthesis results from *one* side of that

---

[3]C.P.E. Bach, *Versuch über die wahre Art das Clavier zu spielen*, part 2 (Berlin, 1762), p. 330; *Essay on the True Art of Playing Keyboard Instruments*, trans. William J. Mitchell (New York: Norton, 1949), p. 434. Earlier in the *Versuch*, Bach advises the performer to play "deceptive progressions" (*Betrügereyen*) loudly; see *Versuch*, part 1 (Berlin, 1753), p. 130; *Essay*, p. 163. From the corresponding example (Fig. 179b in the Mitchell translation), it is clear that Bach includes enharmonically reinterpreted chords among the "deceptive progressions."

enharmonic (namely, the F♯). But there is, as noted above, an inherent ambiguity in the F♮ when it first appears. The motion to C major *seems* to resolve that ambiguity in favor of the notated meaning. As it turns out, the C major is the deception, and the subsequent appearance of E♯ in the bass going to F♯ resolves the ambiguity definitively in favor of E♯. Only by hearing F♮ as really E♯ is it possible to read the C-major tonicization (and the ensuing four measures) as a parenthesis.

But simply to assert that the *true* meaning of the F♮ is E♯ would be somewhat misleading. For the word "true" in that case would be valid from a middleground perspective, but not with respect to a sensitive hearing of the piece, which includes a conflict between F♮ and E♯ on foreground, and even late middleground, levels.[4] The C-major parenthesis illustrates an important point about many tonal pieces, and about development sections, in particular: that the structural status of a chord, or even several measures of music, as in this case, is not necessarily an adequate measure of its dramatic or rhetorical significance. Structurally subordinate phenomena—like this highly unusual parenthesis—can shape our perception of a piece's structure in vital ways. The C-major passage serves a rhetorical function—to masquerade (briefly) as a tonal goal—though it turns out not to have a structural function in the larger context. To describe a chord, in structural terms, as "decorative" or "parenthetical," is often not enough; analysis that stops short at such terms can be misleading, even if basically correct. Recognizing the dramatic or expressive importance of structurally subordinate material is just as fundamental to analysis as identifying the structure itself.

Symphony No. 102: Modal Shifts and Thematic Returns

The first movement of Symphony No. 102 in B♭ contains the lengthiest development section of any London symphony or, indeed, of any Haydn symphony. Seventy-five measures into this development, at bar 185, there is a "false recapitulation" in C major. The major supertonic is a rather unusual choice of key for such a procedure; I know of only two other examples in Haydn, the first movements of the Piano Trio in E♭, Hob. XV:11, and Symphony No. 84 in E♭.[5] The supertonic's closeness in pitch to the tonic could deceive an inattentive listener into hearing a return to tonic. However, the instrumentation and other aspects of this passage (discussed in detail below) do not suggest a true recapitulation.[6]

---

[4]Carl Schachter expresses similar thoughts about the ambiguity of the Fx/G♮ enharmonic in "Nacht und Träume" in his essay "Motive and Text in Four Schubert Songs," in *Unfoldings*, ed. Joseph N. Straus (New York: Oxford University Press, 1999), pp. 209-20; see also his remarks on p. 13.

[5]Compare Beethoven, Piano Sonata in C, Op. 2 No. 3, first movement, bars 109-12.

[6]Two recent dissertations treat the topic of "false recapitulations": Peter A. Hoyt, "The 'False Recapitulation' and the Conventions of Sonata Form" (Ph.D. diss., University of Pennsylvania, 1996); Mark Evan Bonds, "Haydn's False Recapitulations and the Perception of Sonata Form in the Eighteenth Century" (Ph.D. diss., Harvard University, 1988).

This C-major passage, like the one in Symphony No. 93, occurs late in the development. But here C major has a structural, rather than parenthetical, function. As a chord, it constitutes the main middleground harmony prolonging the structural dominant reached in the exposition. It is really more accurate to say that the *bass* C is a structural tone, but that C major, as a chord—and, more emphatically, as a key—conflicts with the diatony of B♭ major.

The false recapitulation is striking for several reasons. It is the first appearance of the main theme since bar 117 (the seventh measure of the development). More importantly, it contrasts strongly with the preceding music. There is a modal contrast between the half cadences in C minor and the false recapitulation in *major*; the dynamic shift from *forte* to *piano*; and the drop in texture from strings and winds to just flute and violins. C major soon yields to its minor (diatonic) form in bar 192, at the end of the consequent phrase of the false recapitulation. This shift to minor coincides with a striking phrase overlap that is marked by a reversion to the loud, tutti sound that preceded the false recapitulation. The orchestration is also enriched by the addition of horns and trumpets at bar 192.

The conflict between C major and the global key, B♭ major, is thus alleviated by C minor, the diatonic form of II. Motivations for the initial conflict can be identified in both the design and structure of the music. With respect to design, the main theme demands to be stated in *major*. Moreover, it would sound odd in C minor.[7] And while it is idle to debate whether Haydn wanted the C-major passage to be heard as a false recapitulation, its dramatic effect undoubtedly has to do with its air of sounding both right and wrong, in two senses. Viewed as a "recapitulation," this passage is in the wrong key (a whole step above the tonic), but in the right mode. Conversely, when viewed as a structural event, the C-major passage prolongs the right *Stufe*, but in the wrong mode.

Before considering the deep structure of the development, and the role of this pivotal C-major passage within that structure, let us consider certain aspects of the foreground. As the graph in Example 4 shows, the opening phrase of the development prolongs the dominant of C minor (until bar 116). Haydn unexpectedly follows this half cadence with a statement of the main theme in E♭ major (bar 117). This abrupt shift from a G-major chord to E♭ major is a "remote harmonic juxtaposition," to use James Webster's apt term.[8] The juxtaposition relates to bars 81–92 from the second group, where there is a broadly articulated motion from A-major harmony to F major (the second key which was previously established). The opening phrase of this passage (bars 81–86) is stated at the start of the development,

[7] A similar phenomenon occurs in the first movement of the Piano Sonata in E♭, Hob. XVI:52: the horn-fifths theme from the second group (bars 27-29) returns twice in the development, first in C major (bar 46), then in E major (bar 68), both times preceded by a half cadence (marked by a fermata) in C *minor*. But the theme is always in the major mode. (Mixture is a pervasive feature of this movement, incidentally.)

[8] James Webster, *Haydn's "Farewell" Symphony and the Idea of Classical Style* (Cambridge: Cambridge University Press, 1991), pp. 134-8; this progression exemplifies Webster's Type 1.

slightly varied and transposed up a whole step. But the continuation (bars 87–91) does not appear transposed in the development. The elision of these measures results in a juxtaposition of V of C minor and the new key of E♭, instead of a smooth modulation to E♭. An important effect of the elision is that the implied opening key of C minor has been abandoned without any cadence on a C-minor chord. The remainder of the development is devoted, in large part, to the fulfillment of its initial implication of C minor.

The essential tonal path of the development up until the false recapitulation may be seen in Example 5a. The bass gradually arpeggiates from F (V) at the end of the exposition, to C (II) at bar 185. The first important goal within that arpeggiation is A♭ (bar 132). On the foreground, A♭ major is preceded by a C-major chord (see Example 4); this progression echoes the development's initial juxtaposition of G and E♭. A♭ is prolonged until bar 147, and then begins ascending chromatically in bars 148–54 (see Example 5b). (The chromatic ascent is somewhat obscured by registral shifts, shown by the diagonal lines between the staves.) The emphatic arrival on C minor in bar 154 might seem at first to fulfill the prophecy of the development's opening measures. But the bass soon begins to descend, as if to undo the approach to C from A♭. The bass descends only as far as A♮ (in bar. 158), supporting V⁷ of D minor. This harmony sets up a stretto passage that starts in bar 161 and lasts until bar 184, just before the false recapitulation. (Interestingly, in both this symphony and in No. 93 the C-major passage is preceded by a stretto, though in No. 93 the juxtaposition is less immediate.) The half cadence at bar 180 (shown in Example 5c) arouses the expectation of an arrival in C minor for the third time in the development. But the false recapitulation, as we know, is in major, and C minor is thus thrice denied. Only at bar 192 is C major corrected to C minor—and with quite a vengeance.

This "correction" is shown in three graphs (Examples 5a, 5b, and 5d). But at a deeper level of reduction, only the diatonic form of II (C minor) would be shown where C major appears on the foreground. Such an interpretation is valid, and conforms to Schenker's view that diatony takes priority over chromaticism (or, more generally, tonality). But it would be meaningless if viewed apart from the other levels. I believe the C major passage is structurally governed by the diatonic *Stufe* C minor; but, in saying so, I do not deny that the conflict between C major and C minor is essential to the piece.

The adjustment of E♮ to E♭ has the specific effect of a change of mode, but when viewed more generally as a chromatic semitone, the motive E♮– E♭ may be heard to resonate with other prominent semitone adjustments in the development and elsewhere in the movement. The *Largo* introduction, a graph of which is shown in Example 6, plants the seed of the conflict between E♮ and E♭. The introduction begins softly, and indeed does not exceed a *piano* dynamic until just before bar 14, where a tonicized A♭-major chord appears, marked *forte*. The top voice's A♭ eventually presses upward to A♮ supported by dominant harmony. The motion from A♭ to A♮ differs from the E♮–E♭ shift in that it is a rising, rather than a descending,

Example 4. Foreground graph of Haydn, Symphony No. 102 in B♭, first movement, beginning of development.

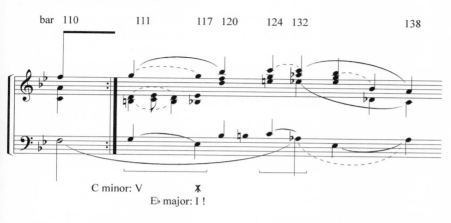

semitone. Yet this very rising semitone is a prominent feature not only of the development (noted above the staff of Example 5a), but also of the second group (bars 71–72). Although the shift from A♭ to A♮ occurs beneath the surface of the development, the tonicized A♭ must surely be an intended echo of the same remote key in the introduction.

Another chromatic adjustment occurs across the boundary between the *Largo* and the *Allegro vivace*, where D♭ is corrected to D♮. This chromatic shift is indirect, of course, because of the intervening E♭ in bar 22; furthermore, D♭ is a neighbor to C, and thus occupies a lower structural level than D♮, the primary tone of the movement. Finally, the E♭ in the oboe at bar 21 comes from an E♮, as a result of elision.

There are also foreground instances of the E♮–E♭ motive toward the end of the development (see Example 5d). The bass motion E♮–E♭ in bars 204–206 results from an elision of F. The retrograde motion E♭–E♮ (continuing to F) occurs in bars 210–11 and again in bars 216–17, marking the structural dominant. Within the retransition, the dominant is decorated by applied diminished sevenths on E♮, which eventually descends chromatically to E♭ in bar 221. The retransition thus recalls the concluding measures of the Largo introduction.

The role of C major in this symphony is ultimately rooted in a motivic idea established in the introduction—an idea that may be described as a basic conflict between flat and natural forms of the same note. The motive manifests itself in various harmonic contexts, but is most often projected through mixture. The false recapitulation is a focal point of the development because it recalls the previously established rivalry between natural and flat pitches by means of thematic contrast, rather than just local harmonic or modal contrast. The contrast between the C-major false recapitulation and the subsequent C minor thus magnifies the motivic idea of altering E♮ to E♭, and brings to a dramatic conclusion the development's quest for a structural C minor.

C major thus has quite different meanings in the two symphonies. In Symphony No. 93, it is a parenthetical key, a consequence of the enharmonic

Example 5a. Deep middleground graph of Haydn, Symphony No. 102 in B♭, first movement.

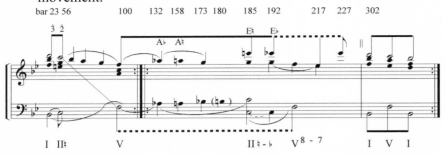

Example 5b. Middleground graph of Symphony No. 102, first movement.

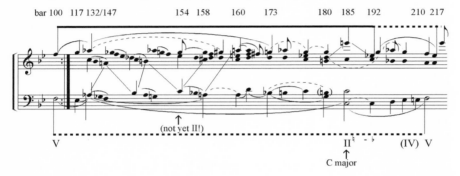

Example 5c. Graph of bars 160-180.

Example 5d. Detailed graph of bars 185-226.

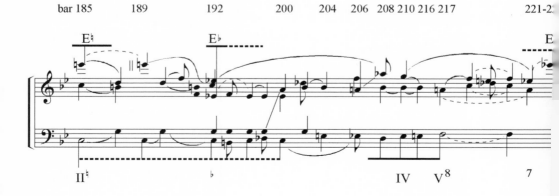

F♮/E♯. In Symphony No. 102, C major has a structural function that is qualified by the need to correct E♮ to E♭. Despite the differences in context and function for C major in these developments, in both cases the subversive role of that key is underscored thematically. The meaning of the key in each case results from the interaction between structure and design. These developments are shaped by the interaction between disruptive and stable elements, or centrifugal and centripetal forces. Haydn's ability to establish tonal tensions in this manner, and then to restore balance so compellingly, is indeed one of the hallmarks of his style.

Example 6. Graph of Haydn, Symphony No. 102, first movement, slow introduction.

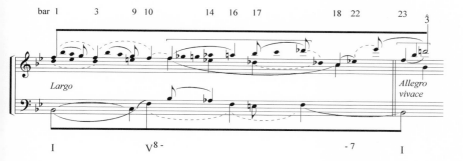

Aspects of Structure in Bach's
F-Minor Fugue, *WTC II*

William Renwick

Music, intangible by nature, is difficult to write about at any time, but Bach's biographer, Johann Nicolas Forkel, was indeed challenged when he attempted to describe how Bach's fugues transcend those of his contemporaries:

> He who is not acquainted with Bach's fugues cannot even form an idea of what a true fugue is and ought to be. In fugues of the ordinary kind, there is nothing but a very insignificant and sloppy routine. They take a theme, give it a companion, transpose both gradually into the keys related to the original one, and make the other parts accompany them in all these transpositions with a kind of thorough-bass chords. This is a fugue; but of what kind? It is very natural that a person acquainted with only such fugues can have no great opinion of the whole species. How much art does it, then, require to make oneself master of such commonplace?
>
> Bach's fugue is of quite another kind. It fulfils all the conditions which we are otherwise accustomed to demand only of more free species of composition. A highly characteristic theme; an uninterrupted principal melody, wholly derived from it and equally characteristic from the beginning to the end; not mere accompaniment in the other parts, but in each of them an independent melody, according with the others, also from the beginning to the end; freedom, lightness, and fluency in the progress of the whole; inexhaustible variety of modulation combined with perfect purity; the exclusion of every arbitrary note not necessarily belonging to the whole; unity and diversity in the style, rhythm, and meters; and, lastly, diffused through the whole, so that it sometimes appears to the performer or hearer as if every single note were animated—these are the properties of Bach's fugue, properties which necessarily excite admiration and astonishment in every judge who knows how much power of mind is required for the production of such works.[1]

Schenker, too, took up the challenge of describing Bach's fugues, but in a more technical manner that connects his impressions with his own theoretical approach:

---

[1] "On J.S. Bach's Life," trans. in Hans David and Arthur Mendel, *The Bach Reader* (New York: Norton, 1998), pp. 449-50.

> Despite the fact that each one exhibits a different design, the fugues of J. S. Bach are genuine fugues in the strictest sense; they are always determined by the subject, by its dimensions and harmonic content, and are controlled by a fundamental structure . . . Without improvisational gift, that is, without the ability to connect the composition to the middleground and background, no good fugue can ever be written.[2]

Each author in his own way affirms that Bach's rigorous and thorough technique controls all levels of a fugue, uniting motivic and formal aspects in a unique masterwork.

A key point in Schenker's view is that form develops essentially out of tonal structure and voice leading—an inner sense of form—rather than from a schematic plan of subject entries and imitative techniques:

> The textbooks and analyses always describe the organization of the fugue in terms of exposition, restatement, episode, and every other device imaginable: e.g. contrary motion, retrograde motion, augmentation, stretto, etc. The only thing they never mention is most important of all: the fundamental hidden relationships that bind the fugue into an organic whole, into a true work of art.[3]

I think that Schenker would claim that it is the voice-leading progressions of the various structural levels that are the "fundamental hidden relationships that bind the fugue into an organic whole." With this in mind we can examine these hidden relationships in a relatively straightforward Bach fugue: the F-minor Fugue from the *Well-Tempered Clavier*, Book II, which is arguably one of the most clear-cut of all the *WTC* fugues in terms of imitation, rhythm, and transparency of voice leading.

An unusual characteristic of the subject that is worth noting is its use of an anacrusis (Example 1). More frequently, Bach's subjects—like most Baroque fugue subjects in general—begin on or after (rather than before) a strong beat. As with many Bach subjects, this one contains two rhythmic ideas: the first a repeated quarter-note motive, the second a flowing pattern of sixteenths. The rapport of these two rhythms is played out throughout the course of the fugue.

The voice leading of the subject is characterized by a two-voice framework elaborated by D♭ and E♮ neighbors. These pitches form a diminished seventh and provide boundaries of tension for the theme, giving it a particular chromatic character frequently found in Bach's minor-key subjects. This character is especially pronounced by the thwarted resolution of the D♭. Soon after the conclusion of the subject (with its descent to 3̂), this D♭ is countered by the appearance of a D♮ in bar 4 (see Example 2). The D♮ combines with F and A♭ of the tonic chord in a beautiful continuation of the

---

[2]Heinrich Schenker, *Free Composition*, trans. Ernst Oster (New York: Longman, 1979), pp. 143-44.

[3]Schenker, "The organic nature of fugue," from *The Masterwork in Music*, Vol. 2, trans. Hedi Siegel (Cambridge: Cambridge University Press, 1996), p. 42.

Example 1. J. S. Bach, Fugue in F Minor from WTC II, voice-leading sketch of foreground.

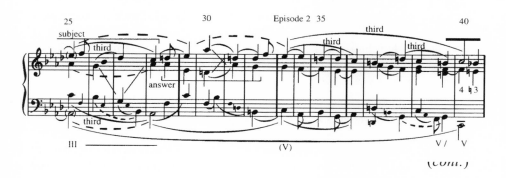

(cont.)

meander that ends the subject. These notes of the tonic chord are thereby
transformed to form part of a diminished triad, in turn helping to lead to the
C-minor harmony of bar 5.

Since no overlap occurs between the subject and the answer, the answer
(except for its first note) can lie wholly within the dominant. Because the
subject is fully polyphonic, containing two complete voices ($\hat{5}$–$\hat{4}$–$\hat{3}$ and $\hat{8}$–
$\hat{7}$–$\hat{8}$), the counterpoint to the answer uses the remaining contrapuntal voice,
$\hat{3}$–$\hat{2}$–$\hat{1}$. This prolongs the initial $\hat{5}$ of the subject, as shown in Example 2.
The answer introduces a new diminished seventh, B♮–A♭, a transposition
of the E♮ and D♭ of the subject, which are themselves contrasted by
appearance of the supporting D♮ and E♭ in the upper voice of the answer.

The bridge that follows accomplishes the return to the tonic key,
necessitated by the presence of the emphatic $\hat{1}$ at the beginning of the

Example 1. cont.

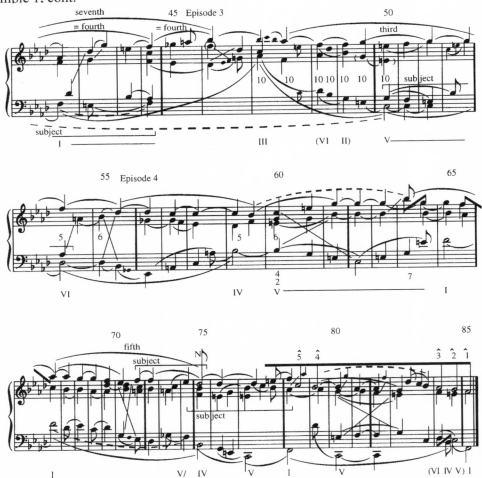

subject. The bridge takes the motivic idea of the half-step resolution of bars 4–5 and 8–9 as a basis (note in Example 2 the A♮–B♭, G–A♭, E♮–F in the lower voice in bars 8–12), as the upper voice outlines a descending fifth, originating in the higher octave established in bar 8.

Whereas the first two subject statements each occupy a four-measure group, the bridge contains only three measures, as the cadence to I overlaps with the beginning of the third entry at bar 12. Elisions are of course not unusual in fugue. As Schenker has argued, the continual elision that is characteristic of fugues works against the development of any metric grouping at deeper levels.[4] Yet in the F-minor Fugue, the elision in bar 12 of the exposition is actually somewhat of an anomaly. For the most part, there is an avoidance of elision throughout the rest of the fugue, thereby allowing a deeper sense of measure groupings to emerge. Example 1 illustrates my interpretation of the metrical groupings through heavy bar lines. The subject

[4]See Fig. 149, 8a of *Free Composition*, which shows how the overlapping entries in the exposition of the C♯ minor fugue from the *WTC* I cause continual disturbance and reinterpretation of the metric groupings.

Example 2. Middleground.

itself, with its eighth-note anacrusis, seems to express an unambiguous four-measure metrical group, and this is reinforced by the lack of overlap at the entry of the answer. To a great extent this pattern is carried through the remainder of the composition, providing an underlying metric regularity to the piece.[5]

The third entry then follows the usual tonic-prolongation plan for subjects that begin with an emphasis on Î. The upper voice returns to its original register through a descending fourth which, taken with the preceding fifth during the bridge, represents a full octave descent (bars 9–14). By this means, the upper voice prolongs C in an expansive and dynamic manner. The "incompletion" of the upper neighbor D♭ in the subject referred to earlier is resolved here by the assertion of the D♭–C neighbor at the conclusion of the octave descent (in bars 13–4) and by the repeated D♭–C motive in the upper part in bars 15–6, which coincides with the arrival of the root-position tonic at the close of the exposition.

The episode that follows (bars 17–24), the first of four episodes, provides for the customary motion to the relative major through a recomposition of the C–D–E♭ third which previously occurred in bar 4 (see Example 3, bars 17–24). Here the D♮ is hidden in the inner voice, rather than exposed in

---

[5]Only two subsequent occurrences of the subject involve a redistribution of the four-measure metrical scheme. In bar 51 the subject appears in the inner part, one measure after the beginning of a bass prolongation of V, and at a weak metric placement. The structural context of the subject at this point is unusual since it occurs within a prolongation of V rather than I. The second instance is again in the middle voice (bar 75), and again without transposition. But here the subject is interpreted within a prolongation of IV moving to V, and in an altered rhythmic guise—altered through its overlap with the preceding entry in the upper voice. In both instances these rhythmic conflicts develop tension prior to resolution—to the deceptive cadence in bar 54, and to the tonic arrival in bar 78.

the upper voice. It acts essentially as a harmonic factor, rather than a melodic factor, part of a D diminished triad that hearkens back to the harmony suggested in bar 4. The reuse of the D diminished triad in bar 23 realizes a potential inherent in bar 4, as the harmony that first led to C minor now leads in another direction, to the relative major. Note that the return of the D♮ and its resolution to E♭ allows this episode to end atypically in a half cadence (on the dominant of A♭, rather than leading directly to A♭). The character of the half cadence complements the dance-like character of the piece and emphasizes the anacrusis at just this point, which contributes to the sense of metric solidity. (Had the episode led directly to A♭, an elision would have occurred at the beginning of the next subject statement, thereby breaking up the metric regularity here.)

Example 3. Deep middleground.

The A♭ section (bars 25–32) supports a temporary upper voice of E♭, an expansion of the projected inner voice E♭ in bar 5 (see Example 4). In bar 28, D♮ is again prominent in the upper voice, where it introduces E♭ as 5̂ of A♭. The deceptive resolution to a C-minor chord in bar 29 makes the associative connection to bar 5 explicit here. As such, one could say that the opening tonic-minor section alludes to the relative major and the major section alludes back to the tonic minor, with the diminished triad binding the keys together as a type of *Grundgestalt*.

Example 4. Subject of the fugue.

The upper-voice E♭ remains prominent in the following C minor section (bars 33–40), where it initiates a 3̂–2̂–1̂ third progression in the key of V. A perfect authentic cadence in V at bar 40 articulates the midpoint of the composition. The extreme low register of the bass emphasizes the deep structural significance of this dominant arrival.

Following this cadence to V, a brief return to the tonic provides for a subject statement (in the bass) to begin the second part. The D♭–D♮ conflict, which has helped guide the discourse in the first half of the work, ceases to have a role in the second half. Instead, the music focuses on the D♭ and neighbor tone function at the background level.

The music beginning at bar 41 (especially bars 45–6) expands upon the E♮–D♭ diminished seventh. This leads through a continuous sixteenth-note passage in the bass to an emphatic presentation of V (bar 50), which is underlined by a return of the eighth-note rhythm of the subject. The breadth of register and the prolonged pedal point of bars 41–53 set up a striking deceptive cadence to VI in bar 54, all of which occurs as support for a broad upper-voice fifth-progression, C–F (see Example 3). Incidentally, the subject that appears in the middle voice over the dominant pedal has no particular structural importance, for it does not articulate a significant point of arrival nor departure in the larger voice-leading framework.

From a motivic standpoint, the deceptive C–D♭ motion in the bass is an expansion of the original upper-neighbor idea in the subject. This concept is very important in understanding how motive and structure together promote an organic sense of unity. Certainly, the move to D♭ at bar 54, about two-thirds of the way through the piece, is the dramatic center towards which the preceding music drives and from which the following music recedes.

The next goal of the bass is IV (bar 59), followed by a broad sequence to V and I in bar 65. Significantly, the bass of bars 50–65 follows the profile of the subject. This motion supports a third-progression $\hat{5}$–$\hat{4}$–$\hat{3}$ in the upper octave, which links registrally with the high C of bar 8 (see Example 4).

Throughout this passage, Bach maintains the broad harmonic motion that thus far has characterized the second half of the piece, somewhat in the character of the Italianate *Brandenburg Concerti*. As though in compensation for the slower rate of harmonic change here, the bass spins out a dramatic arpeggiated pattern that provides motion within each prolongation. The most vigorous part of this passage is the wonderful voice exchange in the dominant-seventh harmony of bars 60–4, by which a third inversion with the root on top becomes a root position with the seventh on top. The ensuing tonic resolution in bar 65 is by no means final, since the bass is so high, and since the treble descends only to $\hat{3}$, in the upper octave.

The fourth episode, bars 66–75, contains a recomposition of episodes 1 and 2. The upper register connects through a descending fifth from A♭ to a pivotal upper neighbor, D♭. The D♭ is supported by IV, as the termination of a subdominant subject statement in bar 75. This D♭ represents the largest expansion of the original upper-neighbor motive of the subject, while its subdominant harmonic support—coupled with the return to the main register—heralds the ultimate conclusion of the composition. The IV–V–I of bars 75–8 leads the D♭ back to the *Kopfton* C and returns the harmony to I, via the depths of the low C that recalls bar 40.

At this stage in the composition the main harmonic events have taken place, but the *Urlinie* remains on $\hat{5}$. In the final eight measures of the fugue, based again upon episodic material, the upper voice descends to $\hat{1}$.

That the *Urlinie* descends only after the essential harmonic events of the fugue are complete is not an unusual feature for a fugue, but in fact represents one of the ways in which fugal structure differs from other models of tonal composition. This final melodic descent once again embodies the motivic D♭–C upper neighbor (in bar 83). Likewise, the bass states the upper neighbor a final time in bar 84, as part of a stretto with the upper voice. This closing music thus represents a union of subject and episode materials as it incorporates the upper neighbors of the subject within the texture of the episode.

At a deep level, the first half of the fugue (bars 1–40) outlines the tonic chord, F–A♭–C (I–III–V) and the second half (bars 41ff.) integrates the D♭ upper neighbor through large-scale harmonic and melodic events (Example 4). Both the diminished seventh and the upper-neighbor D♭ of the subject play important roles in the overall structure of the composition and provide characteristic elements that help unify the composition. In this respect, although the episodic material forms a contrast, it nevertheless relates to the subject through the melodic sixth that originates in the F–D♭ of the subject.

One ought not to conclude a discussion of this fugue without referring to its dearth of subject statements. There are only nine statements in all: three in the exposition, two in the relative major, one at the beginning of the second part, one at the dominant pedal, and two more in bars 71–8. It is especially noteworthy that the bass has only two statements, both at the identical pitch. Despite the small number of entrances, there is no question that they blend with the fabric of the piece in an impressive way. While the subject is often absent in its entirety, it is hardly ever absent in its parts. This is especially true for the bass voice, where the lack of direct subject statements is more than compensated for by the broadly arpeggiating reiterations of the eighth-note motive in the developmental passage work of bars 50–65. Likewise, the concept behind the episodic material is the combination of the eighth-note and sixteenth-note motives of the subject, so that the spirit of the subject is always present.[6]

In discussing this work, Johann Friedrich Reichardt noted that "This fugue is full from end to end of such expressive melody, the restatements of the theme are so clear and penetrating in all transpositions, and the progression of all the voices is so natural and unentangled, as in few fugues except those of Handel."[7]   Indeed, this is counterpoint at the service of music, rather than music at the service of counterpoint. As much as Bach's genius encompasses the complex artifices to *The Art of Fugue* and *The Musical Offering*, much more this elegance and freedom demonstrates Bach's mastery of *musical* composition.

---

[6] I add here a word about the connection of this fugue to its prelude, which is also in 2/4 time and which is an Italianate dance movement in three parts. The conclusion of the prelude in particular displays important characteristics of the fugue: the diminished seventh, the prominent D♭, the deceptive cadence, and the play of eighth-note and sixteenth-note rhythms.

[7] Johann Friedrich Reichardt, *Musikalisches Kunstmagazin*, Vol. 1 (1782), p. 196., trans. in David and Mendel, *The Bach Reader* (first edition, New York: Norton, 1972), p. 456.

The wonderful associations of the subject to the background through the upper-voice connections and through the neighbor development in both upper and lower voices help us recall the remarks of Forkel and Schenker cited at the beginning of this essay. Surely the sense of improvisational gift is what allows the second half of the piece, the developmental part, to blossom. Bach achieves his mastery largely through hidden voice-leading connections that convey a sense of unity and conviction in perfect rapport with his contrapuntal processes.

The Andante from Mozart's Symphony No. 40, K.550: the opening theme and its consequences

Eric Wen

In his once-popular "Master Musicians" biography of Mozart, Eric Blom notes a feeling of anxiety beneath the surface calm of the Andante from the composer's Symphony No. 40 in G minor:

> In symphonies cast in a minor key a slow movement in the major gener-ally makes for some sort of alleviation. This, however, does nothing of the sort. There is a kind of brooding restlessness about it, produced by various devices, such as strong accents on weak beats, little fluttering, detached figures and more especially by semitonal clashes as well as a cross-rhythm of 3–4 against the prescribed 6–8 . . . The tranquil end, which would be heart-easing in its loveliness in another context, here achieves just that quality of pathos which is characteristic of the sym-phony as a whole."[1]

Blom is sensitive to the underlying tension beneath the movement's serene demeanor, but it is more than the surface articulations that contribute to this. The agitation that he recognizes lies deep within the organization of the movement itself. With regard to sonata design, there are some surprising anomalies. Between the two B♭ themes of the second subject in the exposition, the opening theme of the movement reappears unexpectedly in the distant key of D♭.[2] Later, in the recapitulation, the principal theme of the second subject makes an unconventional appearance: instead of returning in the expected E♭ major, it initially comes back in F minor. This paper will examine the structural meaning of these unusual events and show how they relate to motivic details presented in the opening theme.

---

[1] Eric Blom, *Mozart* (London: J.M.Dent, 1935), p.205

[2] The term "second subject" used here follows Donald Francis Tovey's definition in his essay "Schubert," *The Main Stream of Music and Other Essays* (London: Oxford University Press, 1944). Tovey states that "whatever is contained in or about the tonic key, from the outset to the first decisive changes of key, shall be called the first subject, and that whatever is contained from that decisive change of key to the end of the exposition shall be called the second subject." With characteristic humor, he remarks further that "there are no rules whatever to determine how many themes a sonata exposition shall contain, nor how its themes shall be distributed . . . Haydn may run a whole exposition on one theme, Mozart may reserve one of his best themes for the development, and Beethoven may have one-and-a-half themes in his first subject, a very definite new theme for his transition, five-and-a-half themes in his second subject, and still a new one in the course of his development" (p.120).

The first subject of the movement spans bars 1–19 and is constructed as a parallel period. The articulation of this opening theme demands close examination in itself. The pulsating repeated melodic notes are stated initially in the violas and continue in the second violins before appearing in the first violins in bar 3. Indeed, the positioning of the separate voices changes with each successive bar. The viola, which initiates the opening melody, first appears as the top voice in bar 1, then becomes the alto voice in bar 2, and finally the tenor part in bar 3. There is a buildup of textural sonority in each successive bar as the two parts grow to four. From this succession of chords, a melodic line emerges, outlining a rising third, E♭–F–G (Example 1a), in not one, but three different parts.

Example 1a. Mozart, Symphony in G minor, K. 440, II: the opening theme (bars 1 - 4).

Example 1b. The chromaticization of II⁶₅ in bar 2.

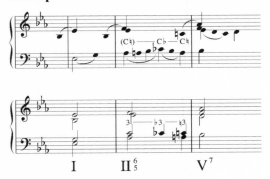

Another distinctive feature of the opening theme is the chromatic bass line elaborating the II⁶₅ chord in bar 2. Example 1b shows the difference in meaning between the two appearances of raised $\hat{4}$ (A♮) in this bar. The first A♮ is a chromatic passing tone between the A♭ at the beginning of the bar and the diatonic passing tone B♭ which leads to C♭. The A♮ at the end of the bar, however, is the midpoint within a larger chromatic motion connecting the A♭ at the beginning of bar 2 to the dominant B♭ in bar 3. The C♭ in the middle of the bar results from mixture (that is, a borrowing of $\hat{6}$ from E♭ minor). Despite its fleeting appearance, this transformation of ♮6 to ♭6 creates a memorable effect. However, when the bass descends a diminished third to A♮ at the end of the bar, C♮ is reinstated in the first violins' upbeat. As we shall see, this juxtaposition of C♭ and C♮ will be played out dramatically later in the movement.

After the motion from E♭ to G in bars 1–4, the melodic line continues up another third from G to B♭ (Example 2). The IV that appears in bar 5 serves to embellish the tonic and supports C as a neighbor-note decoration of B♭ (5̂).[3] As we shall see, this apparent surface detail will be of significance in the movement as a whole. This motive is itself decorated by the chromatic lower neighbor notes, B♮ and A♮. Through these chromatic embellishments of the neighbor-note figure, Mozart recalls and focuses attention on the chromatically-inflected notes of bar 2, C♭ and A♮.

Example 2. The antecedent phrase of the opening theme (bars 1 - 8).

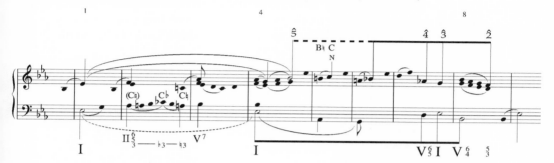

In the consequent phrase (Example 3), the opening theme is stated initially by the cellos and basses before moving up through the violas to the second violins. In counterpoint with this melody, the first violins introduce a new countersubject. As shown in Example 4, this derives from the bass line of the antecedent phrase. Despite the longer note values, the melodic shape of the bass line is preserved. The chromatic passing tone A♮ now lasts half a bar, and C♭ appears as an appoggiatura. Particularly charming is how the bass motion B♭–E♭ in the cadence of bars 3–4 is recast in bar 12 as a melodic skip of a fourth over tonic harmony.

Example 3. The consequent phrase of the opening theme (bars 9 - 19).

[3]In his graph of this movement, Heinrich Schenker connects the IV in bar 5 to V in bar 7. In his reading, the I⁶ chord in bar 6 supports the passing note B♭ between C and A♭. Although a tonic chord can serve as a passing chord between IV and V, I interpret these bars differently. Bars 5 and 6 are grouped as a pair, and are separate from bar 7 which enters as a new idea. More importantly, IV in bar 5 functions as a decoration of I⁶ in bar 6. The melodic outline of B♮–C–A♮–B♭ over bars 5–6 recalls C♭–(C♮)–A♮–B♭ in bars 2–3. Reading B♭ in bar 6 as a passing tone leading to A♭ in bar 7 weakens this motivic connection. See Schenker's "Mozart's Symphony in G minor, K.550," *Das Meisterwerk in der Musik* II (Munich: Drei Masken Verlag, 1926), trans. William Drabkin, *The Masterwork in Music* II (Cambridge: Cambridge University Press, 1996).

Example 4. Comparison of bass, bars 1-3, and first violin, bars 9-11.

In the consequent phrase, as in the antecedent, Mozart juxtaposes the two different forms of 6̂. However, the inflection of C♮ to C♭ and back again occurs over the span of three measures (bars 10–12) in the consequent phrase, as opposed to just one in the antecedent. In the consequent, C♭ is more prominent, appearing in the top voice and lasting half of bar 11. Its "correction" back to C♮ occurs, in the following bar, as a fleeting thirty-second note decorating B♭. The succeeding bars of the consequent phrase continue to repeat the antecedent in invertible counterpoint. Not only does the bass voice of bars 13–15 articulate the melody of bars 5–7 of the antecedent, but the new top-voice countersubject derives from the bass line. The basic melodic motion over bars 13–14 outlines a stepwise descent from a♭² – g², and this echoes the bass A♭¹ – G¹ in bars 5–6. Following the cadential II⁶–V progression in bar 16, the consequent phrase is extended by three bars. In place of the expected arrival of the tonic, an auxiliary cadence is introduced. Here the wind instruments appear for the first time, providing a clear statement of the neighbor motive B♭–C–B♭ as a closing gesture in the top voice.

Another significant motivic idea expressed in this opening theme is the rising linear progression of a third interpolated by a neighbor note. As shown in Example 5, the shape of the melodic line, rising up from 1̂ to 3̂ (e♭¹ to g¹) at the beginning of the antecedent phrase is recalled by the same figure from 3̂ to 5̂ (g² to b♭²) in the consequent.

Example 5. Voice-leading sketch of bass, bars 1-3, and first violin, bars 9-11.

Example 6. Bars 1-27.

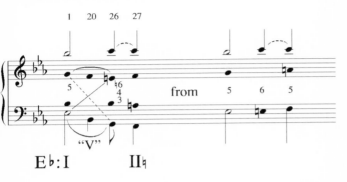

Most listeners would agree that the second subject begins in bar 20.[4] Certainly, the new melody introduced here is in marked contrast to the first theme. The pulsating flow generated by the repeated eighth notes of the opening theme is now arrested by a hemiola, resulting from the new theme's articulation of the first, third, and fifth beats of the bar. Furthermore, this rhythmic conflict greates a static, almost halting quality which expresses a sense of uncertainty. As shown in Example 6, the articulation of B♭ here does not establish the structural dominant of the exposition. Rather, the passage beginning in bar 20 is a step en route to a more definite arrival point: the F major chord in bar 27.

The F major chord in bar 27 would appear to be the dominant of B♭ major, preparing the contrasting key of the exposition. In fact, it would not be implausible for the second B♭ theme of bars 37ff. to follow immediately after this cadence. The expected resolution to B♭ is denied, however, as the F major chord leads instead through a 5–6 contrapuntal motion to D♭ major (Example 7).

Example 7. Bars 27-29.

(a)   (b)   (c)

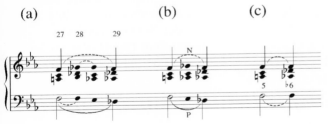

Upon the arrival in this distant key, the opening theme with its repeated eighth-note pattern returns. At this point in the exposition, the restatement of the first theme in a different key from the tonic might imply the formal design of a monothematic sonata movement, so favored by Haydn. But D♭

---

[4]Besides Schenker, several distinguished Mozart scholars have also read bar 20 as the start of the second theme. See Otto Jahn, *W. A. Mozart*, 5th edition, rev. Hermann Abert (Leipzig: Breitkopf und Härtel, 1919–21); trans. Nathan Broder, *Norton Critical Score of Mozart Symphony in G Minor*, K.550, p.69. See also Georges de Saint-Foix, *Les Symphonies de Mozart* (Paris: Mellottée, 1932); trans. Lesley Orrey, *The Symphonies of Mozart* (London: Dennis Dobson, Ltd, 1947), p.117.

Example 8. The recollection of the opening theme (bars 29-34).

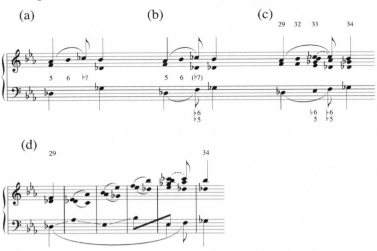

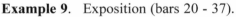

is far removed from the home key of E♭, and it is barely established as a key area before becoming subsumed by an ascending sequence in fifths. With the appearance of C♭ in the top voice this sequence is broken, and a new tonal goal of G♭ is reached. Example 8 demonstrates how the D♭ chord of bar 29 is transformed, in bar 33, into an applied dominant of the G♭ major chord. This G♭ chord itself is short-lived, however, and ultimately serves to prepare the augmented sixth that leads into the cadential $^6_4$ over F, in bar 35.

Example 9 presents the tonal meaning of the remarkable succession of events over bars 27–35. The F major chord in bar 27, initially set up as the dominant of B♭, is in fact a passing chord that connects the opening tonic to

Example 9.   Exposition (bars 20 - 37).

the augmented sixth chord of bar 34. Only at bar 35, with the arrival of the cadential $\frac{6}{4}$, do we reach the true dominant of B♭. The second B♭ theme that appears in bars 37ff serves as the exposition's closing theme. As shown in the graph, it is this closing theme, not the second theme in bars 20ff, that finally articulates the dominant key area.[5] This large-scale reading is supported by the expansion of an important motivic idea: the neighbor-note decoration of B♭. The long-range registral connection of the neighbor-note figure b♭²–c³–b♭² embraces the motion from the opening tonic, through the appearance of the second theme, to its ultimate destination of B♭, the contrasting key of the exposition.

The closing theme is articulated in a period structure whereby a melodic descent from $\hat{3}$ is interrupted. This $\hat{3}$ appears initially in the bass voice, where it resolves the dissonant seventh e♭² (scale degree $\hat{4}$ in B♭) over the dominant in the preceding bar. The consequent phrase is twice the length of the antecedent, and it is expanded by the chromatic inflection of ♮$\hat{3}$ to ♭$\hat{3}$ in bars 44–46 (Example 10). In the progression IV⁷–♮IV$\frac{6}{5}$ supporting ♭$\hat{3}$, the chromatic F–G♭–G♮ motion in the bass echoes the melodic line of bar 43 and evokes the chromaticization of the neighbor-note motive, B♭–B♮–C.

Example 10. The closing theme (bars 37 - 48).

Finally, this closing theme recalls the motivic linear progression of a third decorated by a neighbor note (see the brackets in Example 10). There are two statements of this motivic idea: from $\hat{5}$ to $\hat{3}$ and $\hat{3}$ to $\hat{1}$. This figure, which formed the basis of the opening theme, now descends a fifth, inverting the ascent from $\hat{1}$ to $\hat{5}$, as presented at the beginning (compare with Example 5).

The motivic ideas presented in the opening theme are also echoed in the voice-leading framework of the development section (Example 11). In this section, the bass outlines a descending arpeggiation in thirds from the dominant B♭, at the end of the exposition, through the mediant, G major, before returning to the tonic key of E♭ major at the recapitulation. Above this large-scale bass arpeggiation is an expanded statement of the neighbor-note idea in the top voice. The notes B♭–B♮–B♭, supported by the progression

[5] For other examples where the tonal goal of the exposition is expressed by the closing rather than the second theme, see Carl Schachter, "The First Movement of Brahms's Second Symphony: the opening theme and its consequences," *Music Analysis* 2/1 (1983), pp. 55-68, and Lauri Suurpää, "Continuous Exposition and Tonal Structure in Three Late Haydn Works," *Music Theory Spectrum* 21/2 (Fall, 1999), pp. 174-199.

Example 11. Development (bars 53 - 73).

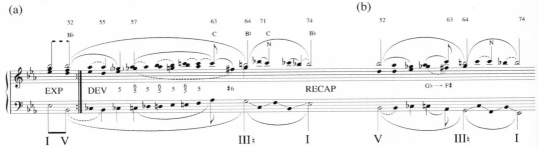

V–III♮–I, are enharmonically equivalent to the neighbor-note figure B♭–C♭–B♭. The chromatic half steps from B♭ to B♮ and back again are each further decorated by a neighbor-note motion to C♮. Note that the G♭ in the ⁶₄ chord, which initiates the sequence beginning in bar 57, prepares the F♯ of the augmented sixth in bar 63. The enharmonic change of G♭ to F♯ over these bars recalls a similar transformation at the end of the exposition in bars 45–46, where the bass G♭ recalls the F♯ in the top voice of bar 39.

The expansion of the motives from the opening theme has its greatest impact in the recapitulation, where it helps give rise to unusual features in the form. In the recapitulation one would expect the two B♭ themes of the exposition (that is, the second and closing themes) to be cast in the tonic key of E♭, thereby resolving the tonal conflict between I and V in the exposition. In this movement, however, the recapitulation does not follow this typical plan. Although the opening theme (bars 74ff.) and closing theme (bars 108ff.) are cast in the tonic key of E♭, the principal theme of the second subject initially returns in F minor (bar 86ff.). Four bars later this theme is stated again, this time in the expected tonic key. In order to investigate the significance of the F minor statement of this theme, we need first to look closely at the beginning of the recapitulation and see how it is prepared.

Although the antecedent phrase of the first theme is presented exactly as in the opening of the movement, the consequent phrase is recomposed. The most noticeable difference is the top-voice countersubject in bars 82–85 (compare with bars 9–12). Instead of the A♭–A♮ succession in dotted quarter notes, bar 83 articulates a series of eighth notes rising up chromatically from A♭ to C♭, before descending back to A♮. This is, of course, a note-for-note repetition of the bass of bar 75 (as well as bar 2 in the exposition) and thus a literal presentation of the opening theme in invertible counterpoint. But hereafter, a subtle change deflects the tonal motion. A comparison of the succeeding bars of both passages (that is, bar 84 with bar 11) reveals that the order of dotted quarter notes is reversed. They are moreover enharmonically renotated: bar 84 is written as B♭–B♮ (instead of C♭–B♭). This unexpected enharmonic change alters the course of the consequent phrase, and leads to the dominant of F minor, instead of closing back in the tonic (Example 12).

Example 12. The transition into the second theme (bars 82-85).

This diversion to F minor seems to be temporary as the second subject returns in E♭ in bar 90. Furthermore, in bar 94-96, three bars missing from the recapitulation of the opening theme are now recalled. This rearrangement of the chronological sequence of musical ideas from the exposition places the second subject within a disjunct statement of the first. The re-establishment of E♭ over these bars, however, is not a structural return to the tonic.[6] Ultimately the tonicized F minor chord (II in the tonic key of E♭) in bar 86 is transformed into a second inversion F seventh chord that serves as an applied dominant to the B♭ chord in bar 98 (Example 13). The "omitted" part of the first theme in E♭, which is reinstated in bars 94-96, does not re-establish the tonic, but serves instead to prepare the E♭ of the F seventh chord of bar 97.[7]

With the subsequent resolution of the dissonant seventh, the C–B♭ neighbor-note idea recurs in the bass, but the B♭ chord in bar 98 does not represent the arrival on the dominant that leads back to tonic. As in the exposition, the expected resolution of this dominant chord is denied. Instead of resolving to the tonic, there is now a diversion to G♭, which ultimately leads to the augmented sixth chord in bar 105. In fact, the tonal motion

---

[6]Op. cit., pp.80–83. According to Schenker's analysis of this passage, the F minor statement of the second theme is an upper neighbor preceding its eventual arrival back in the tonic of E♭. This reading conforms to our expectations of the overall sonata design. Despite the formal logic of Schenker's reading, however, the F minor statement of the second theme is an event of far greater import than the return to tonic in bar 90. Its "interruption" of the tonal motion of the consequent phrase is highly significant, and merits greater recognition; far from functioning merely as a neighbor-note decoration, it is crucial to the movement's tonal structure.

[7]A similar voice-leading situation occurs at the recollection of the "new theme" of the development section in the coda of Beethoven's "Eroica" Symphony, bars 581–603.

Example 13. The second theme in the recapitulation (bars 86-98).

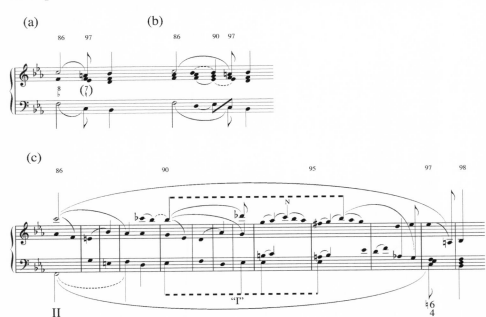

Example 14. Recapitulation (bars 84 - 108).

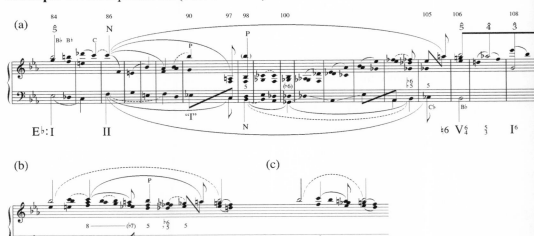

from bar 98 onwards parallels bars 27ff. of the exposition, but transposed down a fifth. As shown in Example 14, the B♭ chord in bar 98 serves to support a b♭² passing note, which connects a large-scale descending third motion in the top voice: c³ (supported by the F minor statement of the second theme) to a♮² (the top voice of the augmented sixth chord in bar 105). Only at the appearance of the cadential ⁶₄ in bar 106 does the true structural dominant finally appear. Like the corresponding point in the exposition, an

Example 15. The connection between bars 86 and 105.

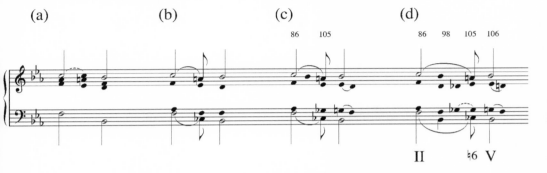

augmented sixth chord heralds the arrival of the structural dominant. Here, the C♭–B♭ bass motion in bars 105–6 not only answers the C♮–B♭ in the bass of bars 97–8, but recalls the conflict between C♮ (♮6̂) and C♭ (♭6̂) initially presented as early as bar 2.

Example 15 reveals the deep connection between the F minor statement of the second theme and the augmented sixth chord in bar 105. The notes which comprise the augmented sixth derive from chromatic inflections of the third (A♭ becoming A♮) and fifth (C♮ becoming C♭) of the II chord which forms the basis of the F minor second theme. In fact, the transformation of F minor into this structurally important augmented sixth recalls the very opening of the movement: the chromatic alterations of C♮ to C♭ and A♭ to A♮ in the II⁶₅ chord of bar 2 (see Example 1b). Incredibly, the same chromatic inflections that occurred in just one bar at the beginning of the movement have now been expanded over the course of twenty bars in the recapitulation.

The chromatic alterations of scale degrees 4̂ and 6̂ are echoed again at the end in the expansion of IV over bars 115–7 (Example 16). In terms of the movement's overall structure, it is this closing theme in the recapitulation that brings the work's fundamental melodic line to a close. Unlike most sonata-form structures that are defined by the technique of interruption, in this Andante movement 5̂ is retained throughout the exposition and

Example 16. the closing theme (bars 108 - 119).

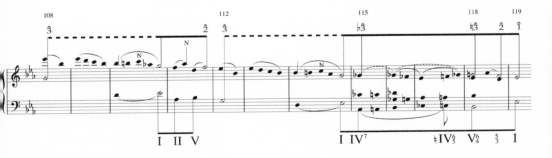

development before making its structural descent in the recapitulation.[8] The $\hat{4}$, which initiates the final melodic descent appears over the V^7 in bar 107, and at the appearance of the closing theme this dissonant seventh is resolved by the articulation of $\hat{3}$ in the bass.[9]

*   *   *   *   *

After the strife and pathos of the first movement, the Andante of this Symphony provides a welcome respite. Despite its tranquil atmosphere, however, the second theme projects a feeling of instability. In both the exposition and recapitulation, it appears initially as a stable key area, yet ultimately defers in structural significance to the closing theme. This changing meaning acts as a metaphor for the restlessness that undercuts the movement's stillness and calm, before the propulsive drive of the Minuetto and the feverish excitement of the last movement to come.

[8]Compare Schenker's reading of this movement, as well as the first movement, where $\hat{5}$ is prolonged through exposition and development before making a melodic descent in the recapitulation. See also Ernst Oster's extended footnote to the section on "Sonata Form" in Chapter 5 of *Der Freie Satz* (Vienna: Universal Edition, 1956); translated by Oster as *Free Composition* (New York: Longman, Inc, 1979), pp.139–41.
[9]For other examples where the fundamental melodic line descends in the bass voice, see my "Bass-line articulations of the Urlinie" in *Schenker Studies* 2, edited by Carl Schachter and Hedi Siegel (Cambridge: Cambridge University Press, 1999).

Motive and Motivation in Schubert's Three-Key Expositions

Deborah Kessler

The three-key exposition is a special type of sonata form by Schubert, one in which the exposition seems to have three key areas instead of the more usual two. The ensuing discussion focuses on two movements with three-key expositions, the first movements of Schubert's E♭-major Piano Trio, D. 929 and the B♭-major Piano Sonata, D. 960, and considers relationships involving Schubert's own songs and Beethoven's instrumental works with these movements.[1]

Schubert cultivated movements with "three-key expositions" throughout his career. His work in this area reached an apex in nine first movements from works written between 1824 and 1828, beginning with the Octet, D. 803 and ending with the B♭ Piano Sonata.[2] The expositions in these movements are difficult to understand in terms of the traditional binary paradigm developed by Adolph Bernhard Marx, in which two contrasting theme groups are aligned with two contrasting key areas.[3] In contrast to this paradigm, Schubert's three-key expositions often exhibit dissociation between thematic and harmonic alignment. In these pieces the middle key area is sharply defined by a memorable theme that contrasts dramatically with the preceding first subject. Yet the local tonic of this second theme does not serve as the exposition's structural goal; its ephemeral nature is conveyed through an abrupt onset and short-lived prolongation. Conversely, the third key area is thematically formulaic, like closing material, yet its

---

[1]This article is a conflation of two papers. The first, "Motive and Motivation in Schubert's Three-Key Expositions," was given at the Third International Schenker Symposium," on March 13, 1999; the second, "A Tale of Two *Schichten*: Schachter and Schubert," was given at the Aaron Copland School of Music celebration in honor of Carl Schachter, on May 2, 1999. Both papers draw from my doctoral dissertation, *Schubert's Late Three-Key Expositions: Influence, Design, and Structure* (City University of New York, 1996). Carl Schachter was my dissertation adviser.

[2]The other examples are from the D-minor Quartet, D. 810 (1824-1826); C-major Piano Sonata (four hands), "Grand Duo," D. 812 (1824); the unfinished C-major Piano Sonata, *Reliquie,* D. 840 (1825); the C-major Symphony, "Great," D. 944 (1825-1828); the Piano Allegro (four hands), *Lebensstürme,* D. 947 (1828); and the C-major String Quintet, D. 956 (1828).

[3]See Adolph Bernhard Marx, *Die Lehre von der musikalischen Komposition, praktisch-theoretisch,* 5th (unaltered) ed., Vol. 3 (Leipzig: Breitkopf u. Härtel, 1879), p. 282. See also Birgitte Plesner Vinding Moyer, *Concepts of Musical Form in the Nineteenth Century, with Special Reference to A. B. Marx and Sonata Form* (Ph.D. dissertation: Stanford University, 1969), pp. 112-113; and my Ph.D. dissertation, *Schubert's Late Three-Key Expositions,* pp. 10-13.

local tonic *does* serve as the structural goal of the exposition: it firmly establishes and prolongs the background dominant. In short, the middle key area is emphasized by design, whereas the third key area is emphasized through its structural role.[4]

Many of Schubert's movements with three-key expositions involve extensive motivic use of $\hat{5}$–$\flat\hat{6}$–$\hat{5}$ neighbor-note motion, and they are tonally structured around dramatic contrasts that relate to this motive. The motivic exploitation in these works relates to similar procedures found in various Schubert lieder, many of which also explore the structural and expressive role of the upper neighbor $\flat\hat{6}$. In a number of these songs, the $\hat{5}$–$\flat\hat{6}$–$\hat{5}$ neighbor motion is found in passages that evoke the supernatural and death and that contrast present misery with past happiness.[5] The compelling use of this motive in Schubert's songs can in turn help provide insight into the three-key exposition.

The first movement of the D-minor Quartet is revelatory because it presents a direct transferal from a Schubert song into one of his movements with three-key expositions. Not only does Schubert's song "Der Tod und das Mädchen," D. 531, provide the theme for the variation movement of this quartet, but it also informs the deep structure of the first movement.

---

[4]Sources on Schubert's three-key expositions include David Beach, "Harmony and Linear Progression in Schubert's Music," *Journal of Music Theory* 38/1 (Spring 1994), pp. 1-20; Richard L. Cohn, "As Wonderful as Star Clusters: Instruments for Gazing at Tonality in Schubert," *Nineteenth Century Music* 22/3 (Spring 1999), pp. 213-32; Mi-Sook Han Hur, *Irregular Recapitulation in Schubert's Instrumental Works* (Ph.D. dissertation: City University of New York, 1992); Irene Montefiore Levenson, *Motivic-Harmonic Transfer in the Late Works of Schubert: Chromaticism in Large and Small Spans* (Ph.D. dissertation: Yale University, 1981); Charles Rosen, *Sonata Forms*, rev. ed. (New York: W. W. Norton, 1988); Felix Salzer, "Die Sonatenform bei Franz Schubert," in *Studien zur Musikwissenschaft*, ed. Guido Adler, Vol. 15 (Vienna: Universal-Edition, 1928), pp. 86–125; Carl Schachter, "The First Movement of Brahms's Second Symphony: The Opening Theme and its Consequences," *Music Analysis* 2/1 (March 1983), pp. 55–68; and James Webster, "Schubert's Sonata Form and Brahms's First Maturity," Parts 1 & 2, *Nineteenth Century Music* 2 (July 1978), pp. 18–35; 3 (July 1979), pp. 52–71.

[5]See Eytan Agmon, "Music and Text in Schubert Songs: The Role of Enharmonic Equivalence," *Israel Studies in Musicology,* Vol. 3, ed. Roger Kamien (Jerusalem: Israel Musicological Society, 1987), pp. 49–58; Charles Burkhart, "Schenker's Motivic Parallelisms," *Journal of Music Theory* 22/2 (Fall 1978), pp. 145–75; Steven Laitz, "The Submediant Complex: Its Musical and Poetic Roles in Schubert's Songs," *Theory and Practice* 21 (1996), pp. 123–59; Walter Everett, "Grief in *Winterreise*: A Schenkerian Perspective," *Music Analysis* 9/2 (July 1990), pp.157–75; Oswald Jonas, *Introduction to the Theory of Heinrich Schenker [Einführung in die Lehre Heinrich Schenkers]*, trans. & ed. John Rothgeb (New York: Longman Inc., 1982); and Carl Schachter, "Motive and Text in Four Schubert Songs," in *Aspects of Schenkerian Theory,* ed. David Beach (New Haven: Yale University Press, 1983), pp. 61–76.

Felix Salzer, in his 1928 essay (cited in n. 4), indirectly points to the relevance of vocal models to Schubert's instrumental movements. Here Salzer finds Schubert's instrumental movements, including those with three-key expositions, to be flawed because of their lyrical nature, holding that the use of song-form construction in these works causes static expansion rather than creating the dynamic improvisatory style characteristic of great instrumental pieces. Salzer later came to view Schubert's instrumental output more positively.

As shown in Example 1, the bass line of the song's first section, in which the Maiden begs Death to spare her, outlines the tonic triad, D–F–A; the bass line of the second section, in which Death persuades his conquest, is a descent: D–B♭–A–D. Embedded in Death's bass line is the half step from ♭6̂ to 5̂, a lament motive that, as Carl Schachter has shown, saturates the entire song.[6] Significantly, the exposition and recapitulation of the quartet movement mirror the structure of the sections of the song devoted to the Maiden and to Death, respectively. As may be seen in Example 2a, the bass line of the exposition travels the same path as the Maiden's. This correspondence underlies the exposition's "extra" key area, resulting in the exposition's "three-key" plan, with the F-major key area providing a striking respite from the surrounding minor tonic and dominant areas. The bass line of the recapitulation, on the other hand, traverses Death's bass-line journey (Example 2b). Although the "death-related" motion from B♭ to A is found throughout the movement, this semitone descent is especially prominent in the recapitulation, where it governs the large-scale tonal motion.

Example 1. Schubert, "Der Tod und das Mädchen," D. 531 (Op. 7, No. 3).

(a)   Bars 1-19, the Maiden's plea.

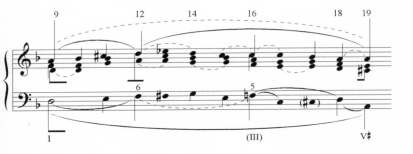

(b)   Bars 22-37, Death's reply.

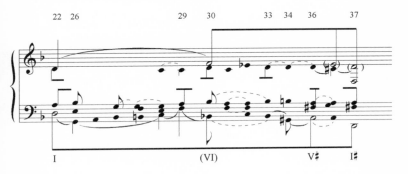

[6]Carl Schachter discusses this lament motive in "Motive and Text in Four Schubert Songs," pp. 67–70. The association between various versions of this motive and death is explored by William Kimmel in "The Phrygian Inflection and the Appearances of Death in Music," *College Music Symposium* 20/2 (1980), pp. 42–76.

Example 2,

(a) Bars 1-134.

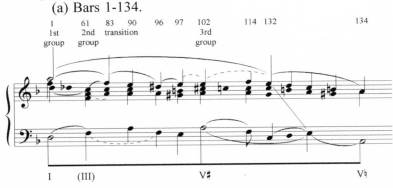

(b) Bars 198-292.

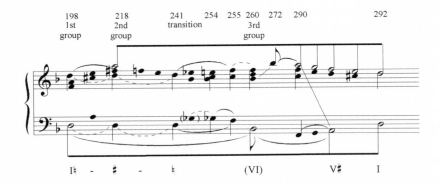

Elements seen in the first movement of the D-minor Quartet continue to be found in Schubert's later works that have three-key expositions. In particular, (♭)6̂ continues to play an important role in these later compositions. However, whereas ♭6̂ was most prominent in the recapitulation of the Death and the Maiden Quartet, in certain later works the structural function of ♭6̂ is more directly manifest in the exposition.[7] Furthermore, the lyrical element exerts an influence in these later works as well, much as was seen in the D-minor Quartet. Yet the relation to specific songs by Schubert is less direct in these later compositions, which exhibit the increasing influence of Beethoven.

---

[7]The use of 6̂ as a structural element within a three-key exposition is featured in the first movement of Schubert's Octet, a work which was composed in 1824, close to the time that Schubert began composition of the D-minor Quartet. The three key areas in the Octet movement are F major, D minor, and C major; in this major-mode exposition, diatonic 6̂ provides the minor-key dramatic contrast with the surrounding major-mode tonic and dominant areas. At times in the Octet, ♭6̂ plays an important and magical role as a foil for ♮6̂, but its structural role is limited.

For an overview of Schubert's three-key expositions with regard to the role of (♭)6̂, see my dissertation, *Schubert's Late Three-Key Expositions*, pp. 404–9; see also Mi-Sook Han Hur's dissertation, *Irregular Recapitulation in Schubert's Instrumental Works*.

The E-flat Piano Trio, D. 929

All of these features may be seen in the first movement of the E♭ Piano Trio, a work which represents a dramatic evolution in Schubert's development of the three-key exposition. Here ♭VI♭ is prolonged in the middle key area of the exposition. And this striking feature appears to result not only from the influence of Schubert's songs, but even more from the influence of Beethoven's instrumental music, in particular from the first movement of Piano Concerto No. 5, the "Emperor."

Certainly the kinship between these movements is easily apprehended through surface similarities. For example, the Concerto's introductory gesture and the expositions in both works begin with majestic arpeggiations of E♭ major, and both principal themes feature double-neighbor motion and highlight C♮ as upper neighbor to B♭. But further comparison, involving the Concerto's solo exposition and the Trio's exposition, yields the most important similarity: both principal themes, after culminating in scalar outbursts, collapse into hushed C♭-minor processionals (see bars 144ff. in the Concerto and bars 44ff. in the Trio). The ensuing unstable middle groups provide the main source of dramatic contrast in their respective movements and highlight the importance of ♭VI, so that both expositions feature the apparent "three-key" plan E♭–C♭–B♭.[8]

The dimensions of the Trio's exposition are gargantuan and its form is difficult to pin down. I locate the exposition's three large sections as follows: the principal group (bars 1–48), the middle group (bars 48–116), and the dominant group (bars 116–86). But a series of motions toward a structural dominant by means of various thematic transformations counteracts this segmentation into large formal blocks. Typically, the quest to achieve the dominant B♭ is disrupted by a foray into the domain of $\hat{6}$ (either ♭$\hat{6}$ or ♮$\hat{6}$). These disruptions are composed out through 5–(♭6)–5 motions. The resulting upper-neighbor motive itself derives from the double-neighbor figure $\hat{5}$–(♭)$\hat{6}$–$\hat{4}$–$\hat{5}$, which is stated at the beginning of the movement and figures prominently in subsequent thematic transformations and in the movement as a whole. In the exposition, the double-neighbor motive informs thematic design, while the shorter upper-neighbor figure associated with 5–♭6–5 motions informs structure.

The melodic insistence on B♭ and the double-neighbor motive throughout the exposition is suggested by the thematic listing in Example 3. The double-neighbor motive is enshrined in the opening motto (3a); the principal group's transformations of this motto (3b–d) show how the double-neighbor figure, often in conjunction with motion through a third, shapes these themes.

---

[8]Notwithstanding their close relationship, the two expositions do not exhibit identical tonal structures. For a fuller discussion of the relationship between Beethoven's "Emperor" Concerto and Schubert's E♭ Trio, see my previously cited dissertation, pp. 187–207.

Example 3.

(a)

(b)

(c)

(d)

(e)

(f)

(g)

(h)

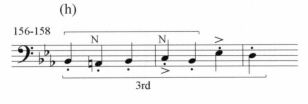

The structural expressions of the $\hat{5}$–$\flat\hat{6}$–$\hat{5}$ motive within the principal group occur within the sphere of the dominant. The motive is activated with repeated motions to a provisional V that is derailed by motion to G♭. Asterisks in Example 4 point to these derailments, which involve $\hat{5}$–$\flat\hat{6}$–$\hat{5}$ motions above B♭ (F–G♭–F). The first move to V occurs with the semicadence in bar 15 and the cello's "false second theme" of bars 16–23 (3b).[9] The prolongation of V here is disrupted by the loud G♭ chord in bar 24 (3c; first asterisk in Example 4). Following the principal group's surprising return to the tonic E♭ in bar 32, there are landings on B♭ in bars 34 and 40; these are again disrupted by G♭ in bars 38 and 44 (3d; second and third asterisks in Example 4). The last G♭, mutated into F♯, assumes the role of $\hat{5}$, ultimately leading to the middle group and the onset of B minor (in Example 4, this F♯ is represented as an inner voice).

Example 4.

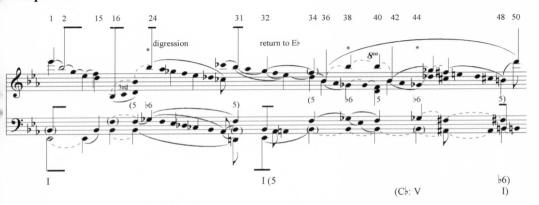

Example 4 shows that, from a broader perspective, the 5–♭6 motions in the principal group occur on two levels: at the foreground, allusions to G♭ form 5–♭6 motions in the sphere of B♭; on a deeper level, the motion to B minor in bar 48 forms a 5–♭6 motion above the tonic E♭. The latter motion underlies the exposition's progress from its principal group to its middle group.

The abrupt arrival at B minor (♭VI♭ in the sphere of the tonic) is the exposition's first large-scale derailment of V, and the adversity suggested by this event is dramatized through the modal shift from major to minor. The contrasting group's ensuing meanderings in search of the thwarted dominant feature repetitive circular gestures with modal shifts, as though portraying a bad dream from which the lost protagonist looks for a way out.

Despite the dramatic arrival of the new B-minor theme at bar 48, the tonic E♭ continues to hold sway throughout the middle group (Example 5).

---

[9] In a Classical movement, the cello's melody might initiate the dominant group of a "bifocal" exposition. See Robert Winter, "The Bifocal Close and the Evolution of the Viennese Classical Style," *Journal of the American Musicological Society* 42/2 (Summer 1989), pp. 275–337.

This may not be apprehended immediately, because the bass line seems to set off from B minor through an apparent inverted arch forged by thirds (B♮–G–E♭–C–E♭–G–B♭) that appears to lead from B♮ down to C and back up to B♭. But the persistent touchdowns of E♭ in bars 66 and 75 suggest that the arrival of B minor in bar 48 and the allusion to C♯ minor in bar 67 arise from 5–(♭)6 motions above E♭. Thus the first and middle groups together move from I to V within the sphere of the tonic, landing on V (bar 84) in the way that a principal theme would end in a "bifocal" exposition.

Example 5.

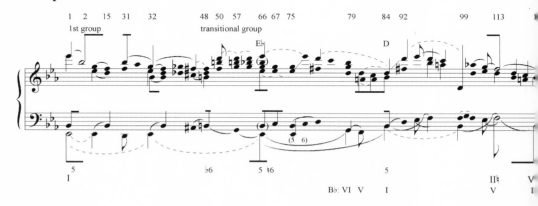

But the struggle to reach structural V continues. After the middle group ends on V in bar 84, there are three more significant arrivals at V in bars 99, 116, and 140, each of which might be considered as structural V and the beginning of the dominant group. As shown in Example 6, I interpret the material following bars 84 and 99 as increasingly desperate attempts to establish a structural dominant that is only achieved with the *Seitensatz*-like cello theme at bar 116; the theme at bar 140 is a codetta. Although the dominant group does not feature ♭6 harmonically, its melodies (Example 3f–h) continue to highlight B♭ and its neighbor notes on the local level. Through these local motives, the 5̂–(♭6̂)–5̂ relationship (with reference to the movement's E♭ tonic) remains active.

Example 6.

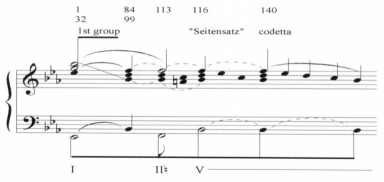

The full potential of ♭6̂ as a threat to V is unleashed with the onset of the development. The juxtaposition of the B♭ at the end of the exposition with the C♭ at the beginning of the development section recreates the B♭–C♭ connection of the principal and middle groups of the exposition. The development is formed mostly from three enormous blocks: the first section in B/C♭ (bars 195–247) is transposed to F♯/G♭ (bars 247–99) and D♭ (bars 299–337), forming an apparent trajectory of ascending fifths (Example 7).

Example 7.

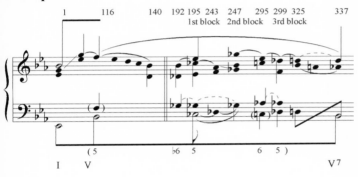

Example 8 shows the first of these three large blocks, each of which recalls the middle group of the exposition in its labored and sectionalized meanderings. Each block recasts the exposition's codetta theme (Example 3g): first in its original chordal guise; then in a rhapsodic continuation featuring sudden shifts from minor to major and leading in the bass through two minor thirds; and then with imitative entries leading in the bass through the four ascending thirds of a "V9." But whereas the first two blocks end with a common-tone diminished-seventh chord and a cadence leading to the next section, the last block departs from this model. This third transposed block, rather than leading to the expected common-tone diminished-seventh chord on A♭, moves toward D minor (third above B♭) and the sphere of the structural V.

Example 8.

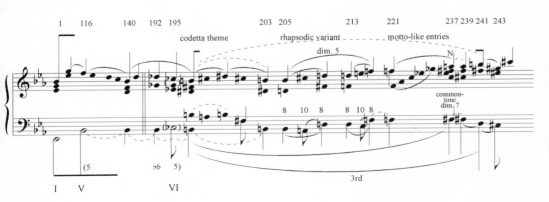

Comparing Example 7 with the music, one sees that the apparent trajectory of ascending fifths formed by the three transposed blocks (beginning with bars 195, 247, and 299) fleshes out a stepwise motion from Cb to Db. These fifths participate in a series of 5–(b)6 motions that embellish a larger stepwise ascent from Bb (end of the exposition) through Cb (beginning of the development) and Db (beginning of the third transposed block) to Db (before the retransition). From a deep middleground perspective, the D-minor prolongation preceding the retransition constitutes an inner voice. The Cb at the onset of the development, however, is a true bass tone, and as such forms a large-scale neighbor to the framing dominants at the ends of the exposition and the development. The neighbor-note motive 5̂–b6̂–5̂ is thus granted large-scale structural status in the development.

The retransition hammers home Cb's essential role in the development section. In bars 337–84, Bb is repeatedly embellished by Cb (together with Ab or A♮). The emphasis on Cb rather than C♮ here produces an edgy and tension-ridden structural dominant, making the arrival of Eb major in the recapitulation seem an even greater victory.

Cb does not figure prominently in the recapitulation. Much of the recapitulation prolongs the subdominant, thus granting structural status to Bb's lower neighbor, the other member of the double-neighbor motive. As part of this subdominant prolongation, the middle group of the recapitulation begins on E /Fb, a fifth below its counterpart in the exposition and the upper neighbor to the tonic. But in the final domain of the structural tonic, Cb asserts itself more and more as the movement tries to close. After reaching a point analogous to the exposition's final cadence, the recapitulation's codetta opens out into an expansion of Cb as bass support for an augmented-sixth chord (bars 571–80) that drives toward the codetta's close. Cb/B♮ appears in the coda, in bars 596–8. Although the movement closes with a jubilant return of the principal theme in Eb major, a chromatic voice exchange from Ab to A♮ and C♮ to Cb (bars 625–8) gives Cb final ascendancy over C♮.

The remarkable saturation of the first movement of the Eb Trio with b6̂ relates not only to practices of Beethoven, but also to motivic usage found in Schubert's songs. Suggestive in this regard is "Letzte Hoffnung" from Part II of *Winterreise*. This song, which is also in the key of Eb, was probably written in the summer of 1827, a few months before composition of the Eb Trio. In Müller's text, the protagonist pins his last hope upon an autumn leaf clinging to its tree; when the leaf falls, he confronts the death of his hope. Schubert's setting features neighbor notes b6̂ and 4̂ as tonal agents of this catastrophe. Both the piano introduction and the vocal line begin with Cb and Ab, unstable members of a diminished harmony that—requiring resolution to Bb—represent uncertainty and dread. Throughout the song the hero's vocal line tends to gravitate toward Bb from Cb or C♮.

In terms of large-scale bass motion, the song's first two stanzas, spanning bars 1–24, together outline the tonic triad Eb–G–Bb.[10] After the dominant

---

[10]This bass ascent is similar to the triadic ascent D-F-A in the Maiden's plea from "Der Tod und das Mädchen"; in both songs, the middle member of the tonic triad represents respite from death, while arrival at the dominant leads to dreaded resolution.

arrives in bar 19, the accompaniment's twitchings from B♭ to C♭ and A♮ mirrors the hero's trembling in the face of imminent disaster. The turn to E♭ minor in the final stanza (bar 26) signals the hero's tragic fate. His intonements of upper neighbor C♭ in bars 27 and 33, both setting the word "Boden" (ground), lead, with a precipitous decline in the accompaniment, to B♭ and a final apotheosis in the tonic major. Despite the song's poignant major-mode ending, the C♭ inexorably persists; it is not supplanted by the more expected C♮. Both the hero's final utterance and the accompaniment's closing gesture feature the motion from C♭ to B♭.

Significantly, this song demonstrates an association between grief and the descending half step in a *major-mode* context. It is true that at the moment of tragedy ("Ach, und fällt das Blatt zu Boden, fällt mit ihm die Hoffnung ab. . .") C♭ sounds within the context of E♭ minor (bars 25–30). But when the hero weeps for his lost hope at the end, the hero's resignation is conveyed by a poignant motion to E♭ major, with a C♮ that darkens to C♭ en route to B♭.

There have long been associations connecting ♭6̂ with grief and death or with entry into dreams and sleep.[11] In both associations, ♭6̂ represents realms remote from living or conscious experience. Perhaps, then, it is not entirely unreasonable to experience the arrival of the Trio's middle group as a nightmarish distancing from the desired path. Awakening from this chromatic minor-mode nightmare into diatonic major-mode reality (the achievement of V) here seems pleasant indeed. Certainly, the motion from a dark B minor (bar 48) to a sunny B♭ major (bar 84) in the Trio's first movement, while indirect, is joyous. In three-key expositions like that of the E♭ Trio, where the opening I (major) moves quite directly to ♭VI (minor), the adversity that might be associated with the underlying 5̂–♭6̂ motion above the tonic is palpable in the arrival to (rather than the exit from) the middle key area. Yet for me, in the Trio, the completion of the neighbor-note motive involving the drop from ♭6̂ to 5̂ does not eradicate the disturbing aura carried by ♭6̂.

The Piano Sonata in B♭ Major, D. 960

The great Piano Sonata in B♭ major was written in September 1828, only two months before Schubert's death. (Henceforth, allusions to the Sonata and Trio refer to the respective first movements of D. 960 and D. 929, unless otherwise indicated.) Unlike the heroic opening of the Trio, with its emphasis on 5̂, the Sonata begins with an elegiac hymn-like theme, which has a quiet stillness redolent of death. The Sonata's principal theme emphasizes 3̂, with its opening tones B♭–A–B♭–C–D; the lower-neighbor

---

[11]Regarding the association of the descent from ♭6̂ to 5̂ with grief and death , see Carl Schachter's previously cited article, "Motive and Text in Four Schubert Songs," p. 70. Regarding the association of sleep with ♭VI see J. H. Thomas, "A Subconscious Metaphor?" *The Music Review* 43/3-4 (August-November 1982), pp. 225–35; see also Carl Schachter's interpretation of "Nacht und Träume" in "Motive and Text in Four Schubert Songs," pp. 71–6.

motion and rising third therein form a motto-like configuration that shapes the rest of the movement.

Despite the B♭ Sonata's distinctive qualities, it resembles the E♭ Trio in its emphasis on ♭6̂ and the neighbor-note configuration 5̂–♭6̂–5̂ to which it belongs. In the Sonata, as in the Trio, ♭VI♭ is prolonged at the onset of the contrasting middle group; the respective middle groups in both recapitulations begin with ♭II♭. In this regard, the Sonata, like the Trio, seems indebted to Beethoven's "Emperor" Concerto.

In addition, Schubert's Sonata relates to three works in B♭ by Beethoven that seem to have a family relationship with one another: the Trio Op. 97, "Archduke," the Sonata Op. 106, "Hammerklavier," and the Quartet Op. 130. In the three first movements by Beethoven, as in Schubert's Sonata, the principal themes outline the third between B♭ and D in conjunction with a neighbor note. Furthermore, Beethoven's movements feature structural and motivic use of (♭)6̂: The first movement of Op. 130 prolongs G♭ (♭VI) in the exposition's second group, and the exposition's first and second endings close with implied F harmony, thus hinting at Schubert's three-key plan. Op. 97 and 106 each prolong G major (VI♮) in the second group of the exposition (F♯/G♭ and B♮ achieve tonicization in the Hammerklavier's restated principal group, bars 240–68), and both of these movements feature the conflict between G♮ and G♭.[12] Indeed, at the end of the "Hammerklavier" (bars 386ff.), G♭ supplants G♮ with obsessive F–G♭ alternations that, especially in their lower-register manifestations, seem a likely progenitor of Schubert's ominous bass trill.[13]

The formal layout of the exposition in Schubert's B♭ Sonata is clear: the principal group (bars 1–48), contrasting middle group (bars 48–80), and dominant group (bars 80–117/125) are marked in Example 9. As shown in Example 10, ternary organization also shapes the principal group; for in this exposition, ♭VI is prolonged as a middle key area *twice,* first as G♭ major within the principal group and second as F♯ minor at the onset of the contrasting middle group. Because of these major/minor prolongations of ♭VI, ♭VI seems to project a dual persona—a "Jekyll/ Hyde" identity. Nevertheless, comparison of Examples 9 and 10 shows that in both contexts, G♭ arises from 5̂–♭6̂ motion over the governing B♭ tonic.

The principal group comprises a virtual song form, whose three sections are a closed parallel period in B♭ (bars 1–18); a passage that prolongs G♭ (bars 20–36); and a recasting of the original consequent phrase (bars 36–

---

[12]This conflict surfaces in the retransition of the "Archduke" Trio (bars 170ff. ; see bars 205–15 in Schubert's retransition) and in the recapitulation of the "Hammerklavier" (bars 332–405).

[13]For more detailed discussion of Beethoven's three movements and their relationship to Schubert's Sonata, see my previously cited dissertation, pp. 284–310. For an analysis of the first movement of Beethoven's "Hammerklavier," see Roger Kamien, "Aspects of the Recapitulation in Beethoven Piano Sonatas," *The Music Forum*, Vol. 4, ed. Felix Salzer; assoc. ed., Carl Schachter; ed. asst., Hedi Siegel (New York: Columbia University Press, 1976), pp. 196–205.

Example 9.

Example 10.

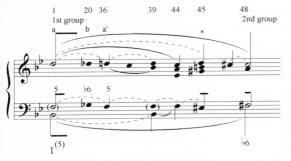

48).[14] In the parallel period's opening melody, the importance of 6̂ is not immediately apparent: it features the motto-like rise from B♭ to D, decoration of main-tone D by upper neighbor E♭ (bar 5), and the fall of D to C (bar 7). Scale-degree 6̂ (G♮) first enters unobtrusively in a subsidiary alto voice that connects B♭ to F (bar 4). But the introduction of ♭6̂ (G♭) in the bass is, by contrast, very obtrusive and justly famous: G♭ embellishes F in the sinister trill at the end of the theme's first phrase (bar 8). This trill recurs at crucial junctures: in the exposition's first ending, at the end of the development, and shortly before the end of the movement. Here the threatening aspect of G♭ and its role as upper neighbor to F are clearly etched.

The drop to G♭ at the onset of the principal group's middle section (bar 19) evokes the descent into a dreamlike state historically associated with the I–♭VI progression,[15] and the first phrase of the G♭ area (bars 20–7), a lovely recasting of the opening melody with an undulating accompaniment, is serene and lovely (Dr. Jekyll). But soon there is a gradual intensification, as the melody in the section's second phrase (bars 27–35) features progressively shorter rhythmic values within ever-shorter subphrases. At the end of this intensification, the G♭ triad is transformed into an augmented-sixth chord, with its powerful pull to F. The fulfillment of this imperative, through the direct bass-line descent from G♭ to F in bars 35–6, brings the

[14]See Salzer's essay (previously cited in n. 4), "Die Sonatenform bei Franz Schubert," pp. 99–100. See, also, Salzer's analysis and more favorable commentary on the Sonata's principal group in *Structural Hearing: Tonal Coherence in Music* (New York: Dover Publications, 1962) Vol. 1, pp. 183–5 and Vol. 2, pp. 161–4.

[15]See, for example, the article by J. H. Thomas previously cited in n. 11.

return of the opening B♭ melody, now over V, and reenacts the semitone descent introduced by the disturbing trill in bars 8–9. The onset of the principal group's third section, with its return to B♭-major harmony, brings a renewed sense of solemn grandeur—the turmoil associated with the motion to ♭VI minor is yet to come.

As in the E♭ Trio, the disruptive potential of ♭VI erupts with entry into the exposition's contrasting middle group. The approach to F♯(G♭) minor is a sudden and loud derailment accomplished by means of the pivotal diminished-seventh chord on E♯ in bars 45–7. As shown in Example 10, this chord is a connecting link in a larger 5–♭6 motion over B♭, from F through E♯ to F♯/G♭.

The turbulent new theme, in the tenor range, is a stepwise fall and rise from C♯ to F♯ and back. But this theme does not remain long in F♯ minor, for it gravitates to A major, momentarily in bar 52 and more seriously in bar 58. (This kind of instability is typical of Schubert's middle key areas.) As shown in Example 11, a tug of war ensues in the bass between A and F♯ that ends when F♮ supplants F♯ in bar 70: note the motions from A to F♯ and back in bars 58–66 and the pair of motions from A to F♮ in bars 67–70. Thus A mediates in a struggle between F♯ and F♮ that ends with the victory of F♮. In my interpretation, F♯/G♭ harmony governs the middle group until bar 70; the intervening A-major triad in bars 58–69, while persistent, represents an inner voice.

The belabored path leading to F♮ in bar 70 vanquishes F♯ but still does not bring the structural dominant. For the chord in bar 70, approached as a deceptive VI in the key of D minor, is immediately reassessed as a cadential $\frac{6}{4}$ in the key of B♭. This B♭ chord testifies to the continuing rule of the tonic; as in the exposition of the E♭ Trio, here the principal and contrasting groups together prolong I. Thus, the tonic's sphere continues into bars 72–3, where the inverted diminished-seventh chord, D–F–A♭–B♮ (a chromatically inflected I chord) completes a chromatic voice exchange originating from the Sonata's opening sonority.[16] The inflected tonic in bars 72–3 is enharmonically equivalent to the chord encountered in the approach to the middle group (Example 10, bars 45–7). But now, instead of leading to F♯/G♭ as it did in the earlier context, it leads to V of V in bars 74–9. The interpretation of an overriding tonic voice exchange spanning bars 1–72 is supported by the motivic emphasis accruing to the diminished-seventh chord B♮–D–F–A♭ (in addition to its pivotal role in bars 45–7 and 72–3, the diminished-seventh chord later plays a significant role in the second movement, in bars 62–6 and 82–5). The third between its bass and soprano tones D and B♮ (bar 73), related to the opening theme's rise from b♭¹ to d², is foretold in the principal group's afterphrase (d²–c²–b♮¹ in bar 14). Also, the extraordinary emphasis given to the V of V in bars 74–9 retroactively enhances the importance of the diminished harmony that precedes it.[17]

---

[16]Carl Schachter discusses a similar tonic chromatic voice exchange in "The First Movement of Brahms's Second Symphony: The Opening Theme and its Consequences," pp. 62–5.

[17]For alternative interpretations of this exposition, see Mi-Sook Han Hur, *Irregular Recapitulation in Schubert's Instrumental Works,* pp. 196–8; Richard Cohn, "As Wonderful as Star Clusters," pp. 222–5; and Peter Pesic, "Schubert's Dream," *Nineteenth* (cont.)

Example 11.

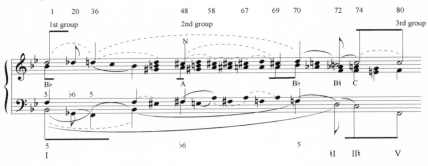

The F#-minor harmony of the contrasting middle group is of relatively humble structural status, subsumed within a larger tonic voice exchange. Yet the turn to F# minor not only permits Schubert's characteristic change in dramatic affect but has motivic ramifications. It makes possible a beautiful motivic parallelism, shown in Example 11: the middleground line b♭¹–a¹–b♭¹ ("alto" line, bars 1–70) joined with b♮¹–c² (the upper voice, bars 72–4) recasts the work's opening melodic gesture; the motion to F# minor (bar 48) provides B♭'s lower neighbor .

Neither the exposition's dominant group nor the development prolongs G♭ in a significant structural role. But the recapitulation does so most dramatically within its principal group. Remarkably, the restated principal group (bars 216–67) retains not only the ternary form it had in the exposition but also the key and design of the outer sections, which remain virtually intact, except for the very end of the final section. Comparison of Example 12 with Example 10 shows that despite harmonic changes to its middle section, the restated principal group also keeps much of the middleground it had in the exposition—its melodic profile, d^2–$d♭^2$/$c\#^2$–d^2 is imported intact and even the large bass motion remains closely related until the very end of the group. The recomposed middle section (bars 235–55) begins in G♭ major and for four bars remains faithful to its analogue; the sudden turn to minor in bar 239 is graphically represented by the juxtaposition of G♭ and F#. This notational enharmonic switch dramatizes the essential unity of "Jekyll" (G♭ major, in the exposition the key of the principal group's lovely middle section) and "Hyde" (F# minor, in the exposition the key of the dark second theme). Yet the turn to F# minor is brief; the bass ascent of a minor third in bar 240 leads from F# minor to A major. From bars 241–54 , the

Century Music 23/2 (Fall 1999), pp.136–44. Mi-Sook Han Hur's large-scale reading of the exposition, in which the chromatic voice exchange governs bars 1-72 of the exposition, is the same as mine; she credits Carl Schachter and Charles Burkhart for her interpretation. Cohn presents an analysis that is premised on a theory of voice leading efficiency, i.e., by semitone; this voice leading is derived from cycles of "major thirds" in conjunction with modal shift. Peter Pesic's analysis rests upon a circle of sixths construct. His observations regarding the significance of ♭VI in Schubert's works derive in part from a verbal document by Schubert, "Mein Traum." While his analysis of the B♭ Sonata differs from mine, his description of the Sonata's F#-minor theme as "a lonely duet over the abyss" and many of his remarks on the meaning of ♭VI in Schubert's works harmonize well with my findings.

recapitulated material is thematically identical to its counterpart in the exposition but is transposed a minor third (augmented second) higher. The A⁷ chord of bars 253–4, a potential augmented sixth spelled as V⁷ of D, moves deceptively to VI of D—that is, to the tonic B♭—thus leading into the reprise of the group's last section.

Example 12.

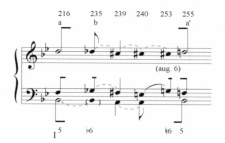

The middle section of the principal group in the recapitulation and the exposition's contrasting middle group are strongly related; certainly the harmonic motions from F♯ minor to A major and from A to B♭ in the middle of the recapitulated principal group recall the expressive and harmonic content of the second group up to bar 70 (compare Examples 11 and 12).[18] From a broader perspective, the restated principal group as a whole almost summarizes, by means of a splicing process, key events of the exposition's principal and second groups. This splicing process simply omits the return to B♭ as it occurs in bars 36/39.

Examples 11 and 12 show different interpretations regarding the relative structural weight of G♭/F♯ (bars 48 and 235/239) and A (bars 58 and 240). In the exposition's second group, the B♭ harmony of bar 70 is in second inversion, suggesting F♮ as local governing bass tone. And, as indicated earlier, I believe that the F♯ of bar 48 moves to the F♮ of bar 70, thus surpassing the intervening A-major harmony in structural importance. (Note the high tessitura of A in bars 58ff.) In the later passage, the B♭ harmony of bar 255 is in root position. This root-position tonic does not necessitate but seems to suggest the other choice, shown in Example 12: G♭/F♯, as upper neighbor to F♮ forms a 5–♭6 motion above B♭, while A♮, as lower neighbor to bass B♭ itself, outranks inner-voice embellishment F♯. (Note the low tessitura of A in bars 239ff.) The inner-voice line above B♭ continues when G♭/F♯ rises to G♮ and falls back to F♮ (coinciding with the return of tonic harmony). Subsequently, the dangerous power of G♭/F♯ seems to be safely subordinated. Yet G♭'s power reerupts at the bitter end with the ominous trill's final iteration in bars 352–3.

The striking prominence of ♭6̂ in the principal group of the first movement of the B♭ Piano Sonata relates strongly to similar prominence in Schubert's

[18]This relationship is also noted by Mi-Sook Han Hur, *Irregular Recapitulations in Schubert's Instrumental Music,"* pp. 212–3, and Richard Cohn, "As Wonderful as Star Clusters," pp. 228–30.

song "Ihr Bild" from *Schwanengesang, D. 957*. The song, in B♭ minor, was written a month before the Sonata, in August 1828. The respective opening phrases of the Sonata and song are melodically related through the opening upbeat, the outlining of the third î–(♭)3̂, and the embellishment of î by its lower neighbor. Also, "Ihr Bild," like the Sonata's principal group, is in ternary form.

Framed by a chilling introduction (two bare octave intonements of B♭) and postlude, each of its three main sections sets a stanza of Heine's text depicting a despairing lover who contemplates the image of his lost love. The song's outer sections (bars 1–14 and 24–36) move from B♭ minor to B♭ major as the protagonist's mood shifts from grief to joyful remembrance or poignant acknowledgment. As Carl Schachter has noted, these outer sections feature descents of a fourth from B♭ to F; embedded within these descents are motions from G or G♭ down to F.[19] The first such descent, in the bass line of bars 1–8, results in a familiar bass oscillation between G♭ and F. The local relationship between this oscillation and the sinister trill in Schubert's B♭ Sonata is unmistakable and has been acknowledged by other authors.[20]

In "Ihr Bild," as in Schubert's B♭ Sonata, ♭6̂ has a dual identity: G♭ embodies both dreamlike and threatening personas. Thus the song's middle section (bars 15–24), like the middle of the Sonata's principal group, prolongs lovely G♭-major harmony. In "Ihr Bild," this prolongation projects the protagonist's memory of happier times. Although the song's G♭-major prolongation conveys emotional relief, the relief is only momentary; as in "Der Tod und das Mädchen," ♭VI inevitably moves to V in a large progression associated with death.

Carl Schachter's Influence

Now for the "background" of this essay—namely, how my studies with Carl Schachter allowed me to look for structural affinities between Schubert's three-key expositions, Schubert's songs, and Beethoven's instrumental works. And so I will focus on an aspect of my teacher's work that is crucial to me, that is, his interest in music as human expression.

His analyses are inherently dramatic, uncovering breathtaking musical dramas. They often follow the evolution of a particular motive; within this evolution there may be a dualistic struggle between diatonic and chromatic variants of a special scale degree or between enharmonic spellings of one pitch. When the

---

[19] See Carl Schachter, "Structure as Foreground: 'Das Drama des Ursatzes,'" in *Schenker Studies 2*, ed. Carl Schachter and Hedi Siegel (Cambridge: Cambridge University Press, 1999), pp. 299–303. See also Heinrich Schenker's detailed analysis of "Ihr Bild" in *Der Tonwille* I (Vienna: A. Gutmann Verlag, 1921; reprint, Universal-Edition).

[20] See Joseph Kerman, "A Romantic Detail in Schubert's *Schwanengesang*," *The Musical Quarterly* 48 (1962), p. 46, reprinted in *Schubert: Critical and Analytical Studies*, ed. Walter Frisch (Lincoln: University of Nebraska Press, 1986), p. 59. See also John Reed, *The Schubert Song Companion* (London: Faber and Faber, 1993), p. 261.

music is texted, then his analyses show how the composing-out of the musical drama parallels and supports the more concrete human drama.[21] His analyses of instrumental works may also attach a dramatic significance to musical events. Such analyses may be found not only in his discussions of programmatic works but in his discussions of "absolute music" as well. [22]

In this essay, I have tried to show how Carl Schachter's approach informed my understanding of Schubert. It was his analysis of "Der Tod und das Mädchen" that set me to wondering whether the lament motive from ♭6 to 5 might give life to the first movement of Schubert's D-minor Quartet and to other three-key expositions by Schubert. The idea that, even in an instrumental work, a prominent motive with structural ramifications might have narrative and expressive content was not unthinkable. And even the far less controversial idea that one composer might be influenced by another acknowledges the human dimension of musical creation. When I first suggested the relationship between Beethoven's "Emperor" and Schubert's E♭ Trio, Carl called my attention to a possible musical "grandparent," C. P. E. Bach's Fantasia in E♭, W. 58. As long as his students retained their rapport with the music, he would give consideration to their poetic musings.

This brings me to some final thoughts, the deep background. All of us who know Carl Schachter know that he is a humanist in every sense. His concern with human experience extends well beyond its role in musical masterpieces and his analyses of them. For he is a most devoted teacher who nurtures his students with lavish gifts of time, attention, and support. I will forever consider myself to be one of the most privileged people to be the recipient of these gifts.

---

[21]See, for example, Carl Schachter, "The Adventures of an F♯: Tonal Narration and Exhortation in Donna Anna's First-Act Recitative and Aria," *Theory and Practice* 16 (1991), pp. 5–20; this article and those cited below are reprinted in Carl Schachter, *Unfoldings: Essays in Schenkerian Theory and Analysis,* ed. Joseph N. Straus (New York: Oxford University Press, 1999). See also Carl Schachter, "Motive and Text in Four Schubert Songs."

[22]See Carl Schachter, "The Triad as Place and Action," *Music Theory Spectrum* 17/2 (1995), pp. 149–69, especially pp. 150–2 and 158–69.

VII — Tributes and Reminiscences

As was the case with most of us, Carl Schachter's early studies were in the field of performance. In Chicago, where he grew up, he studied piano and violin. In the summer of 1948, not yet graduated from high school, he came to New York to attend the master classes of the brilliant pianist and musician Carl Friedberg; in the fall of the same year he began his studies with the famous (or perhaps infamous) pedagogue Isabel Vengerova. A horrifying but entertaining account of his studies with her can be found in Carl's own contribution to *Beloved Tyranna*, a collection of reminiscences by some of her former students. If Vengerova's teaching was in many ways destructive, it did have one positive side for Schachter: it lead to his connection with Mannes and thereby to Schenker. During his time at Mannes he also studied conducting with Carl Bamberger, and some time after freeing himself from Vengerova he took additional piano lessons with Israel Citkowitz.

Although Carl's professional career was in theory and Schenkerian analysis, his interest and involvement in performance never left him. When I studied with him in the late 60's, he went to all of Arthur Rubinstein's concerts along with those of other famous artists and, of course, went to many of the student recitals at Mannes. And not just Mannes: when I played the Goldberg Variations at Juilliard for the first time, he came; from his comments afterward I began to get some indication of what he had to offer as a teacher and critic of performance. The range of what he heard and thought was truly remarkable. Not only were there observations that grew out of his exceptional analytical skills, but also insights into piano technique (both in the mechanical sense and in relation to interpretation), sound (subtle, imaginative), tempo, and rhythm. After that, playing for him became an important part of my life.

Most of the time Schachter's work in other areas kept him away from doing any performing himself. For many years there were his duties as Dean of Mannes, and there was the writing: *Counterpoint in Composition* with Salzer, the rhythm articles for *The Music Forum*, and later *Harmony and Voice Leading*. There were some breaks, however. In the early-mid 70's he returned to conducting, and gave two superb concerts with chamber orchestra devoted to Haydn and Mozart. I remember Felix Salzer expressing concern that conducting would take Schachter away from his analytical and theoretical work, but there were those of us who would have been very happy had there been more of these wonderful events. In any case the pressures of writing and teaching made it necessary for him to abandon his conducting. It may have been a kind of compensation for not conducting that he later took on the organization of the series of annual benefit concerts for Amnesty International, concerts that continue to this day.

But perhaps the most important expression of Schachter's background in performance is his playing in class, his elegant pianism beautifully illustrating his insights into the music. His skill at the piano is an important part of his more public presentations as well. Eloquent demonstrations of the Scherzo from the Schubert B♭ Sonata, several Mendelssohn Songs Without Words, Chopin's Fantasy and F♯ major Impromptu come to mind, along with expert renderings from orchestral and vocal literature. Whenever I heard him, I was always struck by the naturalness of his playing, both physically and musically as well as by the lack of pretension. Nonetheless, in the late 60's and early 70's a certain conscious virtuosity showed itself in his stunning renditions of Mozart's K. 545 and the development section of Beethoven Op. 14 no.1, both which he performed standing with his back to the piano!

Carl's unusual combination of abilities in the fields of performance, Schenkerian analysis, and pedagogy led naturally to his creating a class in analysis for performers. This class has gone on for many years at Mannes and is currently a one-year course for students in the Master's Degree program. It was given throughout Schachter's professorship at Queens College and is now a one-semester required course in the doctoral program at Juilliard. Not surprisingly many of the students in these classes have sought coaching from him, coachings that have covered quite a range: piano, strings, voice, and all manner of ensembles, including guitar and brass.

The intensity and breadth of Schachter's involvement in performance calls to mind that of Heinrich Schenker. In his early days Schenker performed; throughout his lifetime he taught piano and his diaries are filled with comments on performances he had heard. His treatise *The Art of Performance* (Oxford: Oxford Univ. Press, 2000) has recently been published. The work is incomplete, almost certainly because Schenker felt his projects in analysis had to be given priority. Once Carl's book on Analysis for Performers is finished, we will have a book which could not only bring about a big change in the way performers approach their work, but also provide a valuable continuation of what Schenker had to leave undone.

—Edward Aldwell, pianist

* * * *

I had met Carl in April, 1964, when I started working in the development office at the Mannes College of Music. He had been the Dean of the College for two years, and also taught twelve hours of theory and analysis each week. My first impression and most distinct memory of Carl is of his delicious sense of humor and his virtuosity in telling a story. And his phenomenal ear, whose brilliance was not restricted to music. He would fall silent at dinner and one would realize that he was listening to a conversation two tables away. His ear for accented and inflections of particular voices was incredible. One need never have met the famed Mme. Vengerova to experience her terror, or the inner hilarity of some of her pupils.

Carl had been working with Felix Salzer on a text of counterpoint that would include Schenkerian insights. McGraw-Hill had become interested in publishing the book, but informed the authors it would be much too expensive to produce: it would have to be published in one volume, instead of the boxed two-volume edition planned. Though miffed, the authors did cut the text, taking the opportunity to rewrite it while doing so and thus, in their opinion, making it a better text. The completed book *Counterpoint in Composition*, was published in 1969 to immediate and enduring success.

During the next several years Carl's reputation was slowly building. Twice he taught a course at Hunter as a visiting professor, and also taught as a visiting professor at SUNY Binghamaton. In 1971 he was offered a tenured position at Binghamton, followed by a similar offer from Queens College, CUNY. Ultimately he chose to stay in New York and accept the Queens position, which would mean that he would take Dr. Salzer's place in the music faculty the following year when Dr. Salzer would retire. His choice was due partly to his wish to remain in New York City, where he had lived since he was a senior in high school, and partly because he wished to continue his teaching and long-standing connection with Mannes.

After the counterpoint book was published, Carl and Ed Aldwell had discussed writing a possible harmony text. Probably nothing would have come of this, except that Carl was on jury dury early in the summer of 1973. Sitting in the jury room for two weeks, he started to sketch out a workbook for elementary harmony and voice leading—and he and Ed continued to work on it during the summer. McGraw-Hill had an option on the book, but they felt that the book was too expensive and would take too long to recoup their investment, so Carl and Ed went to Harcourt Brace Jovanovich, who published the book—*Harmony and Voice Leading*—in 1979 (subsequent revised editions have since appeared in 1989 and 2003).

—Gretchen Clumpner

* * * *

I was eight years old when Carl Schachter was born. We grew up in the central western area of Chicago called Austin. Carl's brother Jerry was my peer and initially we didn't pay much attention to baby Carl.

My first vivid memory of Carl was when he was about seven years old and was becoming a legend around Austin. His I.Q. had "broken the machine" and his prodigious attention to music was very evident. I was already playing some advanced pieces and young Herk would sit next to the piano giving my performances a remarkably intense concentration for a child his age.

Yes, "Herk" was Carl's nickname! When Jerry saw his baby brother for the first time, he said "he's as big and strong as Hercules." So, to this day, his relatives and I still call him Herk. And I still get messages on my answering machine saying "It's Herk."

Hercules is an apt name for this remarkable man who has had such a powerful a magnificent influence on so many young musicians.

—Marshall Izen

* * * *

In the early 60s, Mannes College of Music suffered the attrition of a succession of senior administrators. Felix Salzer, having with Leopold Mannes established the Bachelors program at Mannes, migrated to Queens College. His intended successor died very suddenly. Leopold Mannes, in one of the last acts of his abruptly curtailed life, had the foresight and wisdom to appoint Carl, the *junior* member of our executive committee, as the Dean: Carl was not yet 29. Carl's youth and brilliance inspired us, his intelligence, sense of responsibility, administrative abilities, his sense of respect—not only for the school's traditions, but also for his colleagues— and above all his integrity inspired confidence and trust in all of us. Carl set us on the path to becoming the current Mannes. With appreciation and love: thank you, Carl.

—Miriam Kartch, piano teacher and former Director of the Mannes Preparatory Division

* * * *

"While Mr. Schachter's breadth of knowledge, musical and otherwise, is truly inspiring, it is rather his ability to understand the bits of knowledge in relation to each other and to see therefore their true meanings which seems to separate him from the vast majority of those in the academic world. Furthermore, he has an innate ability to communicate these crystalline insights to the students around him. Finally, it is not to his discredit that he seems to be a warm and approachable person as well." This statement by one of his students comes from a reference letter addressed to the Queens College, dated 1972. Well, we hired the guy, and he spent the next 25 years demonstrating that sometimes letters of reference are bang-on.

—David Speidel, Provost, Queens College

* * * *

I want to reminisce about a single episode that sums up Carl Schachter and why I regard him so very highly. Carl became a member of the Personnel and Budget Committee of the Queens College Music Department at the very same time that I became the Chairman, and I relied on him more than I can acknowledge. At this time, the school was hit by a terrible budgetary crisis; the budget cuts were so horrendous that our scholarship fund was cut to a tiny fraction of what it had been. The idea of cutting stipends for existing graduate students was seriously considered in order to provide some moneys for incoming students. I was uncomfortable with that prospect: I thought it was wrong, and I thought it was important to maintain our commitments to those students we had before we took anybody else. But in those terrible times we were all somewhat uncertain and so I consulted Carl. He immediately and firmly responded that of course we could not lower the scholarships to any current graduate student who was doing the job properly. That was all we needed to maintain that course of action, and his support meant a great deal to me. This is Carl to the core; along with all the other things we value him for, this is what makes us love him.

> —*Joel Mandelbaum, Professor Emeritus of Music at the Aaron Copland School of Music, Queens College*

* * * *

I may be the only one to have studied with both Nadia Boulanger and Carl Schachter. Everyone is aware of their influence on our profession through their training of generations of students. Other similarities between them—their respect for craft, their sense for middleground structure, their teaching styles and their roles as standard bearers—are less well understood. Are Boulanger and Schachter, as is sometimes thought, as far apart as Schenker from Rameau, or is there a common ground?

My Schenker studies with Carl began twenty years after working in Paris with Mlle Boulanger. I was immediately impressed by the affinity between Mlle's bass reductions and Schenker's prolongations: each of her partimento exercises strings together a dozen or so middleground progressions. Mlle's deep respect for voice leading was attested to by her insistence that we write our realizations in open C clef score, that we play them at the piano for her with each voice legato and that we sing one of the voices while playing the rest. Moreover, she taught us to intertwine canons among the upper part, a further manifestation of her insatiable love of counterpoint. (How many other harmony teachers require overtly contrapuntal realizations of figured basses?) I'll always remember the moment when, in one of Carl's elegant, middleground graphs, there reappeared some of Mlle's voice leading. "Here it is," I smiled, "Boulanger's keyboard harmony in Schenker's notation. How glad am I to have spent all that time in Paris writing out all those exercises!"

Respect for craft and sensitivity to structure were two aspects of the musicianship that Boulanger and Schachter shared; in addition, the highest standards, coupled with keen artistic temperament, characterized their teaching styles. Who hasn't been amazed by their pulling out of the blue at the piano another just-right example of a topic at hand? Extraordinary ears, fluent keyboard skills, and broad-ranging repertoire were their standard fare. Mademoiselle, on the one hand, was apt to explain things away with passages from her favorite poets, this one from Pascal: "The silence of the infinite spaces frightens me." Carl is more down-to-earth. One day while discussing the challenge of analysis, he observed: "The difficulties have to do with the fact that it's difficult."

I remember well the day I arrived for a private lesson. He greeted me with, "So, how did you find *Winterreise*?" "I listened to it all in one sitting for the first time," I replied, "It's beautiful, of course, but I'm not sure I can bear to hear the whole thing through again. It's so desolate." I sat motionless afterward. He responded quietly, "Yes, I know . . . but, the hurdy-gurdy man . . ." Then I remembered what Schenker declared at the end of the Introduction to *Free Composition*: "[even] if . . . only one person is once more capable of hearing music in the spirit of its coherence, then even in this one person music will again be resurrected." I realize now that, in addition to their extraordinary musicianship, something else Boulanger and Schachter have given me is a sense of community. Even when I'm hibernating (as I am wont to do), I am sustained by the knowledge that when I surface, Carl will understand what I hear and see and love in music. And knowing that he cares helps me bear the trials—along with the joys— of a life in our profession.

—*Donna Doyle, music theorist and pianist*

* * * *

A great teacher can by both precept and example make you more yourself—even if that means disagreeing with the teacher. Carl's devotion to an analytical approach that can take ten or more years to really understand—in contrast to most of what surrounds us—has been a valuable example to me as one pursuing an unfashionable muse. When I began to study Schenkerian analysis, it was still widely dismissed as nonsense, not yet having achieved the status of being dismissed as what everybody knew all along. I had never heard of it, but I'm sure that on first looking into this way of hearing, my face must have had a Keatsian look of "wild surmise." It made immediate profound sense, even if it did then take years to really understand.

As a composer, I find that Schenkerian analysis has a special value for one's craft (and of course a danger), but ideally it reinforces one's confidence in one's intuition. As paradoxical as it might seem, Carl's teaching has helped me persist in writing a kind of music he doesn't recognize as tonal and analyzing repertoire that falls outside the Schachterian purview (such as Gershwin, Berg, and Ives). Such is the generosity of a great teacher.

—*Arthur Maisel, composer*

* * * *

In his recent interview with Joseph Straus published in the introduction to *Unfoldings*, Carl Schachter noted that "tracing the sources of the tonal system and how it developed . . . requires a kind of connection between analysis and theory on the one hand and history on the other. That's gone far less than I think it ought to have. . . There are a few younger scholars who are working along these lines, but there is a signal lack of interest on the part of most musicologists in analysis, James Webster being an outstanding exception." That equation really ought to be reversed, it seems to me. Without meaning to give offense, I would say that in the present professional climate in music theory, the majority of its practitioners seem not to evince a great deal of interest in music history, an outstanding exception being Carl Schachter. Music theory and history are not two disciplines, but one. Both have to do with what I believe we all are interested in, namely understanding music, both in the sense of pieces of music and in the sense of musical traditions and practice. I don't believe that these can be disassociated, and I believe that Carl doesn't feels they can be disassociated either.

Here I'd remind people that Schenker was one of the first musicologists, particularly in the sense that he was one of the first persons to understand the importance of studying original sources for pieces of music. His studies and interests in this area had a considerable influence on the development of source studies among musicologists.

In my own work, I do a certain amount of Schenkerian analysis, though I am not what I would refer to as an orthodox Schenkerian. More than once, I engaged Carl in conversations about what I was doing or hoped to do. He always encouraged me and never evinced any degree of defensiveness or sectarianism about what he was doing or what I was doing: that was something for which I was and remain very grateful.

—James Webster, Professor of Music, Cornell University

* * * *

I began and ended my doctoral studies in Carl Schachter's care, and it's probably fair to say that that no one "labored" so much as I in a class of his. In fact, in hindsight it seems that my first year of doctoral study and my second pregnancy moved in parallel motion. May 6 of 1986, a good two to three weeks before my due date, was also a week away from the final exam in Carl's "Introduction to Schenkerian Analysis" class at Queens College. I was sitting in the first row of the classroom, and it was already past 7 when the beginning of labor became obvious to me and would be soon enough to everyone else. I quickly scribbled a note—"I have broken water! Please dismiss the class!"—and thrust it in Carl's face. "Really?" he said, puzzled and surprised, and then immediately ended the class, giving me the opportunity to make a semi-graceful exit to the hospital. Alexandra Sabine was born was born at 12:02 a.m., May 7. Carl got the first phone call. I took the final on time.

Of the many classes I had with Carl Schachter, the best were my weekly lessons as his private student over the course of a year. I would arrive in the afternoon, usually after having walked the whole way up Madison Avenue from Penn Station—a good 30 minutes to an hour for me—time to ponder what was about to take place. After a long cup of tea, we studied Schubert and then Schumann and some Wolf. Those hours were a musical idyll, timeless and mind shaping. And, like the most wonderful cello lessons I ever had, they altered forever the way I heard and thought about music.

—*Helen M. Greenwald, Chair of the Department of Music History and Musicology, New England Conservatory*

* * * *

BUTTERFLY

In his final essay on rhythm, Carl Schachter calls the opening movement of Mozart's A major Sonata, K. 331 "that most overanalyzed piece" and compares it to Lavinia in *Titus Andronicus*. I confess when I first read Carl's remark I didn't know who Lavinia was. But knowing Carl, I decided I would find out.

Mozart's piece is a gem. The number of staves on the single surviving sheet of the original manuscript suggests he probably composed it while visiting Salzburg in 1783. The form is not a sonata allegro as expected, but rather a theme with variations. The lilting 6/8 tune has been traced inconclusively to a work by Scarlatti, a German melody, a Czech folk song, and even a Neapolitan Christmas carol. Its simple didactic quality, lack of modulation, and curious use of the soprano clef all hint this may have been a teaching piece for some Viennese student, jotted down perhaps on the master's stagecoach ride home.

Mozart takes the purest musical material—a rudimentary theme, sparse texture, transparent form—and imbues it with the miraculous. If this piece was intended to teach, it still does its job. But who, I wondered, was Lavinia?

Titus Andronicus, I discovered, is an early and particularly bloody Shakespearean tragedy. Titus's beautiful daughter Lavinia is kidnapped and brutally raped. The perpetrators mercilessly slice out her tongue and chop off her hands, so she can't identify them or reveal what happened. Lavinia's secret remains sealed inside of her, so poor Titus, her father, can only guess at the truth. Horrible, no doubt, but what's the connection with K. 331?

It turns out that like innocent Lavinia, Mozart's innocent little tune has also been carved up, by musical analysts in search of its secret, yet each with a conflicting account of the truth. Schenker, for instance, interprets the first four bars shown above as an interrupted $\hat{5}$-line from E prolonged to a rapid structural descent through D-C$\sharp$-B in bar 4. E-D-C$\sharp$ on the afterbeats of bars 1-3 comprise a motion to an inner voice embellished by lower thirds on the downbeats composing out the headtone E over tonic harmony. Others disagree, however, and see the initial E-D-C$\sharp$ in bars 1-3 not as a prolongation of E, but as the true structural descent from $\hat{5}$ down to $\hat{3}$, with the D at the end of the phrase representing an upper neighbor to the prolonged C$\sharp$ before passing to $\hat{2}$.

A third faction contends that this simple passage really unfolds a $\hat{3}$-line from C$\sharp$ on the downbeat of bar 1 instead of a $\hat{5}$-line from E. The initial C$\sharp$-B-A descent in bars 1-3 moves to an inner voice, but here the structural downbeats are embellished by upper thirds on the afterbeats prolonging C$\sharp$ to bar 4. Still another contingent claims that the B over dominant harmony in bar 2 is a prolonged lower neighbor returning to a structural C$\sharp$ in bar 4, instead of passing down to A within a tonic prolongation.

All in all, some of our best analysts have torn this tiny tune asunder, note by note, to reveal its secret—but they don't agree. And like the hapless Lavinia, lacking fingers to point or tongue to speak, Mozart's innocent little melody can't just tell us the truth. Like Lavinia, its mystery remains locked inside. And like Titus, we can only wonder.

Besides learning a bit of the bard though, I also learned a bit about Carl—and about music too. I decided that in the end, he cares more about music than he does about discovering "the truth." Carl sympathizes with music's analytic fate, even at his own hand, as if it were a person like Lavinia. He probes the notes, but only to embrace them more. Maybe that's what Carl means when he says he's deeply interested in Schenker, but more interested in Mozart. And maybe that's what Schenker himself means when he calls tones creatures with a life of their own. To analyze music, yes, but never to chop out her tongue.

I've learned more about music from Carl than anyone else, and this above all. Carl, like so few of us, has what Martin Buber calls an I-Thou relationship with art. Music for him is a Thou instead of an It. Analysis is a love affair, not a dissection. Carl wants to engage music as an end in itself, not as a means to the truth. He cradles each piece in his hands like a butterfly, admiring the intricacy of its wings, only to let it flutter away again, honoring the mystery of flight.

Perhaps like Lavinia, music's secret always remains best unknown, so that like Titus, we are always left wondering. I have a vision of Carl walking with Shakespeare across a field of butterflies, pondering Schenker's remark—"where there is no wonder, there can be no art."

—*Wayne Alpern, Director, Mannes Institute for*
Advanced Studies in Music Theory

VIII—BIBLIOGRAPHY OF WRITINGS BY CARL SCHACHTER

"The Two Versions of Mozart's Rondo, K. 494," with Hans Neumann. *Music Forum* 1 (1967), pp. 3-34.

Review of *Fugue and Invention in Theory and Practice* by John W. Verrall. *Journal of Music Theory* 11/1 (1967), pp. 157-59.

Review of *Creative Counterpoint* by Maurice Lieberman. *Journal of Music Theory* 11/1 (1967), pp. 169-71.

Counterpoint and Composition: *The Study of Voice Leading*, co-authored with Felix Salzer. New York: McGraw-Hill, 1969. Reprinted, New York: Columbia University Press, 1989. Translated as *Contrappunto e composizione* by Mario Baroni and Elena Modena (Torino: EDT, 1991) and as *El contrapunto en la composición: El estudio de la conducción des voces* by David Bruno (Barcelona: Idea Books; 1999).

"More about Schubert's Op. 94, No. 1." *Journal of Music Theory* 13/1 (1969), pp. 218-29. Reprinted in *Readings in Schenker Analysis and Other Approaches,* ed. Maury Yeston. New Haven: Yale University Press, 1977, pp. 193-201.

"Schubert's Moments Musicaux, Op. 94, No. 1." *Journal of Music Theory* 12/2 (1969), pp. 222-39. Reprinted in *Readings in Schenker Analysis and Other Approaches,* ed. Maury Yeston. New Haven: Yale University Press, 1977, pp. 171-84.

"Landini's Treatment of Consonance and Dissonance." *Music Forum* 2 (1970), pp. 130-86.

"Bach's Fugue in B♭ Major, *Well-Tempered Clavier*, Book I, No. 21." *Music Forum* 3 (1973), pp. 239-67. Reprinted in *Unfoldings: Essays in Schenkerian Theory and Analysis*, ed. Joseph N. Straus. Oxford: Oxford University Press, 1999, pp. 239-59.

"Introduction" to *Beethoven Piano Sonatas*, ed. Heinrich Schenker. New York: Dover, 1975. Adapted in *Five Great Piano Sonatas*, ed. Heinrich Schenker with performance notes by Anton Kuerti. Mineola, NY: Dover, 1999.

"Rhythm and Linear Analysis: A Preliminary Study." *Music Forum* 4 (1976), pp. 281-334. Reprinted in *Unfoldings: Essays in Schenkerian Theory and Analysis*, ed. Joseph N. Straus. Oxford: Oxford University Press, 1999, pp. 17-53.

"Diversity and the Decline of Literacy in Music Theory." *College Music Symposium* 17 (1977), pp. 150-53.

"Ernst Oster (1908-1977) In Memoriam," *Journal of Music Theory* 21/2 (1977), pp. 347-49.

Harmony and Voice Leading, co-authored with Edward Aldwell. New York: Harcourt Brace Jovanovich, 1978-79; 2nd ed., 1989; 3rd ed., New York: Thomson/Schirmer, 2003.

Interview in *The Music Makers*, ed. Deena Rosenberg and Bernard Rosenberg, pp. 130-41. New York: Columbia University Press, 1979.

"Rhythm and Linear Analysis: Durational Reduction." *Music Forum* 5 (1980), pp. 197-232. Reprinted in *The Garland Library of the History of Western Music*, vol. 14: *Approaches to Tonal Music*. New York: Garland, 1985, pp. 223-58; and in *Unfoldings: Essays in Schenkerian Theory and Analysis*, ed. Joseph N. Straus. Oxford: Oxford University Press, 1999, pp. 54-78.

"A Commentary on Schenker's *Free Composition*." *Journal of Music Theory* 25/1 (1981), pp. 115-42. Reprinted in *Unfoldings: Essays in Schenkerian Theory and Analysis*, ed. Joseph N. Straus. Oxford: Oxford University Press, 1999, pp. 184-208.

"Beethoven's Sketches for the First Movement of His Piano Sonata, Op. 14, No. 1: A Study in Design." *Journal of Music Theory* 26/1 (1982), pp. 1-21.

"The First Movement of Brahms's Second Symphony: the Opening Theme and Its Consequences." *Music Analysis* 2/1 (1983), pp. 55-68. Translated by Juan Carlos Lores Gil as "El primer movimiento de la segunda sinfonía de Brahms: El tema inicial y sus consecuencias" in *Quodlibet: Revista de especialización musical* (2001), pp. 90-105

"Motive and Text in Four Schubert Songs." In *Aspects of Schenkerian Theory*, ed. David Beach. New Haven: Yale University Press, 1983, pp. 61-76. Reprinted in *Unfoldings: Essays in Schenkerian Theory and Analysis*, ed. Joseph N. Straus. Oxford: Oxford University Press, 1999, pp. 209-20.

"Analysis by Key: Another Look at Modulation." *Music Analysis* 6/3 (1987), pp. 289-318. Reprinted in *Unfoldings: Essays in Schenkerian Theory and Analysis*, ed. Joseph N. Straus. Oxford: Oxford University Press, 1999, pp. 134-60.

"Mozart—the Five Violin Concertos: A Facsimile Edition of the Autographs." *Strad* (June 1987), pp. 448-49.

"Rhythm and Linear Analysis: Aspects of Meter." *Music Forum* 6 (1987), pp. 1-59. Reprinted in *Unfoldings: Essays in Schenkerian Theory and Analysis*, ed. Joseph N. Straus. Oxford: Oxford University Press, 1999, pp. 79-117.

"The Gavotte en Rondeaux from J.S. Bach's Partita in E Major for Unaccompanied Violin." *Israel Studies in Musicology* 4 (1987), pp. 7-26.

"Chopin's Fantasy, Op. 49: The Two-Key Scheme." In *Chopin Studies*, ed. Jim Samson. Cambridge: Cambridge University Press, 1988, pp. 524-29. Reprinted in *Unfoldings: Essays in Schenkerian Theory and Analysis*, ed. Joseph N. Straus. Oxford: Oxford University Press, 1999, pp. 260-88.

"Schenker's Counterpoint." *Musical Times* 129 (1988), pp. 221-53.

"Mozart's *Das Veilchen*: An Analysis of the Music." *Musical Times* 130 (1989), pp. 151-55. Reprinted in *Ostinato: Revue Internationale d'Études Musicales*, 1-2 (1993), pp. 164-73.

"*The Music of Chopin* by Jim Samson and *The Music of Brahms* by Michael Musgrave." *Music Analysis* 8/1-2 (1989), pp. 187-97.

"Either/Or." In *Schenker Studies*, ed. Hedi Siegel (Cambridge: Cambridge University Press, 1990), pp. 165-79. Reprinted in *Unfoldings: Essays in Schenkerian Theory and Analysis*, ed. Joseph N. Straus. Oxford: Oxford University Press, 1999, pp. 121-33.

Introduction to *The Salzer Collection: Fine music and continental manuscripts—Property of the late Dr. Felix Salzer and Mrs. Hedwig Salzer (Thursday, 17th May 1990)*. London: Sotheby's, 1990.

"The Adventures of an F♯: Tonal Narration and Exhortation in Donna Anna's First-Act Recitative and Aria." *Theory and Practice* 16 (1991), pp. 5-20. Reprinted in *Unfoldings: Essays in Schenkerian Theory and Analysis*, ed. Joseph N. Straus. Oxford: Oxford University Press, 1999, pp. 221-35.

"Mozart's Last and Beethoven's First: Echoes of K. 551 in the First Movement of Op. 21." In *Mozart Studies*, ed. Cliff Eisen. Oxford: Oxford University Press, 1991, pp. 620-26.

"Twentieth-Century Analysis and Mozart Performance," *Early Music* 19/4 (1991), pp. 620-624.

"The Prelude in E Minor, Op. 28, No. 4: Autograph Sources and Interpretation." In *Chopin Studies* 2, ed. John Rink and Jim Samson. Cambridge: Cambridge University Press, 1994, pp. 161-82.

"Chopin's Prelude, Opus 28, No. 5: Analysis and Performance." *Journal of Music Theory Pedagogy* 8 (1994), pp. 27-45.

"The Sketches for Beethoven's Piano and Violin Sonata, Op. 24." *Beethoven Forum* 3 (1994), pp. 107-25.

"The Submerged Urlinie: The Prelude from Bach's Suite No. 4 for Violoncello Solo." *Current Musicology* 56 (1994), pp. 54-71.

"The Triad as Place and Action." *Music Theory Spectrum* 17/2 (1995), pp. 149-69. Reprinted in *Unfoldings: Essays in Schenkerian Theory and Analysis*, ed. Joseph N. Straus. Oxford: Oxford University Press, 1999, pp. 161-83.

"Idiosyncratic Features of Three Mozart Slow Movements: The Piano Concertos, K. 449, K. 453, and K. 467." In *Mozart's Piano Concertos: Text, Context, and Interpretations*, ed. Neal Zaslaw. Ann Arbor: University of Michigan Press, 1996, pp. 315-33.

"La reconciliación de opuestos: Elementos cromáticos en los dos primeros movimientos de las sonatas para piano op. 31 núm. 1 y op. 53 de Beethoven," trans. David Bruno. *Quodlibet: Revista de especialización musical* 6 (1996), pp. 47-59.

"Schoenberg's Hat and Lewis Carroll's Trousers." In *Aflame with Music: 100 Years of Music at the University of Melbourne*, ed. Brenton Broadstock et al. Melbourne: Center for Studies in Australian Music, 1996, pp. 327-41.

"El impromptu en fa sostenido mayor op. 36 de Chopin: Analisis e Interpretacíon," trans. Isabel García Adánez. *Quodlibet: Revista de especialización musical* 14 (1999), pp. 116-26.

"Structure as Foreground: 'das Drama des Ursatzes.'" In *Schenker Studies 2*, ed. Carl Schachter and Hedi Siegel. Cambridge: Cambridge University Press, 1999, pp. 298-314.

Unfoldings: Essays in Schenkerian Theory and Analysis, ed. Joseph N. Straus. Oxford: Oxford University Press, 1999.

"Counterpoint and Chromaticism in Chopin's Mazurka in C# minor, Opus 50, Number 3." *Ostinato rigore: Revue internationale d'études musicales* 15 (2000), pp. 121-34.

"Entrevista a Carl Schachter," interview with Cecilia Medina and Juan Pablo Medina. *Pauta: Cuadernos de teoría y crítica musical* 74 (2000), pp. 18-24.

"Playing What the Composer Didn't Write: Analysis and Rhythmic Aspects of Performance." In *Pianist, scholar, connoisseur: Essays in honor of Jacob Lateiner*, ed. Jane Gottlieb and Bruce Brubaker. Stuyvesant, NY: Pendragon, 2000, pp. 47-68.

"Elephants, Crocodiles, and Beethoven: Schenker's Politics and the Pedagogy of Schenkerian Analysis." *Theory and Practice* 16 (2001), pp. 1-20.

Preface to reprint of *Free Composition* by Heinrich Schenker, trans. Ernst Oster. Hillsdale, NY: Pendragon Press, 2001.

"Taking Care of the Sense: A Schenkerian Pedagogy for Performers." *Tijdschrift voor muziektheorie* 6/3 (2001), pp. 159-70.

"Deception, Disguise, and Mistaken Identity in the Finale of Mozart's Prague Symphony." *Composition as a Problem* 3 (2003), pp. 5-14.

"Idiosyncrasies of Phrase Rhythm in Chopin's Mazurkas." In *The Age of Chopin: Interdisciplinary Inquires*, ed. Halina Goldberg. Bloomington: Indiana University Press, 2003, pp. 95-105.